TriQuarterly

TriQuarterly is

an international

journal of

writing, art and

cultural inquiry

published at

Northwestern

University

TriQuarterly

issue 134

Editor of this issue: Leigh Buchanan Bienen

Contents

Front and back cover photos by Bill Arsenault.

Leigh Buchanan Bienen

Art, and the Art of Teaching

What do you read, my Lord? —Words, words, words . . .

I

Of course a great artist can't be taught to be a great artist. Why then do we pore so eagerly over their biographies and autobiographical writing, the endless collections of letters (mostly un-illuminating), the scribbling in diaries? To find the mystery, how that work which survives, continues to delight decades or centuries later, was created. What is the relationship between life and art, we ask so stupidly. The secret why that otherwise ordinarily neurotic, pedestrian, unhappy or, perhaps more puzzling, that happy or well-adjusted person became a great novelist, or playwright, actor, or director. Or the great ones among the composers, dancers, painters, architects, and for that matter the chemists, the physicists, and biologists. All who transcend the ordinary, who lift competence and turn it into something else, performing a service, and presenting an unexpected gift.

And the luck of it, the circumstances—there was the time to do it, when it could happen—and who recognizes that, who promotes it, the connections. What if your first novel was published on the day of Pearl Harbor, as was Saul Bellow's *Dangling Man*? Why was everyone crying at Mary Zimmerman's *Metamorphoses* in New York after 9/11? Since we can't even begin address those realities, let's talk about what we can see—the teaching of art, of literature and the theater arts in the universities. Most of the theater artists who have written essays for this volume are serious teachers, as well as working artists.

The eternal questions posed by literature and brought to the stage have changed little:

What matter? Who goes there?[1]
Thy business? How goes it here? All dead.

That controlled uncertainty, the not knowing what is going to happen next is the essence of drama. All art springs from wondering. The common spring is that rush of pleasure, which brings the blood up and the tears.

II

Chicago is in the middle of a theatrical renaissance, with a large diverse community of actors, playwrights, designers, and directors living here and making a living here. The simultaneous presence of Steppenwolf Theatre, Lookingglass Theatre, the Goodman Theatre, the Court Theatre, Victory Gardens, Writers' Theatre, as well as Hypocrites, Greasy Joan, the House Theatre, and many, many others, is living proof of this. The contributors to this volume are not all from Chicago nor are they all trained or associated with Northwestern University, although many of them work together and have long lasting associations, some of them going back to when they were students.

The academic theater tradition at Northwestern has always been text driven, literary—as Frank Galati, Mary Zimmerman, David Catlin, and Virgil Johnson describe—laying performance on unexpected texts, challenging the form by creating theater pieces from texts never designed to be staged. The Department of Theatre at Northwestern began as the Department of Reading Aloud, became, after several transformations, Performance Studies within the School of Speech, and now is embraced in the School of Communication. Literature requires that you speak back. Performances of actors dramatizing the reading of names in the phone book were legendary, a reminder that a gifted theater artist can impose emotion and structure, order and beauty on any series of words, in the

---

1. All *Hamlet* and *King Lear* quotations are from *The Complete Works of Shakespeare Kittredge Players Illustrated Edition* (Gin & Co., 1958).

spaces between words, and in the absence and expectation of words. Unfortunately, the converse is also true, the attempted dramatization of the most poetic, thrilling words will fail when delivered on flat feet.

If the making art or science or invention cannot be taught, if the leap of the imagination must be spontaneous, the foundation can be laid. In the theater where the effort is always a group effort, the role of an individual teacher will always be tempered by the presence of the others necessary to make it happen. And this selection, attention, preparation for the moment is critical.

For literature, for fiction and poetry, there must be at the beginning a single person sitting down to put pen to paper, or to tap out what appears magically on a screen. To pick up a pen, or a piece of charcoal, is an act of hope. The making of art, the experience of art, seems to be inextricable from the need to live with others, to observe and be observed, in villages, towns and cities, the need to hear the news, to talk and whisper.

> We two alone will sing like birds i' th' cage.
> When thou dost ask me blessing, I'll kneel down
> And ask them forgiveness. So we'll live,
> And pray and sing, and tell old tales, and laugh
> At gilded butterflies, and hear poor rogues
> Talk of court news; and we'll talk with them too—
> Who loses and who wins; who's in, who's out—
> And take upon 's the mystery of things,
> As if we were God's spies; and we'll wear out,
> In a walled prison, packs and sects of great ones
> That ebb and flow by th' moon.

Ten centuries later someone will see on a scroll unfurled the carefully drawn carriages carrying gentlemen in robes and the ladies with jewels in their hair, at their necks, as the procession makes its way down a highly stylized, angled projection of a walled road—to a wedding, a funeral of a consul, an offering to an oracle—and there will be the recognition of a portrait of how some people presented themselves to each other, and how they lived a long time ago in a distant place.

So when I moved to Chicago and became part of Northwestern University, it was a delight to find that our university not only had a long and distinguished history of teaching theater, but also provided an intellectual and institutional home to some of the most original and exciting theater artists practicing in America. Watching their work, getting to know them, has been another education and is the inspiration for this volume.

III

As a young person I walked into Vladimir Nabokov's Masterpieces of European Literature class and on the first day recognized that I was in the presence of an extraordinary intelligence. This was before *Lolita*, before *Conclusive Evidence*, the haunting memoir later retitled *Speak Memory*, which Nabokov remarked he called *Conclusive Evidence* because "it was conclusive evidence that I exist."

At the first lecture—and they were lectures, this was long before interactive teaching was in vogue—I sat myself down next to Mrs. Nabokov, the famous Vera, his scribe and muse, and copied down every word he said. I didn't know what else to do. She smiled and nodded approvingly at my scurrying pen. I treasured any notice either of them took of me. It was as if I had been conscripted into service in a strange nameless brigade. Yes, he delivered the same lectures for many years. Some academics criticized Nabokov for that, and for making easy fun of the Constance Garnett translations. Decades later I came to appreciate the crafted performance art those lectures were, even with the seemingly spontaneous digressions and offhand jokes scripted and repeated year after year, as was the assertion of the commonality of the goals of art and science.

When I announced with sophomoric certainty to the then chairman of the English Department at Cornell—Vladimir Nabokov was in the tiny, fractious Department of Comparative Literature—that I wanted to take every course Professor Nabokov taught, the chairman of the English Department replied: that would be a waste of time. There was another lesson, not lost on me and one that served me well. I may have been a greenhorn from California but I knew that was dead wrong.

My freshman English teacher, on the other hand, a recent graduate of the University of Iowa Writers' Workshop, later himself a well known novelist and poet, did not share the chairman's attitude: he directed me to find Nabokov's European novels in the library. So I had another reason to climb those slippery circular iron stairs in the stacks of the beautiful Cornell library tower. Later, I reviewed *The Real Life of Sebastian Knight*, and sat in another class as Nabokov joked about *Lolita* jousting with *Doctor Zhivago* for first place on the *New York Times* best-seller list.

Much later when I was marooned and pregnant in Kampala, I spent hours on weekday afternoons in the tiny and then peaceful university library up the road and found there more pre-*Lolita* Nabokov novels, left as a gift perhaps by some long departed colonial professor of English who may have considered himself a writer. First editions of *Bend Sinister* and *Laughter in the Dark* were in the Makerere University library, I wrote Mrs. Nabokov, receiving months later a very polite reply from Montreux. This long before e-mail and when the international telegraph and telephone were unreliable and unavailable, and the spirits of my undergraduate days were far away.

But soft! Behold! Lo, where it comes again!
I'll cross it though it blast me—Stay illusion!
. . .
Looks it not like the King.

I had earlier abandoned the search for the ghost of my own dead father in the libraries and halls of economics and banking, at the Massachusetts Institute of Technology, leaving, in the middle of a gray eastern winter, the graduate study of economics for the Iowa Writers Workshop to study, following my former freshman English teacher at Cornell, George P. Elliott. Indeed he became my workshop teacher, mentor, friend, and he gave me away at my wedding.

The Cornell English Department then and still publishes a distinguished literary journal, *Epoch*, which I worked on for four years, but the same small group showed up for readings by poets and fiction writers. There was a vibrant culture of undergraduate theater. At the Iowa Writers' Workshop an audience of three hundred people came to hear a poet. Cornell had a few excellent writers as teachers, mostly of Freshman English—this was when only two universities, Iowa and Stanford, offered a graduate fine arts degree in "creative" writing—but at Cornell we were the runts of the department, the people who didn't aspire to graduate school in English at Harvard or Columbia. This brings up another point for the teaching of theater, art, or science: critical mass.

The University of Iowa Writers' Workshop was an entirely different academic endeavor. The writers were important people at the university. The rivalry between the poets and the fiction writers on the softball field was legendary, with the macho poets usually victorious. The University of Iowa champion football and basketball teams were followed avidly in the workshop by students and faculty, and by my new husband. What was not discussed was that the black football and basketball players were housed in separate dormitories. I only knew that because a black poet in the workshop told me, but I didn't know what to do or think about it.

At Iowa a very young Philip Roth, flush with the unexpected success of *Goodbye Columbus* and before the deluge of fame and outrage elicited by *Portnoy's Complaint*, taught a great books course of his own devising and introduced me to Isaac Babel, Italo Calvino, I. B. Singer. Philip Roth was passionate about the books, very married, and very much the protégé of Saul Bellow. Probably he was writing *Letting Go*, not that he talked about his own work, but he did talk amusingly, ironically about his life, his family, and about the curiosity of finding himself at twenty-six living with a stepdaughter at an adolescent stage he still remembered.

Philip Roth was very precise and careful about what we read, about himself, somewhat hypochondriacal, and with my workshop teacher we brought wine in a brown bag to the one steak restaurant and went in together on a purchase of some awful tasting dietary supplement which was to make us all thin. Only Philip Roth succeeded. Charming, serious about his service to the teaching of literature, Roth showed none of the darkness and steely sheen, which was to characterize some of his work after *When She Was Good*. Roth and Nabokov had the same view: a writer must read and identify only with the author, never with the characters. And, of course, don't waste time with any writer who isn't doing something that is worth your full attention.

IV

Some five years later, pregnant with a third child, I was back in Chicago, having lived in Kampala, Uganda, for two years where I worked for the astonishing African literary magazine *Transition*. I wrote a note asking Saul Bellow for a part time job—enclosing a review essay of mine on new American fiction from *Transition*, which argued that *Herzog* was the best of an usually rich crop of new novels coming out with a new identity for themselves and American literature. He hired me for a few dollars an hour for a few hours a week—I only paid my babysitter a dollar an hour—to wade through the hundreds of letters he had received in response to *Herzog*, a book which was a homage to the epistolary novel, and thus the solipsistic circle was complete.

Bellow was teaching then, at the University of Chicago's Committee on Social Thought, like Nabokov perched in a usual academic place.

I did not take or sit in on any of his classes. I was interested in what they were reading, though, and who the students were. He was having them read Theodore Dreiser, a writer whom I did not come to appreciate until returning to Chicago thirty years later. Bellow didn't seem to take his teaching very seriously; and he was puzzled as to why his students had so little sympathy or interest in Dreiser's work, which suited his own dark mood at the time. Soon he was having me read Tanazaki and Mishima and Graham Greene, and writers I had never heard of who wrote one good book and disappeared.

Bellow had not yet won the Nobel Prize for Literature and was pleased and amused by his fame and relatively recent prosperity. He would have laughed at Woody Allen's remark to Studs Terkel: "Having money just means you fail with a higher class of woman." He was grappling with a new public self, shedding his old identity and a wife, and enjoying it all but troubled by whom to serve now that he was a success, as became clear in *The Dean's December* and *Mr. Sammler's Planet*.

Bellow had written a play and had disastrous experiences with the theater. When I was there, he traveled for a day to a university performance of his play, *The Last Analysis*, a theatrical presentation of his preoccupations in *Herzog*, only to find the show had been cancelled and no one had bothered to call and tell him. This to a man who, no matter what, wrote everyday from eight in the morning until noon.

Once again, while considerably absorbed in my own teeming life, I knew immediately that I was in the presence of an extraordinary and original intelligence, someone who cut to the quick, and had an unerring nose for the genuine. He was always in pursuit of a goal, and in service of some higher good, but what? He knew what kind of a man he himself was, too, not just from narcissistic self-reflection. To be in his orbit was itself an education. He was never not thinking like a writer, and if he turned his attention to you or your work, it was a searchlight shining right in your face.

Who's there? Nay answer me! Stand and unfold yourself.

For me, then, the best part may have been that I could climb, huffing and puffing, to his tiny fourth floor Committee on Social Thought office at the University of Chicago, a few afternoons a week, and drink in some silence and have the room to myself, before he would sometimes come and we would go through the motions of going through the huge pile of mail on the tables and floor. They were both a metaphor and a reality, the letters in response to letters, which were themselves imaginary responses in an epistolary novel. The then later real response, or lack of response we crafted was the tangible, intangible bubble of art. That year Bellow never did give any of those letters to the University of Chicago Library, although eventually most ended up in the archives. I read through hundreds of the letters, and they became another part of my education: how readers respond to what novelists write.

Many women, complete strangers, wrote and invited him for lunch or coffee, with a not very veiled invitation for more! Some were from old friends, many from other writers, some from literary critics—he had little use for those, saying he only paid attention to what other writers said about writing—and some from old lovers or companions who wrote in amazement, he said, to ask if he was the same (unwritten: unsuccessful, ordinary) person they had known years ago. That refrain would be reprised later as well. Part of my job was fielding random enquiries, and I met more writers, such as John Berryman, who came to town as a visiting fireman, and Cy Colter, who became a friend, improbably picked up with thirty years later in Chicago.

V

Later, during another stint in East Africa, while living in Kenya, I was hired to be a ghost writer and editor for another powerful, enigmatic man, Bildad Kaggia, the Mau Mau leader in the forest in the 1950s, a defendant in the notorious Kapanguria Trial where he, Jomo Kenyatta, and the others were all sentenced to die on the basis of evidence concocted by the British. Kaggia had decided to write an autobiography, and his editor, an Englishman at East African Publishing, hired me to write the book. For want of the seven pounds (the value of a cow) his father was unwilling to pay, Kaggia never went to the high school for Africans attended by the next several presidents of Kenya and most of the African members of Parliament. Instead he lied about his age, joined the British Expeditionary Force, and was sent to Palestine. Kaggia's life story had more real drama than could be contained in any novel or play and, even in its simple factual retelling, was an astounding narrative.

> Thou art a scholar; Speak to it, Horatio.
> Looks it not like the King? Mark it, Horatio
> Most Like. It harrows me with fear and wonder

It would be spoke to.
Question it, Horatio.

We would sit on a park bench, Kaggia and I—by that time he walked with difficulty with a cane—whether for reasons of security or privacy or convenience, I never knew. I would sit with my pencil and pad, and he would talk looking straight ahead with his hands folded on top of his cane. Kaggia would tell me the stories of what happened to him and what he did, and I would write down every thing he said. Once again, I found myself pressed into a strange service. The stories were extraordinary, but I never doubted they were true.

Sometimes I would ask him questions, and sometimes he would answer. Other times he would be silent in response. Then I would go home and type up what he told me, add some connections, edit it, and the next week he would read it, correct it. I would ask more questions, and we would go down another path. More typing, more editing. No computers, no e-mail, no word processing. Just writing and editing and typing, and copying and copying again. A book, a life story emerged. I did turn the experience into fiction, writing what now seems an unsatisfactory short story titled "The First Secretary."

The publisher who paid me five hundred dollars found the book Kaggia and I produced so readable that he delayed its publication, probably fearing it would jeopardize the status of then president (and former codefendant with Kaggia) Jomo Kenyatta, an African leader who seems benign by current standards. Kaggia had planned that the book would launch his own campaign for president, as the only Kikuyu challenger to Kenyatta, and perhaps that was what the publisher feared. He would be king.

Then suddenly Kaggia withdrew his candidacy and from political life and would answer no questions. This mysterious stepping back from a rather small man who had faced down armed policemen on his doorstep, been thrown into jail by the Kenyans under the same laws as the British used to imprison him, had been beaten and shot, and yet always remained undeterred by threats to his own life and those of his wife and children. He was driven to serve, maniacally selfless.

Bits and pieces of the book were published over the years in bowdlerized form, and then only outside of Kenya. I learned another lesson: I had written the book, but didn't own it, and it was about someone else's life. There was interest in publishing an English edition of a biography of Kaggia in America, but I didn't have the rights to sell the book we had written, although Bildad Kaggia wanted an American edition. The book couldn't be published in America, and never was, although it would have found readers in America in the 1970s. Those rights had been long ago signed away to the Englishman.

VI

Not long after Joyce Carol Oates and her husband Ray Smith, and the *Ontario Review,* had arrived at Princeton, I sent them a piece of short fiction in an interoffice envelope, which prompted Joyce Carol Oates to call my husband at his Princeton University office and say that they wanted to publish his story. Soon we were pals and going for dinner and having parties together. Most of us were university teachers with great freedom, leisure, money, exceptional students, and a life that allowed for social activity, travel, and talk. Joyce Carol Oates herself had the reputation of being a serious and dedicated teacher of writing. Over the years I was to watch, with a sharp intake of breath, that enormous intelligence and long artistic reach transform, sometimes with little disguise, the material of the lives of our friends into novels, plays, and stories. To witness this was startling and amusing and sometimes infuriating, especially since I had always fiercely maintained that as a fiction writer I never wanted to write stories or novels about the lives and loves of people in suburban university towns like Princeton, New Jersey. This was just what Joyce Carol Oates was doing with great glee and aplomb. Certainly I wasn't doing it, although later the book I published with Ontario Review Press did include some forays in that direction.

To see Joyce Carol Oates apparently effortlessly recreate with stunning sophistication the world in which we were at that moment living was arresting, and a challenge, even to observe. There was the hilarious and sometimes hurtful *roman à clef* aspect, and then the larger question of whether that really was us, and our community. I always felt as amusing, as apt, as sharply satirical as her portraits were, she held something back in order to continue to live amongst us. Nor did it feel as if love was the moderating reason for this restraint, although her being a woman was evident everywhere.

He was a man, take him for all in all.

Surely we deserved harsher scrutiny, to be taken to task for falling short in the moral measurement she applied with such fierce precision in those novels about uneducated people in upstate New York in the 1950s, the America of her childhood. She was not deceived, even if taken in by this clever, self-congratulatory group, which took itself and its importance far too seriously. We always knew all the answers, had always been rewarded for that by ourselves and others, and we never were at a loss for words. Even our infrequent self-criticism was entertaining and full of wit.

It would have elicited more than a barking laugh of recognition if her unerring moral compass had been allowed to point and stayed fixed upon that privileged little island in America, made possible by an extraordinarily wealthy university, where we so pompously sat. What if she had considered the responsibility we took or didn't take for our lives there? I suspect I too would have held my punches had I chosen us for the subject of my fiction, and perhaps that is why I looked elsewhere, and why she was braver. For to look closely would have required a harsher judgment, and perhaps a change.

VII

By this time, I had gone to law school, partly because I wasn't earning enough money working—at a job I hated—or writing fiction no one seemed to want to buy or read, and there was nowhere in Princeton at that time where a woman with a degree from the Iowa Writers' Workshop could teach writing. As my husband pointed out, I needed to get a real job. Soon, perhaps not soon enough, I was in the thick of it as a public defender, drowning in the conundrums and contradictions of the criminal law, but soon teaching too, first at the University of California at Berkeley—with great pleasure since it was where my father had been a professor, and I could sense his ghost at the unchanged faculty club where the moose was still on the wall—then at the University of Pennsylvania School of Law, and at Princeton.

If I had gone to law school to find subject, I had found it—ironically first while on leave from law school in Nigeria—although I still didn't know what to do with it. All the teaching turned into the teaching of writing, and the practice turned into the writing of legal reports and articles and academic papers. By then I was writing in, for, and about the law for a professional audience, and that went on for years. In Nigeria I started down a path of doing research on homicide, murder, and capital punishment—with a five-year detour for rape and incest—and there was enough in the law for several writing lives. In fact other writers were starting to take my material. I now think I spent too much time writing for that professional audience.

VIII

Why do we question whether the practice of art can be taught? The practice of law, of medicine, are taught, as is the practice of performance and composition of music, and the quality and content of this teaching is appropriately guarded by the professions. Astronomy is taught, as is engineering, and all of the arts of invention and building. Anyone would be ridiculed who set out to build a computer or a car without looking at what has been done before—isn't that what teaching is, looking at what has gone before?

The essays in this volume are written by artists who are sometimes teachers. The ability to teach someone to play, to draw, to build something, to test a theory, or to write a poem is a great gift. The principle remains the same across the disciplines: to learn to accomplish a complicated human task, the best way is to watch or listen or talk to people who know how to do it well. You can teach someone how to ride a horse, and lay out the rules of Olympic competition, but that wordless communication between horse and rider—and the luck of it, that rider and horse are both healthy, the track firm—that may, after years of training, win a gold can not be taught. However, no one believes that some one should just mount a horse and head for the jumps.

Some artists will be articulate and willing and capable of teaching about what they do, others will not want to or have that ability, choosing not to pierce the protective veil between their work and the talking about it whose existence we all recognize. Some can talk about the game or the ride, but not do it, and mostly they should not be teachers.

IX

And so I was writing about crime, capital punishment, hangings, and lethal injections, and counting murders and studying homicide—having started down that path as a law student while in Nigeria—but not writing murder mysteries and not writing a novel about a woman who was a public defender, in a state where the death penalty was just reenacted, a woman who found no answers to all of the hard questions. Perhaps if I had believed in psychoanalysis I would have figured out why I could not, or would not, write directly about the life I was then living. It was certainly interesting enough, it was full of the stuff of high and low drama, even eerily comic, too full of melodrama, and the existing dramatizations frequently trivialized, marginalized, and cheapened the fact that real people had been killed and real people were going to prison, or death row. There was real work to be done there. So why did it feel like a betrayal to write about what I was experiencing straight on? How could I write a work of fiction when a real person's life was at stake, although I still put myself squarely in Nabokov's camp with those who believe that art should not be in the service of any but itself.

As I published more articles and editorials and books about murder and the death penalty, and increasingly played a public role involving lots of writing and research, my commentary turned away from the scholarly legal questions. Meanwhile the technical research, the proportionality review analysis, was ever changing, hugely challenging, and becoming of interest to the Supreme Court of New Jersey and to other courts and legal observers. My writings were now solicited, and their authorities were raked over by an ever-changing squadron of law student editors. Then, as the commercial legal publishing business outsourced, communication was with faint, accented voices with foreign questions—Is F.B.I. a common acronym?—from India, or the unidentifiable countries where the copyediting was done, but where that work would never be read.

And I was always enjoying and learning from my teaching, ostensibly about the law but always about writing, who was writing, what did they have to say, and how did it fit with what you wanted to write. And how do you reach the audience you need to reach? Not surprisingly, there were many writers and would-be writers in the law. Many of my students in the law schools wanted to be writers, and some of them were. When the academic writing was doing its job of persuading people in the right places, or not, and the legal cases and their supporting writings were doing their work, making their way, or not, through the court system, at that point I knew I had to return to serious writing, not just continue writing in, for, and about the law, for a professional audience of lawyers and judges.

I knew I had to return to fiction because what I wanted to write about—the murderous, destructive heart of man, the web of human interactions we spin, the cruelty and compassion and love between us—these could not be encompassed within the strictures or forms of writing acceptable to the legal profession. The stories I wanted to tell, what I had to say about the law, authority, about who has the privilege to tell whom how to behave, that could not be told within the confines of my adopted profession. In legal journals and books I said what I thought and felt about murder, rape, incest, the application of the law, who made it, who enforced it, about legalized executions and the death penalty, and I did so with increasing force and freedom, especially to my students.

That straight-ahead commentary or expression of opinion did not do the job. It wasn't that I couldn't say what I felt, because I could and did, but I could not express the complicated contradictory nature of my thoughts and feelings outside of the structure of a work of art. Only by transforming these into an imagined world could the truth be told.

I continued to teach law because the protected space of the classroom allowed for an openness of communication not present in other spheres of my life, not within the family where the urgencies of love and the need to protect and preserve structured interactions, not at the office where the collective commitment to our joint effort required everyone to ignore certain obvious and painful truths, nor among my friends where another agenda—maintaining the silhouette of community—took precedent.

When I was ready to move back into fiction writing, after years of studying and writing about the law, practicing law, teaching legal subjects, and puzzling over legal conundrums (mostly just the human inability to admit a mistake, when the technicalities were unraveled) I knew I needed to retool. It had been a long time since the University of Iowa Writers' Workshop. And while I had some friends who were writers, I didn't have an artistic community of trusted colleagues where I could try out new ideas, the kind of necessary, supportive community which several of the theater artists describe in this volume.

X

Theater brought me back to fiction. I went to plays, read plays, thought about plays, and started to read with a playwright's eye, especially after participating in an extraordinary class taught at Princeton by Jean-Claude van Italie, himself a highly original playwright. The class was an undergraduate class in playwriting, which meant the nine of us wrote every week, dramatizing interactions from our lives, tiny scenes, baby steps, and we read them aloud and talked about what we were trying to accomplish with the writing and acting. Some of the students in the class were already accomplished actors and writers, and some had directed plays. After teaching law for more than a decade, to be in this class was a true and enlightening educational experience, a stepping from air into water.

After that class, and then another one, I wrote a couple of plays which it took me some time to realize were not very good plays, and that was useful because it bounced me right back into fiction where I was at home. The class only met once a week, but I thought about it a lot in between the meetings. I could not have gone to a similar course in beginning fiction writing. The most important thing about the class was that it disarmed me, and put me back into that part of my brain where imaginative work could begin. This gifted teacher created a protected place where art could happen, and I was able to write fiction again. And, as a side benefit, I had a new and life-long interest and appreciation for the art of the playwright and the complicated time-structured beauty of the art of the theater.

XI

And so I wrote *Technician*, a short novel about a young man from Trenton, New Jersey, who through a series of circumstances applies for and gets the newly created job of execution technician with the state of New Jersey. I wrote this novel because the proposed regulations for the job of execution technician started appearing along with other proposed administrative regulations on my desk at the Department of the Public Advocate, not long after New Jersey reenacted the death penalty in 1982. Then I was spending all of my professional time writing about proportionality review in New Jersey, a factual and legal inquiry into who of those eligible were prosecuted for capital murder, when the law made many more eligible for the death penalty than were actually charged or sentenced to death.

This enterprise generated hundreds of pages of opinions of the Supreme Court of New Jersey, not to mention the legal briefs filed by the Office of the Public Advocate, the Attorney General, the thousands of pages of published research, and at least a thousand footnotes in legal journals, most written by me. Each footnote entry, each period, comma and capitalization, and source in each footnote scrutinized by successive generations of law review editors at various law schools. The last such article, written a year ago for a special conference on the role of doctors in executions, circled back to my literary preoccupations in *Technician:* the use of bureaucratic procedures and language to obfuscate and confuse when the state is doing something it wants to camouflage or lie about.

I wrote *Technician* because the legal, professional discourse was too limited, too hidebound, too restricted to allow for the telling of the story I had to tell. Of course brutality, cruelty, and inhumanity were not new topics in the law or literature. Nor was murder on the order of a state something new. But the level of bureaucratic overlay, if not new, felt different. The law was masquerading as something else, as the law carried out this mandate. And no one was calling it out. It was all reality, all the time. And there was no art there. The crudity, the admitted brutality of hanging or the electric chair seemed more honest than the lethal injection administered anonymously behind a curtain to a man strapped on a gurney. Only the larger, freer form of narrative fiction could accommodate such a perspective.

The law prides itself on its objectivity, its ability to rise above decisions based upon feelings or emotion, although emotion is everywhere in the law, especially in criminal law; the emotions of repression, rage, anger, hatred, and revenge are rampant. The hatred wafts off the page of some court opinions. It is not that the law is unemotional; it is that the expression of emotion in the law must be presented as "nonemotion," or as "objective." When a guard beats a prisoner in a cell, we know that is wrong, and we even have a word for it and a statutory formulation of the wrong. It might even result in a criminal prosecution. Here a someone in a white coat was being instructed to play doctor, kill, and then be signed on as a state employee, with benefits, vacation, and Social Security. Who would that someone be?

Ironically, all those academic articles, the hundreds of pages of opinions from the Supreme Court of New Jersey which always went out of their way to declare the statute constitutional, and the scholarly and technical work of the New Jersey Proportionality Review Project probably did influence the legislators to repeal the New Jersey capital punishment statute more than twenty-five years later. Proportionality review delayed the reimposition of executions in New Jersey, and consequently legislators and policy makers could take a step back and evaluate what they had done and be able to move at a propitious moment—to take the jump—when everyone was temporarily sick of all of the debates and the violence and spilled blood of a recent hideous murder was not momentarily in the news.

Art makes nothing happen, and I agree with Bruce Norris's stricture that art should delight and do no more. I find myself simultaneously nodding in agreement with Anna Shapiro's exhortation that the teaching of theater should at least be relevant to the world we live in, and with Bruce Norris's passionate plea that it not be relevant to anything but itself. A lot of art went into presenting those facts and arguments to decision makers and the public in New Jersey. It is paradoxical that some of the greatest art concerns itself with matters of profound morality and yet art mostly stumbles when it carries a message.

I wrote *Technician* because my heart was chilled by imagining an actual person, someone whom I might know, applying for the job whose supposedly objective specifications were neatly displayed in numbered paragraphs on the blue, mimeographed sheets of proposed regulations from the New Jersey Department of Corrections on my desk. Some days I would just stare back at them. There was no place to ask certain questions at that desk in my professional role, and so I asked them of myself in the course of writing the novel: what kind of a person would apply for that job? It was too easy to imagine a brute or a sadist, although there were always those in the system, so I imagined an ordinary person who might find himself applying for that job.

While writing *Technician* I didn't anticipate that psychological and sociological research, as well as the reality of twenty-five years of post-*Furman* experience with state-mandated executions by lethal injection, would support my imagined view that it was just such ordinary people who did apply for those jobs, and, if it came to it, did carry out the executions, often with a mind-numbing lack of preparation or comprehension. Not only were executions going to be done according to fake scientific instructions, but those instructions would be bungled, misunderstood, or ignored. Ordinary people, people like you and me, were going to do this and do it badly. And if this didn't matter, then nothing mattered. The scenes of executions were gruesome, bizarre, and grimly comic. The reality was that imagined in *Bend Sinister, Invitation to a Beheading,* and *Laughter in the Dark,* all written more than fifty years earlier.

I didn't want to think about this conundrum within the confines of the law or another academic discipline—sociology, anthropology, psychology—although I admired what they did and saw the similarity between that work and my preoccupations. I wanted to write about what laws like those imposing capital punishment did to the people whose job it was to carry them out—not the police officers, not the prosecutors or defense attorneys, or even the judges, they had already been turned into stock characters in the entertainment culture—but the people who got up in the morning and went to work and found this was now their job. Actually, people like me. What did this do to the human spirit, and what did it do to the law itself? After all, the law is inseparable from the people who enact it and enforce it.

Already, just the fact of those blue regulations staring back at me was making me feel creepy, as was that I was spending almost every waking minute, and increasingly my nightmares, with thoughts and images of murder, capital punishment, and executions, as I was worrying about who, if anyone, should be killed by the state. It got so I could not walk out into the employee parking lot after dark. I began to notice that the defense attorneys who spent years representing murderers in capital cases tended to be either serious, practicing Catholics or religious Jews. But I had a job to do, too, and that job was trying to persuade a very reasonable court to at least wait to execute people, most of whom had without doubt committed unprovoked, inexcusable acts of murder, with intentionality, brutality, and cruelty, people who deserved to be called evil, if that word had any meaning. And this was something else, which could not be said at the office.

So I spent many months over the course of several years writing and revising *Technician*, until I could do no more with it, even though I was far from happy with it. No one wanted to publish it, but then I started getting notes from editors saying things such as, "This didn't win the prize, but two of the judges thought it should have." Eventually the piece did get published in TriQuarterly and by the Ontario Review Press. Now *Technician* is taught in some law school classes.

Technician accomplished several other tasks for me as a writer, in addition to pointing me away from the audience of courts and lawyers: It was an artistic tribute and nod of gratitude to Saul Bellow. The novel's structure was modeled upon *Seize the Day*, my favorite of Bellow's works. There seemed something fitting in attempting to lay that anguishing subject matter over a borrowed structure of great elegance. *Technician* was also a portrait of Trenton, New Jersey, the city where for fifteen years I worked but did not live, and a portrait of some of the people I worked with who lived there and considered the city their home. I did my best to avoid the melodrama everywhere in the subject. I didn't care if anyone else noticed that *Technician* followed the formal design of *Seize the*

Day; that was a satisfaction and a guidance for me alone. The art itself is an answer, even when it is frustratingly imperfect. I didn't realize that writing about Trenton was to be a warm up for writing about Chicago.

XII

I was brought back to a place where I could write fiction by a class on playwriting. Perhaps that is all that teaching in the arts has to do, or can do, create a space in the heart or head where something can grow, remind everyone in the room that art does matter, even when, or especially when, so many things are making noise and creating distractions as they crash down around us. By putting the teaching of the art of theater, and the art of writing, squarely in the university and art school curriculum we reaffirm that art is as necessary as physics, as important as history.

What schools and universities can do for artists is provide a safe haven, a quiet harbor where artists are nourished and protected. The most important role the university can play is in supporting those parts of the institution where the arts and their disciplines are valued, as well as practiced. Sometimes such institutions are exclusive, or repressive. In recent times, the American research university has been highly competitive, broad-based, internationally oriented, open to all views, all people devoted to learning and teaching. Therein lies its strength. All great civilizations have had as their foundation the library, the storehouse of knowledge, a place where the culture is respectfully preserved so that it may survive to the next generation, and, it is hoped, the next and the next and the next generation. The Internet hasn't changed that obligation.

One of the seven wonders of the ancient world was the Library at Alexandria. One of the wonders of our world is the computer and its miraculous connections. It is a game changer, just like penicillin and the birth control pill. But there still must be something to put in the library, no matter its physical confines. The need to preserve a record of who we are, how we lived, and what we believed and thought is primordial, unchanged. Technology alone can't do that without thought. The mindless archiving of the feed of the daily television news, or the preservation of everyone's e-mail is no solution. The most primitive societies make art; the most sophisticated, luxury driven, spoiled societies make art; need art; teach art.

The record of a civilization may come down to us as 55,000 Chinese scrolls walled up in one of a thousand Buddhist caves in Dunhuang in the western desert of China on the silk road. The testament that a culture leaves may be in crumbling books in trunks in Timbuktu. It may be in the photograph of a dancer in air, or in the retelling of a story whose ending everyone knows. New forms have to be created for new ideas, and for old ones. Or how will we capture the attention of an audience?

The challenge now for fiction writers, poets, and theater artists is to pull people's eyes and attention away from their screens, from the incessant clicks and beeps and those hard-edged images on the screen of the tiny phone. An audience is more than one person paying attention at the same time, unless it is the solitary reader. The magic of the Internet includes the hypnotizing blur of those tireless bouncing cartoons, and the bottomless well of pornography.

The Internet has and will continue to generate new forms of art, and theater artists and novelists will and do use these new images and technologies. The new-found possibility of reaching an audience of millions with the old and the new art is breathtaking. But the ability to reach people is not enough; someone has to have something to say that others want to see or hear.

Perhaps the Internet will force commercial television out of the mire of its obsessive trivialization and make it into the great educational medium it has never become. Why should anyone continue to be trapped by advertisements, when more entertaining content somewhere else can be found with a click? Just as our communal behavior has been forever altered by our interaction with these machines, so our art, and our teaching of it, is irrevocably changed and challenged. New art has been born in the new medium, just as our social behavior has been collectively and individually altered by our relationship with computers. Still, the basic human need for beauty, love, reflection, transcendence, meaning is unchanged. We remain beings who stare out the window and into one another's eyes, looking for the still point in the turning world.

Published books will survive, surprisingly, as books, for high culture, for low culture, for teaching and for history and politics. Books are efficient containers for culture, information, thought, and art. They last, they are easy to carry around. They can't be adulterated. And with a minimum of effort they have been and can continue to be preserved for hundreds of years. Writing will survive, drawing and singing will survive, even as the distribution of music and images and words is forever changed.

If art is going to survive, people do have to stop killing one another, on the small and large scale, and beating up on one another, on the small and large scale, and learn to look at each other and ask who is there. We never have stopped killing one another. The urge to kill seems as fundamental as the others, although heavily gendered. Every study of homicide over every century and society shows men killing men as the dominant pattern, in peace and war. While we can analyze how and why and understand some part of that, we don't seem to be able to stop. We are the richest people to ever inhabit the earth, there are more of us to take care of than ever before, yet we have so few answers.

XIII

The real questions cannot be asked or answered alone, and they are asked most powerfully when we listen knowing that others are listening with us at the same time, in a darkened space, or in the quiet of a class. Then there comes that sense—irrational, foolish, evanescent—that we are serving something outside of ourselves, although artists don't like to talk about that either.

How now? What art thou?

A man, sir.

What dost thou profess? What wouldst thou with us?

I do profess to be no less than I seem, to serve him truly that will put me in trust, to love him that is honest, to converse with him that is wise and says little, to fear judgment, to fight when I cannot choose, and to eat no fish.

What art thou?

A very honest-hearted fellow, and as poor as the King.

If thou be'st as poor for a subject as he's for a king, that art poor enough. What wouldst thou?

Service.

Who wouldst thou serve?

You.

Dost thou know me, fellow?

No, sir; but you have that in your countenance which I would fain call master.

What's that?

Authority.

What services canst thou do?

I can keep honest counsel, ride, run, mar a curious tale in telling it and deliver a plain message bluntly. That which ordinary men are fit for, I am qualified in, and the best of me is diligence. . . .

The essays here are reflections upon the art of the theater, adaptation, performance, writing, and life in the theater by some of the most innovative artists working today. They have been pushed and prodded into putting their thoughts into this unfamiliar form, the unstructured essay. This volume is testament to the vitality of theater in America, and to the vigor and discipline of the teaching theater arts in the university. It is a record of service, tradition, and innovation, and a tribute to the teaching arts. We would be so very much poorer without their diligence.

Frank Galati

Adapting *Kafka on the Shore*

1.

For many years I taught in the Department of Performance Studies at Northwestern University where there has been a long tradition of studying literary texts through performance. Fiction was my special interest as a student and teacher. Storytelling, the performance of fiction, was the focus of my teaching. One of the writers my students really connected with was Haruki Murakami. The six stories that comprise his *after the quake* afforded rich opportunities for both solo performances and group adaptations. It struck me that a full evening of theater might be made out of two or three of the stories. I tried several combinations but settled on the idea of a theater piece with interlocking parts made by braiding together two stories, the final two in the volume. Martha Lavey, artistic director of Steppenwolf Theatre, agreed to schedule a production and, with Murakami's permission, and thanks to the theater artists who collaborated to create it, *after the quake* played substantial runs in Chicago, New Haven, La Jolla, and Berkeley.

The stories held the stage. They played. Their interlocking parts were fascinating in performance. The hero of the final story "honey pie" is a young short-story writer. As his story unfolds (told by an omniscient narrator) he is working on a new story, "superfrog saves Tokyo," the penultimate story in the collection, also seen by the audience. Double-casting increased the sense of the interlocking pieces. The hero of one story becomes the narrator of the other, antagonist plays protagonist, and the two stories alternate back and forth like verse and chorus in a song. These cadences and the tensive pull between two separate stories, each working through the aftershock of the 1995 Kobe earthquake, proved compelling on stage.

Murakami writes in an easy contemporary style. His characters are real, and the world they inhabit is both familiar and strange. His novels are charged with theatrical jolts, adventure, mystery, nightmare violence, deep eroticism, and high comedy. These dimensions of Murakami's writing are the ingredients of good theater—but the proof of the pudding is in the dialogue. The dialogue scenes in Murakami's novels and stories are fraught with tension, deceptively simple, and very often where the action is:

"Sorry for dragging you out in the middle of the night," she said, "but I didn't know what else to do. I'm totally exhausted, and you're the only one who can calm her down. There was no way I was going to call Takatsuki . . ."

"Don't worry about me," he said. "I'm still awake till the sun comes up, and the roads are empty this time of night. It's no big deal."

"You were working on a story?"

Junpei nodded.

"How's it going?"

"Like always. I write 'em. They print 'em. Nobody reads 'em.

"I read them. *All* of them."

"Thanks. You're a nice person," Junpei said. "But the short story is on the way out. Like the slide rule. Anyhow, let's talk about Sala. Has she done this before?"

Sayoko nodded.

"A lot?"

"Almost every night. Sometime after midnight she gets these hysterical fits and jumps out of bed. She can't stop shaking. And I can't get her to stop crying. I've tried everything."

"Any idea what's wrong?"

Sayoko drank what was left of her beer, and stared at the empty glass.

"I think she saw too many news reports on the earthquake. It was too much for a four-year-old. She wakes up around the time of the quake. She says a man woke her up, somebody she doesn't know. Earthquake Man."

(From "honey pie," 2002)

This is a scene from a movie. It feels like a Pinter play or a Hemingway short story. The dialogue floats along a dark current. A moment of crisis brings together two characters with considerable history. In the aftermath of an epic disaster (five thousand people were killed in the Kobe earthquake in 1995), they are feeling psychic shock waves and the dreams of a child are stalked by a killer. All of this is caught in the cadences of speech, the ebb and flow of conversation feeling its way, improvised, with a gradual tensive slide to its close. The scene lands like the padded cursor on a Ouija board.

The process of adapting and directing *after the quake* was a rewarding and exhilarating collaboration with composer Andre Pleuss, lighting designer Jim Ingalls, set designer James Scheutte, costume designer Mara Blumenfield, stage manager Malcolm Ewen, and a talented ensemble of actors. Developing another, larger scale adaptation of Murakami's most recently translated novel *Kafka on the Shore* seemed crazy but irresistible.

I began work adapting the novel in the summer of 2007. Martha Lavey scheduled a major production to open the 2008–2009 season at Steppenwolf. We had several readings of various drafts of the script, extensive meetings to talk about design and music (the creative team remained together), and months of auditions organized and conducted by Steppenwolf casting director Erica Daniels. Though the novel is densely populated, our adaptation of *Kafka on the Shore* would be performed by an ensemble of ten actors. The "double casting" that worked so well in *after the quake* would also work well for *Kafka*. The reverberations have special impact with two particular characters.

In talking about where he gets his ideas for the characters he creates Murakami admits that some of his most outrageous characters have simply popped into his mind full-grown from he knows not where. Two of those characters, both global consumer icons, appear in *Kafka on the Shore*. "Johnnie Walker and Colonel Sanders are . . . performers who appear from the darkness." They are beings, says Murakami ". . . that live in the other world." Jay Rubin, translator of *after the quake*, says, "Murakami has latched onto these familiar—even beloved—symbols of worldwide corporate penetration and imbued them with unimaginable powers of evil, violence, and depravity." It could be argued that both characters/commodities are bad for us even though we crave them.

Whatever they are and wherever they come from, it is because of them that, as Murakami says, "the story is able to move off in a new direction."

While I'm writing, I'm not thinking: I don't know if they are good or evil. I still don't know whether (Johnnie Walker) is good or evil. . . . What he does is surely evil, but I don't know how much of that is true. And Colonel Sanders? I have no idea what he's all about. Both of them give a kick to the flow of the story, help it to move along. Rather than whether they themselves are good or evil, the really big question for me is, What kind of direction do they give the story as they help it to move along? It may be that, depending on how you look at them, Colonel Sanders and Johnnie Walker are the same thing appearing with different faces. This is a very real possibility . . . I think the story would not have proceeded so successfully had those two icons not been present. I think too, though, that there are a lot of people out there who can't accept such things.

(Jay Rubin, interviews with Haruki Murakami, 2007)

Each of these corporate specters is the key to the crisis, the turning point, of a dramatic action in the novel. The crisis in a drama is that event which, more than any other, limits the direction of the action to its conclusion. Finding these strong spinal bones of dramatic action in a sprawling episodic novel is perhaps the most fundamental challenge in the adaptation of fiction for the stage. Johnnie Walker lures the novel's docile dim Mr. Nakata into his darkness and forces the old man to murder in order to reach the next "stage" of his journey. End of act one. In the second act Colonel Sanders is the agent of the action. Through him the magic entrance stone is found and the inexorable conclusion of the archetypal action is reached.

Murakami suggests that these two supersized characters "are the same thing appearing with different faces." This dimension of persona, mask, and performance is featured when the same actor plays both Johnnie Walker and Colonel Sanders. The actor's virtuosity links these archetypal figures in a thrilling way. Each has an exit line of theatrical bravado. The dying Johnnie Walker gasps his congratulations to his murderer for moving the story along and completing his mission: "That's the ticket, Mr. Nakata, wonderful! That's the stuff. You didn't hesitate. Well done." Colonel Sanders takes leave of the story with an analysis of Chekhov:

COLONEL SANDERS

What Chekhov was getting at was this: necessity is an independent concept. It has a different structure from logic, morals, or meaning. Its function lies entirely in the role it plays. What doesn't play a role shouldn't exist. What necessity requires *does* need to exist. That's what you call dramaturgy.

HOSHINO

I should thank you. For showing me where the stone was.

COLONEL SANDERS

No need, just doing my job. Just consummating my function.

COLONEL SANDERS presses a button on the head of his walking stick. He descends below the stage floor with the rattle and grind of a freight elevator . . .

(production draft, 2008)

These two characters bifurcate the action of the story. For me they were keys to the discovery of a play, hiding in plain sight, between the pages of Murakami's panoramic novel.

2.

Kafka on the Shore is a novel woven of two narrative strands; two stories unfold in alternating chapters. Two stories travel on parallel paths. They meet at the horizon line. *Kafka on the Shore* is a doppelganger novel. The word may be translated as "double-goer" and has been applied in literary criticism to the darker (as in shadowed) side of human character, an alter ego; "frequently the appearance of the (doppelganger) presages imminent death," (Bent's Readers Encyclopedia; Harpers). Nabokov is the author of numerous "doppelganger novels" (*Lolita* and *Pale Fire*, but also *Despair*). Melville's Bartleby and Conrad's Secret Sharer are doppelgangers. The doppelganger is the traveling companion of the self. Murakami's fifteen-year-old hero, who calls himself Kafka, after the storyteller of Prague, runs away from home. As he runs he listens to a voice in his head: his doppelganger. The voice—an echo of an echo—has a name, Crow, and a need to cheer the hero on. Crow is a goad and a prod; he lurks where fear lurks and rages. Crow ("kafka" in Czech) visits his alter ego with an invitation:

CROW

How about we play our game?

KAFKA

All right.

CROW

Okay, picture a terrible sandstorm. Get everything else out of your head. Sometimes fate is like a small sandstorm that keeps changing directions. You change direction but the sandstorm chases you. You turn again, but the storm adjusts. Over and over you play this out, like some ominous dance with death just before dawn. Why? Because this storm isn't something that blew in from far away, something that has nothing to do with you. The storm is you. Something *inside* of you. So all you can do is give in to it, step right inside the storm, closing your eyes and plugging up your ears so the sand doesn't get in, and walk through it, step by step. There's no sun there, no moon, no direction, no sense of time. Just fine white sand swirling up into the sky like pulverized bones. That's the kind of sandstorm you need to imagine.

CROW opens a folding knife and hands it to KAFKA.

From now on—no matter what—you've got to be the world's toughest fifteen-year-old.

CROW withdraws. KAFKA turns to the audience.

KAFKA

Cash isn't the only thing I take from my father's study when I leave home. I take a folding knife with a really sharp blade. Made to skin deer. And an old photo of me and my big sister when we were little, the two of us on a beach somewhere. Who took this, and where and when, I have no clue. And how could I have looked so happy? And why did my father keep just this one photo? The whole thing is a total mystery. I must have been three, my sister nine. Did we ever really get along that well? I have no memory of ever going to the beach with my family. No memory of going *anywhere* with them. No matter, though—there is no way I'm going to leave this photo with my father. I don't have any photos of my mother. My father threw them all away.

KAFKA shoulders his backpack into the darkness.

(production draft 2008)

Kafka has no memory of happiness with his family, and Mr. Nakata, Kafka's surrogate in alternate chapters, has no memory at all. "Nakata's like a library without a single book." One hero sets off with his shadow and the other hero sets off in search of his shadow, though he begins looking for lost cats. Mr. Nakata encounters an old tomcat at the start of his journey and tells him he had an accident when he was nine years old.

CAT

What sort of accident?

NAKATA

I had a high fever for about three weeks. I was unconscious the whole time. And when I finally woke up, I couldn't remember a thing.

CAT

But you found yourself able to talk with cats.

NAKATA

That's correct.

CAT

Your problem, though . . .

NAKATA

Problem?

CAT

Your problem is your shadow. Your problem is your shadow is a bit—how should I put it? *Faint*.

NAKATA

I see . . .

CAT

Your shadow looks like half of it got separated from you.

NAKATA

Really?

CAT

What I think is this: you should give up looking for lost cats and start searching for the other half of your shadow.

(production draft 2008)

Kafka's first encounter on his journey is with a chatty young hairdresser he meets on a bus. She is bursting with half-remembered aphorisms, one about the doppelganger.

SAKURA

". . . in traveling, a companion," as the saying goes.

KAFKA nods.

SAKURA

How does that end?

KAFKA

How does what end?

SAKURA

After "a companion," how does it go? I can't remember. I never was very good at Japanese.

KAFKA

"In life, compassion."

SAKURA

"In traveling, a companion, in life, compassion." So what does that really mean? In simple terms?

KAFKA thinks.

The most immediate if not palpable experience of the doppelganger in what we call "real life" is our own reflection in a mirror. We see outselves, our various selves, in a glass darkly. This out-of-body routine warms us up for the reflections, representations of self and doppelgangers in stories and on stage. You could argue that Shakespeare's use of soliloquy is a theatrical metaphor of the hero before his glass reflecting, and of course we, the audience, are his reflection. We are his interiority in performance.

Shakespeare, naturally, made spectacular use of twins, doubles, and doppelgangers in his plays. It seems that the theater is the perfect host for a party of multiple selves. Throw gender and disguise into the mix and you find yourself in a hall of mirrors: a theatrical funhouse.

We've observed that one actor may play multiple roles (Johnnie Walker/Colonel Sanders) but one character may be played by multiple actors (Kafka/Crow). Our hero is bodied forth by two actors. The narration of the Kafka chapters in the novel is double-voiced: Kakfa tells his story in the first person. Crow tells his story in the second person. On stage in performance, the shift of grammatical person, from "I" to "you," has significant impact on the relationship between speaker and audience. When the ego pronoun speaks we the audience receive the message from the other. When the second person pronoun speaks we are the

(Front to back) Steppenwolf ensemble member Jon Michael Hill (Crow) and Christopher Larkin (Kafka) in *Kafka on the Shore* based on the book by Haruki Murakami, adapted and directed by ensemble member Frank Galati. Photo: Michael Brosilow.

other. We become the "you" and there is also a potential imperative, a command implied by the use of the second person.

In the most intimate scene in the novel—indeed, the primal scene, when mother and son mate—the erotic details of the transgression are articulated by Crow to Kafka. The hero's voice-over doppelganger is speaking to him in the second person while he is deflowered by an older woman, the beautiful and enigmatic Miss Saeki. For the reader this creates the illusion of an out-of-body experience, but in the theater it can have the opposite of an alienation effect because when Crow turns the searing light of his "you" upon us, the audience—then *we* become the hero, the addressee, at least in the grammatical construct, and we feel that we are performing the actions the doppelganger describes. We are the other self his persistent voice interrogates:

CROW
(to the audience)
Where does your responsibility begin here? Wiping away the nebula from your sight, you struggle to find where you really are.

But you can't locate the borderline separating dream and reality. You're face up, and Miss Saeki gets on top of you. You're helpless—she's the one who's in charge, she bends and twists her waist as if tracing a picture with her body. Her straight hair falls on your shoulders and trembles noiselessly, like the branches of a willow. Little by little you're sucked down into the warm mud. The whole world turns warm, wet, indistinct, and all that exists is your rigid glistening cock. You close your eyes and your own dream begins. It's hard to tell how much time is passing. The tide comes in. The moon rises. And soon you come. There's nothing you can do to stop it. You come over and over inside her. The warm walls inside her contract, gathering in your semen. All this while she's still asleep with her eyes open. She's in a different world, and that's where your seed goes—swallowed down into a place apart.

(production draft 2008)

At this moment of congress, this mysterious and powerful climax, the young hero releases himself into that other world, that region of dream only reached through the secret tunnels, caves, and conduits hidden in the bright light of the waking world.

And this penetration into the heart of darkness, articulated by our traveling companion, is manifest again at the conclusion of the novel when Miss Saeki, with Mr. Nakata's help, is released from her lived life and travels to the other side. There, deep in a mythic forest, young Kafka will find her again, but not before a final encounter with his doppelganger.

This "confrontation," a version of the "dark night of the soul," where the hero wrestles with his own demon, may be manifest in stage action that is not in the original novel. In our adaptation of *Kafka on the Shore*, the young hero's journey into the heart of darkness leads him to the threshold of the nether world. There he meets himself. Before he is allowed to pass he must do battle with his own violent nature. We staged this as a physical fight between Kafka and Crow. Kafka's mentor and friend Oshima (a transgendered guardian of the Komura library) drives him to a remote cabin in the mountains. The police are looking for Kafka. They are investigating the brutal and mysterious murder of the boy's father. Before Oshima leaves Kafka he offers a clear warning—as if he suspects the boy may be ambushed by some prowling beast, the beast in the jungle, the beast within:

(Left to right) Christopher Larkin (Kafka) and Steppenwolf ensemble member Francis Guinan (Johnnie Walker) in *Kafka on the Shore* based on the book by Haruki Murakami, adapted and directed by ensemble member Frank Galati. Photo: Michael Brosilow.

OSHIMA

Be extra cautious if you go into the woods. If you get lost you'll never find your way out . . . there's another world that parallels our own, and to a certain degree you're able to step into that world and come back safely. As long as you're careful. But go past a certain point and you'll lose the path out. It's a labyrinth. Most definitely a risky business.

KAFKA

Sort of like Hansel and Gretel.

OSHIMA

Right—just like them. The forest has set a trap, and no matter what you do, no matter how careful you are, some sharp-eyed birds are going to eat up all your crumbs.

KAFKA

I promise I'll be careful.

OSHIMA steps into the shadows. KAFKA heads off into the woods. A CLAP OF THUNDER seems to push CROW up from below the stage. KAFKA turns and faces his double.

CROW

Try imagining Miss Saeki as your mother, leaving you behind when you were four.

CROW and KAFKA stalk one another in a wide circle.

KAFKA

Why would Miss Saeki have done that? Why does she have to hurt me, to permanently screw up my life?

KAFKA lunges for CROW. They wrestle to the floor.

CROW

It's not that your mother didn't love you. She loved you very deeply. The first thing you have to do is believe that. That's your starting point.

Fists fly. The two boys are locked in combat.

KAFKA

But she abandoned me. I'm finally beginning to understand how much that hurt. How could she do that if she really loved me?

CROW begins to get the upper hand.

CROW

That's the reality of it. It did happen. You were hurt badly, and those scars will be with you forever. I feel sorry for you, I really do. It's not too late to recover. You're young, you're tough. You're adaptable. You can move on. But for her that's not an option. The only thing she'll ever be is lost.

CROW pins KAFKA to the floor, then releases him and slips into the darkness.

Crow is Kafka's shadow in the novel. On stage he can be an eloquent presence, even when only a silent sentinel. He can also serve as a conduit between the two parallel stories. The reader/audience learns Kafka's father has been murdered at the same time that Kafka does. We know, because we were there, that Kafka had a mysterious blackout and regained consciousness to find himself covered with blood.

CROW

Man alive, how'd you get that blood all over you? What the hell were you doing? But you don't remember a thing, do you? Your memory's frozen shut. No wounds on you, though, that's a relief.

KAFKA

No real pain, either—

CROW

except for that throbbing in your left shoulder.

KAFKA

So the blood's gotta be from somebody else,

CROW

not you.

KAFKA

Somebody else's blood.

(production draft 2008)

In the parallel world of the other story, both audience and reader witness Mr. Nakata provoked into killing Johnnie Walker. As we observed, this is the culminating action of our constructed first act. Mr. Nakata is lured into Johnnie Walker's dramaturgical trap by a dog. "The dog's eyes were totally expressionless and the skin around its mouth turned up, exposing wicked-looking fangs. Its teeth had blood stuck on them, and slimy bits of meat matted around its mouth. Its bright red tongue flicked out between its teeth like a flame." (p. 113 *Kafka on the Shore*, Knopf, 2005, Philip Gabriel trans.) The dog barks at Nakata: "Stand up!" and Nakata follows him to Johnnie Walker's lair.

Early in the rehearsal process it struck me that there would be some value in having the actor playing Crow also play the talking dog who brings Nakata to the evil Johnnie Walker, "infamous cat killer," father figure, and doppelganger of the meticulous and equally methodical Adolf Eichmann. (Kafka has randomly picked out a book on Eichmann. He reads it late into the night at the library.) Dog is in the thrall of the butcher Walker, but, if the dog is embodied by Crow, then Kafka's other self is placed at the scene of the crime. And to firmly seal the link it is Crow/Dog who hands Kafka's folding knife to Mr. Nakata, the same knife used to skin deer stolen from Kafka's father by Crow and given to Kafka in the opening scene. So some part of Kafka is an accomplice in the killing and the murder weapon is a prop that is transported by Crow from one zone of the story to another. The transition for the actor from Crow to Dog is a stunning theatrical transformation. Kafka is summarizing the first week of his sojourn in Takamatsu for the audience:

KAFKA
I spend seven days visiting the library and reading. Every night in my room at the hotel I jot down what I did that day in my diary, read a little and then it's lights out at eleven. Sometimes I masturbate before going to sleep.

CROW
But on the evening of the eighth day—as had to happen sooner or later—this simple centripetal life is blown to bits.

CROW howls wildly and barks. KAFKA dashes into the darkness and MR. NAKATA remains frozen in a shaft of light. CROW transforms himself into DOG. He charges on all fours over to NAKATA who falls to the ground in panic.

DOG
Stand up!

NAKATA
Oh my. This dog is talking!

DOG

Follow me.

(production draft 2008)

In the labyrinth of mirrors, doubles multiply and a mythic destiny is achieved: the accursed progenitor is (unknowingly) vanquished. The prize is his queen who takes the young hero, her son, to bed. In the end the queen swings by a rope to the "other side" and the young hero, now in the know, is led off to finish junior high. *Kafka on the Shore* steps in the footprints of another story: the story of Oedipus.

Story is the engine that drives theater art. Shakespeare drew from other literary sources; so did Greek dramatists. Play structures vary widely and often are crafted from non-dramatic literary modes. Adapting works of narrative fiction for the stage, it is suggested, is a matter of excavation, of editing, of removing everything that is *not* a play so that what's left, probably most of it dialogue, can be "bodied forth" by the actors on stage. Of course some narrative works are better suited to stage adaptation than others. Novels tend to be long and sprawling, abundant often in descriptive detail, analysis of character, and action, anchored in the persona, and from the point of view, of the narrator. The theater, by contrast, craves action, velocity, momentum, inexorable forward motion. Reading seems to imply getting comfortable, sitting back and relaxing, receiving form and story, taking it all in. Theater art, on the other hand, implies turbulence, sitting on the edge of the seat, being wary, suspicious, always on the *qui vive*. The fun of theater is filling in the blanks. Suspecting or guessing the outcome. Knowing beyond the knowledge of the hero or even the play. We may derive that same fun from reading but in the theater, in the now of time, we are receiving the story in a group of others and our silence, laughter, murmurs, gasps, or expressed impatience are all part of an energized effort to concentrate and understand what is before us.

In a social construct, like an audience at a play, we don't have the time, frankly, or the patience to endure lengthy description of scene or nuanced analysis of character and theme. We don't want abundance so much as essence. We often get the idea and want to get on with it—see what happens next. In theater we may be fascinated by the "photographic" representation of social reality like a room, but we are ever ready to have that reality swept away and replaced by another. Does the play only stay in this room? I hope it *moves*. How can it move if it stays here?

Let's say the curtain rises on an empty room. There are two doors and a window set into its three walls. Before the appearance of a human being we are speculating about the space before us. Of course both doors will be used. One must open into a closet. The other does not lead off-stage into the wings but to other, unseen rooms in this represented house. The window looks out upon rooftops overhung by a full paper moon. What makes this room drama and each portal alive with suspense is the expectation of who or what might be behind those doors and what human destiny may be played out in this closed-up domestic space. Where we are as spectators when the story begins is in the middle of a world already in motion, rolling to some uncertain destination.

In adapting fiction for the stage one goal would be to reduce the sense of a retrospective view and give the audience a sense that something real is alive now before them, caught in a "situation," tangled in a problem, and heading for some collision with the light, with revelation and possible redemption. The difficulty with an epic narrative is not only the frequent use of the past tense (done before it's begun) but the tremendous energy and effort it takes to get the ball rolling. Square one is a hard place to start. Great drama rarely begins at square one. Susanne Langer reminds us that the temporal condition of narrative is memory and the temporal condition of drama is destiny.

But memory and the act of putting back together, re-membering a narrative dis-membered, fragmented by time, is the implied modality of all imaginative literature including fantasy and dystopia. Nineteen Eighty-Four was once the future, but for George Orwell it was an act of re-membering, of going back, we might say, to the past. The Glass Menagerie announces itself as a memory play and Romeo and Juliet begins in doomed retrospect:

> Two households, both alike in dignity,
> In fair Verona where we lay our scene,
> From ancient grudge break to new mutiny,
> Where civil blood makes civil hands unclean.
> From forth the fatal loins of these two foes
> A pair of star-crossed lovers take their life;
> Whose misadventured piteous overthrows
> Doth with their death bury their parents' strife.
> The fearful passage of their death-marked love,
> And the continuance of their parents' rage,
> Which, but their children's end, naught could remove,
> Is now the two hour's traffic of our stage.

Why would Shakespeare spill the beans at the outset? Why tell the audience that the story is ended before it's begun? Wallace Steven says "Death is the mother of beauty." The shadow of death in Shakespeare's love story makes the beauty of the lovers' youth and passion all the more exquisite and heartbreaking. Truth be told, in a sense all love is doomed by time and the grave. So some plays begin in retrospect and some novels jump-start.

The story of Oedipus, told and retold in numerous versions around cultural campfires all over the world, is, in Jean Cocteau's words, an infernal machine. It presents a clockwork nesting of gears and cogs, turning, grinding, and finally chewing up the hero. Momentum, velocity, inexorable forward motion are the essence of Greek drama and Sophocles's version of the Oedipus story explodes onto the stage in full cry, mid-crisis, and thrillingly close to its conclusion.

Something deep in the legend of Oedipus, upon which Sophocles based his play, profoundly struck the playwright. The jolt of inspiration from that earlier source resulted in a work of musical theater, conceived for performance and aimed perhaps at the public reaffirmation of two fundamental taboos, incest, and patricide: a reaffirmation through the catharsis of an imitated action witnessed by the community. A bolt from the blue must have brought the Sophocles play to Freud's mind while he was deeply engaged in the exploration of social taboos and the human unconscious. He saw the story of Oedipus as the template for everyone. His famous essay "The Oedipus Complex" offers Jocasta's own words from the play as proof of its universal truth.

> Why should the thought of marrying your mother make
>   You so afraid?
> Many men have slept with their mothers in their dreams.
>   Why worry? See your dreams for what they are—
>   nothing, nothing at all
> Be happy, Oedipus
>   (*Oedipus The King*, Stephen Berg and Diskin Clay, trans.)

So, was it a bolt from the blue that brought the story of Oedipus to Haruki Murakami's mind, resulting in the creation of his novel *Kafka on the Shore*? Did lightning strike with the notion that Murakami's huge novel might deliver his version of Oedipus in "two hours' traffic of our stage?"

Oliver Sacks's recent book *Musicophilia* (2008) begins with the story of a surgeon in his forties, who is struck by lightning and has a near-death, out-of-body experience. What makes the surgeon's story noteworthy is that some weeks after he survived the strike, the doctor became passionately interested, for the first time in his life, in classical music.

The enigmatic Miss Saeki of *Kafka on the Shore* is the author of a book about people in Japan who have survived lightning strikes. She is a librarian, but also a pianist and composer, the guardian of a precious collection of rare books by Japanese Tanka and Haiku poets. She is something of a spider-woman, a Jocasta figure, who lures Kafka into a terrifying labyrinth of voluptuous incest, farcical patricide, and meticulous genocide. The boy who calls himself Kafka keeps a journal. His favorite short story is "The Penal Colony," and he reveals to the reader that his father was struck by lightning when he was in college working part-time as a caddy at a golf course.

> One day he was following his golfer around the course when the sky suddenly changed color and a huge thunderstorm crashed down on them. They took refuge under a tree when it was hit by a bolt of lightning. This huge tree was split right in two. The golfer he was caddying for was killed, but my father, sensing something, leaped away from the tree in time. He got some light burns, his hair was singed, and the shock of lightning threw him against a rock. He struck his head and lost consciousness, but survived the ordeal with only a small scar on this forehead. It was after he recovered from his injuries that my father got serious about his career as a sculptor. As Miss Saeki went around interviewing people for her book, maybe she met my father. It's entirely possible. There can't be that many people around who've been struck by lightning and lived, can there?
>
> (*Kafka on the Shore*, p. 233)

Murakami has described his first inspiration to write a novel as a bolt from the blue, one afternoon at a baseball game. At the end of "honey pie" Junpei, the short-story writer, is improvising a tale about two bears for the four-year-old Sala. The bears are best friends.

> "They talked about *everything*. They traded know-how. They told each other jokes. Tonkichi worked hard at catching salmon, and Masakichi worked hard at collecting honey. But then one day, like a bolt from the blue, the salmon disappeared from the river."
>
> "A bolt from the blue?"
>
> "Like a flash of lightning from the clear blue sky," Sayoko explained. "All of a sudden without warning."

"All of a sudden the salmon disappeared?" Sala asked with a somber expression. "But why?"

("honey pie," 2002)

The answer to that question is buried deep in the personal relationship between Junpei and his best friend who is Sala's father. The girl's mother, Sayoko, has always been the love of Junpei's life, but that love went unexpressed and Junpei lost his love to his best friend. In the end, Sala's parents divorce and Junpei is united with Sayoko.

> "We should have been like this to begin with," she whispered after they had moved from the sofa to her bed. "But you didn't get it. You just didn't get it. Not till the salmon disappeared from the river."

The lightning bolt of inspiration drives the plot of the story.

MISS SAEKI

Kafka, I wrote a book on lightning once.

KAFKA

A book on lightning?

MISS SAEKI

I went all over Japan interviewing people who'd survived lightning strikes. It took me a few years. Most of the interviews were pretty interesting. A small publisher put it out but it barely sold. The book didn't come to any conclusion, and nobody wants to read a book that doesn't have one. For me, though, having no conclusion seemed perfectly fine.

(production draft, 2008)

The bolt of lightning produces a blinding flash of light. It burns an image in the mind's eye; it is an analogue of the imagination and in its blaze, without warning, is the shadow of an idea. It is this jolt of clarity that delivers to Kafka the true identity of this mysterious woman he loves so much. He asks her why she was interested in the topic of lightning.

MISS SAEKI

I'm not sure. I guess there was something symbolic about it. I came up with the idea and just started researching it. I was a writer then with no money worries and plenty of free time, so I could mostly do whatever sparked my interest.

KAFKA

When by father was young he worked as a caddy at a gold course and was hit by lightning. He was lucky to survive.

MISS SAEKI

A lot of people are killed by lightning on golf courses—big wide-open spaces, with almost nowhere to take shelter. Is your father also named Tamura?

KAFKA

Yes, and I think he was about your age.

MISS SAEKI

Was? Your father died?

KAFKA

Not long ago. Very recently, in fact.

MISS SAEKI

How did your father die?

KAFKA

He was murdered.

MISS SAEKI

You didn't murder him, did you?

KAFKA

No I didn't. I have an alibi.

MISS SAEKI

But you're not entirely sure?

KAFKA

I'm not sure at all.

MISS SAEKI

I don't remember anybody named Tamura. I didn't interview anybody by that name.

KAFKA

My father was in love with you, but couldn't get you back, or maybe from the beginning he couldn't really make you *his*. He knew that, and that's why he *wanted* to die. And that's also why he wanted his son—*your* son, too—to murder him. *Me* in other words . . . It's just a theory.

MISS SAEKI

In your theory, then, I'm your mother.

KAFKA

That's right. You lived with my father, had me, and then went away, leaving me behind. In the summer when I'd just turned four.

MISS SAEKI

And part of your theory is that your father and I met while I was researching the book, and as a result you were born.

KAFKA

Yes.

MISS SAEKI

That never happened. Your theory doesn't stand up.

(production draft 2008)

Kafka's theory links him to the ancient king of Thebes, the solver of riddles, the one chewed up in the infernal machine who screams.

LIGHT LIGHT LIGHT

never again flood these eyes with
your white radiance, oh gods,
my eyes. All, all
the oracles have proven true.
I, Oedipus, am the child

(p. 77 Oxford, 1978, Berg and Clay trans.)

The infernal machine, as Cocteau understood, is the story itself. The infernal machine, a torture device in Franz Kafka's "The Penal Colony" scores the violated commandment on the prisoner's flesh in bitter blood: "HONOR THY FATHER." Patricide is the crime and young Kafka is caught in a narrative machine that dooms him to repeat it because the course of action in *Kafka on the Shore* flows on the riverbed of Sophocles' play. Oedipus, too, is Kafka's doppelganger.

Kafka tells his friend Oshima the story of his blackout and of this uncertainty about this father's murder. Oshima responds:

Listen, Kafka. What you're experiencing now is the motif of many Greek tragedies. Man doesn't choose fate. Fate chooses man. That's the basic worldview of Greek drama. And the sense of tragedy— according to Aristotle—comes, ironically enough, not from the protagonist's weak points but from his good qualities. Do you know what I'm getting at? People are drawn deeper into tragedy not by their defects but by their virtues. Sophocles' *Oedipus Rex* being a great example. Oedipus is drawn into tragedy not because of laziness or stupidity, but because of his courage and honesty. So an inevitable irony results.

(*Kafka on the Shore*, p, 184)

Kafka goes on to reveal that ". . . a few years back my father had a prophecy about me." Oshima is curious; Kafka continues:

"More like a curse than a prophecy, I guess. My father told me this over and over. Like he was chiseling each word into my brain . . . *Someday you will murder your father and be with your mother.*"

(p.186)

The infernal machine has scored its curse on Kafka's back. Kafka quotes a note penciled in the book he has been reading about the infernal mechanic Adolf Eichmann.

"*In dreams begins responsibilities*, right?"
Oshima nods. "Yeats."
"So maybe I murdered him through a dream. Maybe I went through some special dream circuit or something and killed him."

(p. 188)

Korogi, a young women in Murakami's recent novel *After Dark*, has come in contact with the infernal machine.

Korogi pulls her shirt up, exposing her back. Impressed in the skin on either side of her backbone is a mark of some kind. Each consists of three diagonal lines like a bird's footprint and appears to have been made there by a branding iron. The scar tissue pulls at the surrounding skin. These are the remnants of intense pain.

(*After Dark*, p. 192)

Korogi offers this view of these remnants as a gift to a friend. In turn the friend reveals that her older sister had been sleeping for two months. Trading secrets, giving advice. Korogi says:

"Sometimes I feel as if I'm racing with my own shadow . . . but that's one thing I'll never be able to outrun. Nobody can shake off their own shadow."

But Korogi keeps on running and what keeps her running is memory:

> "You know what I think?" she says. "That people's memories are maybe the fuel they burn to stay alive. Whether those memories have any actual importance or not it doesn't matter as far as the maintenance of life is concerned. They're all just fuel. Advertising fillers in the newspaper, philosophy books, dirty pictures in a magazine, a bundle of ten-thousand-yen bills: when you feed 'em to the fire, they're all just paper. The fire isn't thinking, 'Oh, this is Kant,' or 'Oh this is the *Yomiuri* evening edition,' or 'Nice tits,' while it burns. To the fire, they're nothing but scraps of paper. It's the exact same thing. Important memories, not-so-important memories, totally useless memories: there's no distinction—they're all just fuel."
>
> (p. 193)

Shakespeare too compared human life to a fire "consumed with that which it was nourished by." Memories ignite the flame of the present moment. The gorgeous young prostitute encountered by Hoshino, Nakata's traveling companion in *Kafka on the Shore*, says "the pure present is an ungraspable advance of the past devouring the future. In truth all sensation is already memory." She is paraphrasing Henri Bergson. The present moment is a spark on the long fuse of our own personal nuclear weapon. The present moment is a kindred spirit on the highway of life. Kafka glances at his watch and turns to his traveling companion.

KAFKA

It's five-thirty already. Maybe we better be getting back on the bus.

SAKURA

Yeah I guess so. Let's go.

They do not move.

KAFKA

By the way, where are we?

SAKURA

I have no idea.

SAKURA cranes her neck and sweeps the place with her eyes.

SAKURA (con't.)

From the time I'm guessing we're near Kurashiki, not that it matters.

A rest area on a highway is just a place you pass through to get from here to there. What does it matter what it's called? . . . It's all pointless—assuming you try to find a point to it. We're coming from somewhere, heading somewhere else. That's all you need to know, right?

(production draft, 2008)

The audience is always at the intersection, the living moment through which the action of the play flows. In a way, the audience is keeping an appointment. "Meet me at the withered tree this evening. I'll try to be there around curtain time. Please wait. Ever your Godot."

Murakami's erudition is evident in all of his books no matter how plainly he writes. Allusions to myth, legend, music, literature, philosophy, and psychology abound. But he's a very popular writer. His embrace of the narrative and commodities of pop culture delights his fans. On stage in performance his writing casts a spell. Audiences engage on the battlefield of his imagination.

Martha Lavey

A Note on Frank Galati's *Kafka on the Shore* and Steppenwolf Theatre's New Play Initiative

Steppenwolf Theatre Company launched its 2008–2009 season, an exploration of *the imagination*, with the world premiere of *Kafka on the Shore*, based on the book by Haruki Murakami, adapted for the stage and directed by ensemble member Frank Galati. The production, featuring ensemble members Francis Guinan and Jon Michael Hill with Christine Bunuan, Gerson Dacanay, Mary Ann de la Cruz, Christopher Larkin, Aiko Nakasone, Andrew Pang, David Rhee and Lisa Tejero, ran from September 18 to November 16, 2008 in Steppenwolf's Downstairs Theatre at 1650 N. Halsted St. The design team included: James Schuette (sets), Mara Blumenfeld (costumes), James F. Ingalls (lights), Andre Pluess and Ben Sussman (original music and sound), and Joe Dempsey (fight choreography). Malcolm Ewen was the stage manager and Lauren V. Hickman was the assistant stage manager.

In the play, a young boy's coming of age parallels an old man's search for destiny in modern day Japan where the borders between everyday reality, dreams, and imagination are constantly crossed. In this world premiere adaptation of the popular novel, we encounter talking cats on the streets of Tokyo, World War II soldiers trapped in time, Colonel Sanders, and Johnnie Walker. The unexpected is experienced in this fantastical tale about waking up to one's own life.

Tony-Award-winner Frank Galati previously adapted and directed

Haruki Murakami's *after the quake* during Steppenwolf's 2005–2006 Season. This critically-acclaimed production went on to successful runs at Long Wharf Theatre, La Jolla Playhouse, and Berkeley Rep. Haruki Murakami, author of *The Wind-Up Bird Chronicles* and other novels, is an award-winning writer whose work has been translated into thirty-four languages.

Kafka on the Shore was developed as part of Steppenwolf's New Plays Initiative. Steppenwolf is recognized as a national leader in the development and production of new work for the American canon. Through this initiative, the company maintains ongoing relationships with writers of international prominence and rigorously discovers and supports the work of early and mid-career playwrights.

Committed to the principle of ensemble performance through the collaboration of a company of actors, directors, and playwrights, Steppenwolf Theatre Company's mission is to advance the vitality and diversity of American theater by nurturing artists, encouraging repeatable creative relationships, and contributing new works to the national canon. The company, formed in 1976 by a collective of actors, is dedicated to perpetuating an ethic of mutual respect and the development of artists through ongoing group work.

Steppenwolf has grown into an internationally renowned company of forty-two artists whose talents include acting, directing, playwriting, filmmaking, and textual adaptation.

The greatest challenge that Steppenwolf faces in order to thrive in the future is how to be the best conversation partner to our multigenerational audience. We are in the midst of our thirty-third season as an arts organization and we have developed over that thirty-three years a sophisticated, experienced ensemble of artists; a professional, seasoned staff; a dedicated and knowledgeable board of trustees; and an enviably intelligent and devoted audience. The growth of the Steppenwolf as an anchoring cultural institution in Chicago with a national and international reach has afforded us the infrastructure to create programming that reaches a diverse and knowledgeable audience.

The challenge in addressing our multigenerational audience is to speak to them in the manner most urgent and eloquent to their lives. The manner of that address is a negotiated language; a language inflected by the nuances of their historically and socially specific vocabularies. While we are rooted in the conviction that the shared space of theater, and the public square it engenders, creates a common language for human experience, the nuances of that conversation are informed by the technologies of storytelling particular to each generation. How does the contact of shared space shift with the revised technologies of social and artistic networking? How do we continue to maintain that shared space when young artists and audiences, raised on the technologies of the Internet, raised to regard themselves as the co-creators of their experience, meet in the theater? How do we find a gratifying common language through which to negotiate meaning?

We acknowledge that while we have proficiency in reaching our audiences that have matured in step with the lives of our artists and the life of our organization, we find ourselves less informed in our reach to younger artists and audiences. What is the delivery system that young artists (artists in their twenties and early thirties) want for their work? What is the conversation their age-cohort audiences want to have about the work and its articulation with their lives?

Further, what is the contract that these audiences want to create with their theater? The subscription series had been the model for that contract. But young audiences have less inclination to commit their time to a season of work, curated by the organization. They seek a co-creator status with the programming in their lives. What does that imply for the theater? A season subscription commits an audience to the unfolding of a conversation, a dialogue that is cumulative, that accrues meaning over time. Do younger audiences, trained to the rapidities of electronic communication, to the vast access to knowledge and experience afforded by the Internet (et al.) seek the long-arc conversation of a season's programming? How do they want to negotiate the shared space of theater? What sort of conversation do the artists and audiences of this age demographic want to have and how do they want to have it?

Our success in recent years in creating multiple streams of programming and in developing new work provides a store of institutional knowledge in approaching the collaboration with younger artists and audiences. We annually offer more than forty projects and over six hundred and thirty performances on our three stages that draw racially and culturally diverse, multigenerational audiences into the theaters year round.

In addition to the increased array of programming, we have been engaged in new play development in a rigorous way since the inception of our New Plays Lab in 1996; honoring this deep artistic and institutional commitment with an entire season of new work on the occasion of our thirtieth anniversary. As it happened, the final production of our twenty-ninth season was a new play by Bruce Norris that was quite provocative and stirred a controversy in the Chicago press about the use of child actors in the production. We decided that the controversy was something we should negotiate with our audiences and so increased the frequency of our post-show conversations. What we discovered from the experience of *The Pain and the Itch* was that our audiences were deeply appreciative of being taken into partnership in the negotiation of new work. Offered an opportunity to discuss the work, they registered a sophisticated intelligence in response to challenging material. We decided that we would henceforth offer post-show conversations after each performance.

The engagement with our audiences in conversation at our performances activated a larger sensibility within the theater about audience engagement generally. We undertook an engagement initiative, supported by the Wallace Foundation, to understand how our audiences articulate with our multiple programming streams and our artists. Our dialogue with our audiences works off many formats: audio slide shows, photo galleries, video pieces, show programs, blogs, e-mail, post-show discussions, pre-show events, *Backstage* magazine, podcasts, and through new media including YouTube and Facebook.

Our theater is committed to the model of conversation as the fundamental purpose of live performance. We are well-poised to expand that conversation to include the youngest artists and audiences in Chicago. The good fortune of our leadership position permits us the resources to situate ourselves as listeners: we want to hear what our young artists and audiences are saying about the theater they want and need in their lives and are passionate about supporting that voice.

By initiating a partnership with Northwestern University and by adapting our efforts to engage visiting theaters to be more responsive to their needs, we seek to make the platform of our theater more democratic, inclusive, and immediate. We open the platform knowing that we invite challenge, ambiguity, and unchartered processes into our institutional culture.

Steppenwolf's New Plays Initiative is generously sponsored by the Harold and Mimi Steinberg Charitable Trust, the Zell Family Foundation, the Andrew W. Mellon Foundation, the John S. and James L. Knight Foundation, and members of the Director's Circle.

Mary Zimmerman

Adapting Proust:
A Moment in the Red Room

Mary Zimmerman is a Professor of Performance Studies at Northwestern University and a member of the Lookingglass Theatre Ensemble, as well as an Associate Artist of the Goodman Theatre of Chicago. She directs her own adaptations primarily of ancient literature and she begins each production period with no script—writing each night in between the hours of rehearsal. Her work has been widely produced in the United States and overseas. In 2002 she won the Tony Award for the direction of her adaptation of Ovid's Metamorphoses. *In 1998 she directed a site-specific performance entitled* Eleven Rooms of Proust *that was specifically cited by the MacArthur Foundation committee when it awarded her a MacArthur Fellowship soon after. Recently, with her longtime collaborative design team, Dan Ostling (sets), Mara Blumenfeld (costumes), and T. J. Gerckens (lights) she has directed two operas for the Metropolitan Opera,* Lucia di Lammermoor *and* La Sonnambula. *That creative team's production of* The Arabian Nights *is touring in 2008 and 2009 to Berkeley, Kansas City, and Chicago at Lookingglass Theatre.*

I have spent most of my time in the theater adapting old texts derived from even more ancient oral tales, texts such as *The Odyssey, The Book of One Thousand Nights and One Nights, Jason and the Argonauts,* the Chinese epic *The Journey to the West,* and various myths and fairy tales.

Despite the challenges in representation these non-dramatic texts pose for the theater director—challenges I love, such as flying carpets and camels, transmutations from person to bird, epic battles and storms at sea, genies and monsters and the like—they have nevertheless always seemed to me obvious choices for the theater because their original form was oral. It is in their nature, part of their conception, to live in the air, to be told aloud.

But there is one non-dramatic text I've worked with extensively in the theater that is altogether different, and that is Proust's *In Search of Lost Time*. It is not ancient, it was never an oral tale, and it contains no fantastical or epic events. I cannot think of another text that is so *textual*, so bound to its print form. Its sentences are unspeakably long, its ideas so intricate the reader must often retrace his steps. The plot is glacial in pace but not in weight and although there is some dialogue it is neither frequent nor particularly persuasive. Most challenging of all, its almost exclusive concern is the unspoken, invisible, interior life of a person. Its method is to record the smallest of human interactions—a glance, an interrupted phrase, a movement of the hand—and then to dwell on these moments for pages; seeing the thing first one way and then another, taking it through thought after thought, metaphor after metaphor, and finally deducing from it a general rule of human behavior. All of this conspires against an evening in the theater.

So how to embody this text in the gross, material, real-time world of the stage where things must be seen as well as heard? Where the "shot" for the audience is most often a wide angle and not the intense close-up so prevalent in this book? And further, why bother? Is the novel not enough? I could answer that the constant metaphor in the novel, the constant comparison of one thing to another (and then another and another), shares something with the entire theatrical enterprise, whose very existence depends on one thing standing in for another—but then, almost every form of artistic representation has this in common. The more honest answer is that I couldn't help it. My obsession with this particular text is deep, and all my efforts at adaptation are driven by a purely personal desire for an ever-increasing intimacy with a text that I can only achieve through the sustained labor and concentration that adaptation and staging requires. I want to memorize, clothe, and accompany a text. I want to *see* it, and I want others to see it. I want to haul it into three dimensions so that I may dwell inside it for a while. In short, I want to give it a body that I may love it all the more entirely.

Whatever the origins or futility of the task, I've created two distinct theater pieces based on Proust. Neither uses a direct representational approach; neither seeks to "dramatize" the characters and plot of *In Search of Lost Time*, but both bring the language of the book to the stage. The first piece is a one-person show called M. *Proust*, based on the memoir of Proust's indefatigable housekeeper Celeste Albaret. It interlaces selections from the novel with passages from the memoir in a way common to many one-person shows based on literary figures. Although I am fond of this piece, it is not particularly innovative in approach and its adaptive process is apparent. The second piece is a site-specific performance called *Eleven Rooms of Proust*.

The first production of *Eleven Rooms* took place in 1998, in an old mansion on the shores of Lake Michigan. Two years later I staged a second production in a vast, empty, three-story former factory and warehouse in an industrial neighborhood of Chicago. In both cases audiences entered the Proust House (as we called it) every forty minutes, six times a night in groups of fifteen (in the mansion production) or thirty (in the factory). When one audience was stepping up to the third and final floor of the space, the next was filing in on the first. They moved through a series of rooms where they were presented with vignettes—text and images—from all seven volumes of the novel, mostly centered on Swann's love of Odette and the parallel love of the narrator for Albertine. The mansion audiences witnessed scenes in through windows to the outdoors, in a library and stairwell, a hallway, foyer, and attic. The factory audiences saw scenes on stairs and in hallways as well, and in elevator shafts, a loading dock, and in vast colonnaded rooms 150 by 85 feet as well as claustrophobic spaces 10 by 15 feet. The show was not an installation; audiences were not free to wander or linger; they were guided and prodded by various live narrators and a bilingual recorded text that mixed instructions in the form of a French lesson, music, repeated fragments of the text, conversation about the text, and so on.

Eleven Rooms of Proust remains one of the most complete theatrical experiences of my life. The entire production was a dream of collaboration and organic development. All of our rehearsals were on site, all of the designers and all the cast were present at every rehearsal. I went into the project, as I always do, without a script, and the space led the adaptation; the various rooms suggested texts, images, and possibilities for staging. Instead of prettily staging something and then calling my lighting designer John Culbert to come look at it and light it, John lit the architecture of the space, created something dynamic and mysterious for the space, and I staged into and out of the light, using the text that I thought most appropriate, most related to where we were.

In order to give an example of one passage of text passing into one moment of performance, I will dwell, in a close up, Proust-like sort of way, on just one room of the eleven in the second production, paying particular attention to how the image arose and how it was shaped by the space, the text, the experiences of the creative team.

The Red Room

With the warehouse, our approach in terms of design was different than with the mansion. The mansion somewhat resembled the world of the novel insofar as it was old, grand, and decorative, and yet it was actually of the wrong period and country. It was almost too closely representational without being accurate. I was more excited by the warehouse because its physical reality was so starkly different from that of the novel and no one could think we were trying to pass one space off as the other. I thought that this text and these characters in their old-fashioned clothes set in the grim, gray industrial warehouse would be extremely dynamic visually and that the space would become unmistakably psychological rather than "real."

There was a single, windowless, interior room in the warehouse, set inside a much larger room. Cramped, filthy, and pitch-dark, it contained, set close to its far wall, a strange, corroded metal object: a sort of three-sided box, perhaps five by five feet and eighteen inches deep. A sort of miniature stage on tall legs. In its back wall, three-quarters of the way up, there was a torn, jagged hole. This box within a box had an ominous, almost tortured air, an air of confinement and unhappiness, and it suggested to me the shape of Swann's obsessive love for Odette, the cramped space to which his thoughts have become confined, the terrible narrowness of his life. I had already had the thought that it might be beautiful to make one room of the performance unlike any other by giving it some startling element of artificiality; by saturating it entirely with some bright color, for instance, while the rest of the warehouse remained raw and untreated as we found it. This discrete interior room seemed ready made, and to paint it lurid red seemed right: a sign of the wounded heart which has completely overtaken Swann's life, eliminating every other possibility; a torn red heart in the heart of the "Proust House."

We were meeting about the show one night in an old pizza parlor on the south side of Chicago when I noticed that almost every inch of our wooden booth was covered with years' worth of graffiti. I thought: what if, when the audience first entered our red room, the light would be so low that nothing would be visible but the interior of the metal box with Swann already inside, dressed in tails and top hat, illuminated by fluorescent light. Then, as the scene unfolded, a bare lightbulb above the narrator would illuminate and grow in intensity until the audience slowly became aware that on every surface of the room, the walls, the floor, the ceiling, the vents and wiring, in every size and shape, scrawled at random or formed in meticulous patterns, was a single word endlessly repeated: Odette.

My set designer Dan Ostling and I undertook to do the writing, and it became a singular addiction. We could never fill the room enough, never write enough. We went to the room at every opportunity, even continuing to work on it long after the show had opened, visiting the room in between audiences. All members of the cast and team helped out from time to time, but no one beside us could stand it in there for long. I began to write "Odette" hundreds of times in the form of paragraphs, divided into sentences with punctuation and paragraph breaks, quotation marks and headings, as though there were an actual text or a language entirely comprised of one word. Dan made elaborate, graphic patterns, and wrote minutely in places nearly or completely invisible to the audience, writing down the wire of the single incandescent light-bulb, for instance, or inside the doorjamb. The act of representing an obsession became one, and our brains, like Swann's, were as inscribed as the walls with Odette.

The action of the scene was simple. The audience is guided by the taped instructions into the room and the door is closed and locked behind them. It is dark. Then the fluorescent light near Swann flickers on. The narration, spoken by a woman in late-nineteenth-century dress begins. As she speaks, the incandescent bulb hanging above her illuminates and grows in strength. The writing on the walls becomes apparent. The growing light also illuminates a winged, naked figure lying on the warehouse floor beneath the box. Visible through the jagged hole in the back wall of the box there is a small, framed entomological display hanging on the red wall of the room. The narration and action are continuous; neither pauses for the other. Swann's movements are slow, effortful and pained.

> Narrator:
> Even when he could not discover where Odette had gone when she left him,
>
> [Swann looks out towards the audience, then rises from his little stool. He cannot stand fully upright. He begins to move the stool slowly to the other side of the box.]
>
> It would have sufficed him, to alleviate the anguish which he then felt, and for which her presence, the joy of being with her, was the sole cure (a cure which in the long run served to aggravate the disease, but at least brought temporary relief to his sufferings), it would have sufficed him,
>
> [He sits down on the other side of the box in profile to the audience. He stares straight ahead.]
>
> if only Odette had allowed it, to remain in her house while she was out, to wait for her there until the hour of her return. But she would not;
>
> [He looks towards the audience, then slowly stands up and moves the stool back to its original position and sits down.]
>
> he had to return home; he forced himself, on the way, to form various plans, ceased to think of Odette; he even succeeded, while he

undressed, in turning over some quite happy ideas in his mind; and it was with a light heart,

[Swann rises again, moves the stool again to the other side of the box.]

buoyed with the anticipation of going to see some favorite work of art the next day, that he got into bed

[Swann sits down, but then removes his hat and half sinks onto the floor of the box, uncomfortably.]

and turned out the light; but no sooner, in preparing himself for sleep, did he relax the self-control of which he was not even conscious—so habitual had it become—than an icy shudder convulsed him

[The figure on the floor beneath the box convulses, slightly.]

and he began to sob. He did not even wish to know why, but wiped his eyes and said to himself with a smile:

Swann:
This is delightful; I'm getting neurotic.

Narrator:
After which he felt a profound lassitude at the thought that, next day, he must begin afresh

[Swann puts on his hat, arises and moves his stool again. He sits.]

his attempts to find out what Odette had been doing, must use all his influence to contrive to see her. This compulsion to an activity without respite,

[He moves the stool.]

without variety,

[He moves the stool.]

without results, was so cruel a scourge that one day,

[Swan touches his abdomen.]

noticing a swelling on his stomach, he felt genuinely happy at the thought that he need no longer concern himself with anything further,

[He sits.]

that his malady was now going to govern his life, to make a play-thing of him, until the not-distant end. And indeed if, at this period, it often happened that, without admitting it to himself,

[*He moves the stool to the other side.*]

he longed for death, it was in order to escape not so much from the intensity of his sufferings

[*He moves the stool back.*]

as from the monotony of his struggle.

[*Swann continues to move his stool from one side to the other, sitting momentarily each time, as the audience leaves.*]

The winged figure below the box exists nowhere in Proust and is entirely personal for me. Eros appeared in my play *Metamorphoses*, naked, blind, winged, and holding a golden arrow in a story about the triumph of love. Here the very same wings and arrow appear—not copies of the old props, but the old props themselves—filthy and broken. I was marking for myself a change in my life, a change in my experience of love. The figure lies beneath Swann, below the level of his consciousness, unseen by him yet clearly connected to him by the spasm of remembering both figures feel at the same moment. His white, sullied wings form a glancing pun off Swann's name. He is a filthy, broken part of Swann, the burden in his heart that tethers him to this pointless motion, that will not let him rest. He is the double of Swann, the spirit of him, outside the body, trampled on, forgotten, but not lost.

The little entomological display hung on the wall of the red room and visible through a jagged hole in the back of Swann's metal box has no literal place in Proust either. It is something Dan and I came across in a shop near the performance site when we were looking for something else, and it seemed to want to be in the show. Collections are forms of obsession and the butterflies, emblematic of transformation and useless beauty, are pinned up for our inspection, in much the same way that Proust arrests his characters for long pages while he minutely inspects (or makes?) the meaning of a moment. In the room, the framed display outside the metal box figures as the work of art in the gallery that Swann wants to go and see but which lies beyond his capability to engage. It is a mirror of his own condition, as he is on display in a box himself, for us.

No one could mistake *Eleven Rooms of Proust* for an attempt to represent the entirety of the novel. Instead it concentrates, Proust-like, on a few small, fragmentary moments of the whole and asks the audience to dwell on them long enough that the moments begin to blossom, to change under inspection, to multiply in meaning. In each room, the presented image undergoes a complication and deepening through its own small changes and the unfolding narrative accompanying it and, above all, through the attention paid to it. It becomes one thing and then another and then another; and just as the audience slowly becomes aware of the inscribed text on the walls of the red room, so its awareness of the text of the Search itself is heightened. All adaptation of text into performance image is simultaneously grossly reductive and spectacularly enriching. A friend of mine captured the spirit of the Proust House best, I think, when he described it by referring to a Disney ride, "It's exactly like The Pirates of the Caribbean only you're sobbing the entire time."

Note

Eleven Rooms of Proust was originally co-produced by Northwestern University and About Face Theatre in 1998. The 2000 production was co-produced by About Face, Lookingglass, and Goodman Theatres.

Paul Edwards

Into the Abyss:
Adapting *Madame Bovary*

Part of the price Flaubert paid for celebrity was a string of requests from Paris theaters "eager to stage *Madame Bovary*" and cash in on the novelist's *succès de scandale*. Biographer Geoffrey Wall reports that one theater merely wanted to use the title, while retaining the freedom to devise its own story and script. Two other "unofficial versions" reached the variety stage. "One of them sang comic songs and the other one gossiped about her love affairs. Flaubert saw them both—and was not amused." Adaptation of his work into any other medium could make the novelist "frantic": "It was hardly worth the trouble using so much art to leave everything vague," he wrote in reaction to the prospect of publishing *Salammbô* with illustrations, "if some clod is going to come along and destroy my dream with his stupid precision."[1]

As a longtime practitioner of an art of stupid precision, I find myself wondering along with Flaubert why I ever wanted to disturb the vagueness of his dream. The first time I tried was in the summer of 1987, when sixteen student actors at Northwestern University joined me in a project of insane-sounding ambition and complexity: in seven short weeks we staged as much of Flaubert's *Madame Bovary* as we could squeeze into a serial of three two-and-a-half-hour episodes. The following summer, I brought a three-hour reduction of this script to a small playhouse on Forty-second Street in Manhattan, for production by a fledgling company of Equity actors. The *New York Times* reviewer found the parts better than the whole. The narrated play was "an amusing intellectual exercise, but only up to a point": "when the story turns tragic it merely leaves us frustrated and puzzled." Inevitably, the reviewer explained his dissatisfaction with the play through an exercise in "fidelity criticism" (as film scholars call it), by offering a short list of the novel's pleasures that defy translation to another medium.[2]

Perhaps I should have learned my lesson and stopped there. For another two decades, however, the novel accompanied me into performance classrooms, where it provided the basis for student adaptations of various lengths and degrees of irreverence. Adapting *Madame Bovary* became a project without limits. In diverse settings, I practiced a continual, probably unfinalizable rewriting upon pastiche translations of this astonishing old book. My most recent revision took the form of a new three-hour script, which I produced on Northwestern's campus in the winter of 2006.

My frequent return to the novel can be viewed as a desire to repeat it (though hopefully not in the compulsive way that psychoanalysis theorizes), for indeed, questions about repetition live at the heart of my interest in *Madame Bovary*. I wonder first of all whether any performance medium can find stylistic equivalents for the novel's representation of repetitive human behavior; my search for such equivalents in successive productions has led me to appropriate and modify extreme styles, such as that of a museum performance I describe below. I wonder as well whether a performance's exact quotation of a source text constitutes a repetition of that text; among the lessons learned from a 1991 film adaptation, much admired for its fidelity, was the realization that interpretive gaps inevitably open between an appropriated literary text and the competing signs of the new text that performs it. Finally I wonder whether an adaptation constitutes a repetition of any sort. From the example of my own work, I argue that adaptation is neither a repetition nor a neat, one-time-only transformation of a single source, but an ongoing and broadly comprehensive activity. The process of adaptation provides a gathering place for multiple sources and influences, and a progression of fresh contexts for creative reinvention. In saying this, I align myself with a growing body of recent theory about adaptation.

Theoretical

How do we read an adaptation? If we begin by measuring the adaptation against the achievement of a well-known source, whose cultural capital it poaches, we read it as a project doomed to failure. In the growing literature of "adaptation studies," scholars have demanded a move beyond fidelity criticism, as it has been practiced for half a century in a rich but "ancillary" area of film scholarship. In his introduction to the anthology *Film Adaptation* (2000) James Naremore calls for the replacement of fidelity criticism by "a general theory of repetition": "The study of adaptation needs to be joined with the study of recycling, remaking, and every other form of retelling in the age of mechanical reproduction and electronic communication," if it is to "move from the margins to the center of contemporary media studies." Robert Ray, one of Naremore's contributors, is especially harsh in characterizing how scholars "persist in asking . . . the same unproductive layman's question (How does the film compare with the book?)" and "getting the same unproductive answer (The book is better)." Yet contributor Robert Stam, while rejecting fidelity criticism in favor of a more dialogical and intertextual model, continues to practice a complicated form of it. His admiring analysis of *Madame Bovary* as a "protocinematic" novel leads him to describe its various film adaptations as "much less innovative, and much more concerned with adapting the text to a mainstream audience."[3] (Read: the book is better.) My second attempt at staging *Madame Bovary*, in 1988, appears to have been a failure at "mainstreaming," as Stam calls it, whereas my first attempt—nearly three times longer, less audience-friendly, and far more reverent in its intentions—was a failure at fidelity.

"What a fuss people make about fidelity!" declares Wilde's Lord Henry. "Young men want to be faithful, and are not; old men want to be faithless, and cannot." Speaking now as an old man, I find myself desiring not merely to *be* faithless but to *theorize* faithlessness, on behalf of my students. For guidance, I turn to a recent book by Thomas Leitch, *Film Adaptation and Its Discontents* (2007), which begins by challenging humanities educators to stop "teaching our students *books*" and start "teaching them *how to do things with books*." True literacy, Leitch feels, concerns itself with "active, writerly engagement," a "sense of performance and play," and the cultivation of a student's "agency even in the presence of canonical works." Leitch's influences range from Roland Barthes and M. M. Bakhtin to Wolfgang Iser: "whenever the reader bridges the gaps" in a literary text, Iser insists, "communication begins." So does adaptation, if we view it broadly as a competency in the kind of literacy Leitch imagines. From Lindiwe Dovey he borrows the distinction between "appropriational" and "pro-creative" adaptation. The second mode goes beyond mere "borrowing" from a source story. It is a performative mode of critical engagement that can be practiced in any medium, and that respects its source in the very act of changing it: "The pro-creational adaptation claims a kind of freedom for itself, but does not assume dominance over the text," which, after all, is still there to speak on its own behalf no matter what an adapter does.[4] What moves Leitch's book out of film studies (its ostensible area of inquiry) and into adaptation studies is a desire to find in the work of adaptation a model for active interpretation and criticism.

The same desire animates A *Theory of Adaptation* (2006), the wide-ranging book by Linda Hutcheon that seeks to explain how we experience adaptations *as adaptations*, no matter how different they are from their source texts. To qualify as an adaptation, regardless of medium, a new work must be both "announced" and "extended": "allusions to and brief echoes of other works would not qualify as extended engagements, nor do most examples of musical sampling." An interactive narrative like a video game based on a popular movie would count as an adaptation, in other words, whereas a short quotation or near-quotation of the *Dies Irae* (in a concert work by Berlioz or Rachmaninov, or the theme to the television series 24) would not. Elsewhere, I have examined the relationship of Hutcheon's book on adaptation to her earlier writings on parody and irony and have stressed the continuity of certain leading ideas. Notable among these are the very pervasiveness of adaptation in western art-making practices, and the way in which adaptations are "inherently 'palimpsestuous' works, haunted at all times by their adapted texts" in the oscillating perception of their audiences. Like Leitch, she envisions the adapter as "an interpreter before becoming a creator": the active interpreter can view any source text as "a reservoir of instructions" for future creation. But she appears to agree with Dovey that the adaptation claims a kind of freedom for itself. The source text requires critical interpretation, but not fidelity. "Adaptation is repetition," Hutcheon asserts paradoxically, as if in answer to Naremore's call for a general theory of repetition, "but repetition without replication."[5]

What has begun to emerge in recent scholarship is a challenge to respectful, source-centered theories of adaptation. Hutcheon defends the originality of the adaptation when she asserts, for example, that "to be second is not to be secondary or inferior; likewise, to be first is not to be originary or authoritative."[6] And Leitch celebrates the freedom to transform even the canonical classic as a crucial component of literacy itself—or at least the kind of literacy he feels we should be teaching.

By stretching adaptation to include "announced" and "extended" works like video games, Hutcheon provides a framework for discussing one of *Madame Bovary*'s most curious performances, a spectacle so playfully unlike its celebrated source that it might not strike its viewers as an adaptation at all. Local historian René Vérard has documented how the town of Ry, less than twenty kilometers east of Rouen, took advantage of a dubious distinction. In the 1840s, Ry had been home to Eugène Delamare and his wife Delphine, alleged to have been the real-life originals of Flaubert's Charles and Emma. Vérard helpfully reviews the rise of Ry as a literary "place of pilgrimage," due in part to the organization of a "Bovary Committee" in 1954 to advertise Ry as a tourist attraction, the "real" Yonville-l'Abbaye.[7] The Flaubertiste in a rental car, armed with a fold-out map from the Rouen tourist office—"Promenade au pays d'Emma Bovary," the complete plan for a day trip in Emma-land—can take a tour of over a dozen likely candidates for the novel's locations, from les Bertaux to la Huchette, before navigating the identified Yonville sites in Ry itself.

But the highlight of the tour is the work of a diorama hobbyist, Michel Burgaud, who with the help of his family opened a toy-theater spectacle in 1977. On the ground floor of an old press-house, several hundred costumed and automated puppets "perform the principal scenes from the novel by Gustave Flaubert."[8] What the motorized figures at the Galerie Bovary Musée des Automates do very well is repeat something, like a simplified dance step, over and over. The first tableau, from part 1, chapter 1, shows the entire expressive range of the small actors. "We were at prep," the tourist reads on a printed caption, "when the Head came in, followed by a new boy. . . ."[9] Male dolls, dressed as students, sit at school desks. The door swings open, revealing the headmaster and young Charles. The same clockwork causes all heads in the room to turn. The door closes; the heads turn back. When you enter Burgaud's theater, Charles is always already arriving. His curious new classmates "take," and still will be doing so when you leave. Or consider the representation of a passage from part 3, chapter 6. As the affair with Léon continued, Emma began to realize that she felt "nothing remarkable" after her meetings:

> This disappointment would soon disappear beneath a new hope, and Emma would come back to him more inflamed, more voracious. She would undress herself brutally, tearing at the delicate

laces on her corset, which would rustle down over her hips like a slithering snake.[10]

The frank passage is surprising for its late arrival in a novel about adultery that generally avoids explicit descriptions of the characters' lovemaking. Burgaud's tableau is more modest, but in some ways no less surprising. The Emma doll rips open her corset, to reveal two dots of red paint, signifying "nipple," atop two exposed doll breasts. The automated Léon doll responds with a nonstop "take," a kind of no-exit leer.

The nearly thirty scenes are arranged in a big horseshoe shape, so that you can go around as often as you like. On your first circuit, you might be overcome by how silly it all seems, as a response to so venerated a classic—a "serious" book, despite the often cruel humor achieved by its ironic narration. But it is hard to resist a conception so cheerfully perverse as the one on display at the Musée des Automates, and an execution so filled with camp delight. Even its mistakes are charming. A passage about shining stars, great waves of darkness, and the nighttime cold making "embraces the warmer," accompanies a tableau of the Emma doll and the Rodolphe doll caressing beneath a sunny blue sky.[11] The passage of text invites us not merely to interpret and complete the spectacle, but to correct it in some of its chief details.

By your third or fourth pass, perhaps you begin to yearn for additional scenes. Moments in the novel seem suddenly like missed opportunities. Disappointed by her conversation with Bournisien about earthly suffering, Emma "turned on her heel, abruptly, like a statue on a pivot." Disappointed by Léon's response to her audacious suggestion that he steal money from his office, Emma "rose to return to Yonville, like an automaton, obeying the stimulus of habit." Disappointed by her life in Tostes, Emma heard "echoes from another world" in the tunes cranked out by an organ grinder; while "her thoughts were leaping to the music, swinging from dream to dream," little automated dancers "went round and round" on the organ's lid. You begin to realize that Burgaud's theater is one that Flaubert had already imagined, and had deployed in various scales as a device of irony that Tony Tanner relates to the techniques of eighteenth-century satire.[12] Burgaud's harshly reductive vision of Flaubert's novel—as an arena for figures something less than human, whose chief behavioral distinction is mechanical repetition—begins to strike you as oddly appropriate.

Can repetition, of the sort that is so central to the experience of

Flaubert's novel, be represented successfully in any kind of performance? The very alternation of verb tenses, *passé simple* and *imparfait*, signals two distinct experiences of time: "singular or specific time" gives way to "circular time or repetition," as Mario Vargas Llosa observes. "The story moves but does not advance," and eventfulness continually surrenders to routine. The characters' aspirations and yearnings seem constrained by the centripetal pull of circular time. Ross Chambers describes Emma's *bêtise* as her failure "to realize that in trying to escape banality and in searching for something 'new' she is only condemning herself to an existence of repetitions." As Emma struggles to experience difference, novelty, eventfulness, she discovers sameness. "The more she tries to become Emma," Tanner writes, "the more she becomes 'la même'" and "suffers repetition":

> This is what is genuinely tragic in the experience of Emma Bovary. Her very capacity to feel dooms her to an increasing engagement with everything that serves to obliterate difference . . . and to deny originality.[13]

Nothing is "tragic," of course, about the drama at the Musée des Automates, where Emma's sameness arises from the fact that identical, mass-produced doll blanks perform her in every tableau; only the little costumes and the motorized activities change. My *New York Times* reviewer would have felt every bit as "frustrated and puzzled" had I put something like this onstage in 1988. But Burgaud's puppets succeed in foregrounding repetition unbearably and grotesquely, as no human actors could do, at least for very long. At the Musée des Automates, almost nothing else about the novel is perceptible. Is this in fact the ideal theater for staging *Madame Bovary*? If we reduce the complicated book to only one of its leading ideas, then we are forced to concede that the puppets perform the roles better than people.

I have chosen a ludicrous-sounding example to stand Hutcheon's test, and find that it passes. The adaptation is both "announced" and "extended." It maps the entire plot, and even attempts moments (like Binet surprising Emma by emerging from the duck blind) that more "serious" adaptations neglect. While it plays to the strengths of its performers, it uniquely magnifies a dynamic of the novel, the force of repetition, that other adaptations have failed to realize. Much as I would like to laugh it off, I find that the performance at the Musée des Automates is no mere prank or piece of kitsch. It is "palimpsestuous" rather than reverentially faithful, and haunted by the ghost of its source. Ry's puppet theater is repetition, as Hutcheon suggests, but repetition without replication.

Seriously Cinematic

The serious scholarly examination of *Madame Bovary* adaptations appears to begin with George Bluestone's demolition of Vincente Minnelli's MGM film, the final case study of his *Novels into Film* (1957). It is hard to imagine any Hollywood adaptation of *Madame Bovary* succeeding under the constraints still being enforced in 1949 by the Production Code Administration, and of course the plot of Minnelli's film has been euphemized and bowdlerized. "Minnelli 'mines' the novel," as Stam suggests, "not only for possible production numbers but also for potential melodramatic and spectacular scenes." But for Bluestone, the film's signal failure is its inability to draw upon "the power of language to show habitual behavior."[14] No matter how much we admire the histrionic talents of Jennifer Jones or Van Heflin, we acknowledge that they lack the relentless precision of Burgaud's mechanical puppets who do one thing (repeat themselves) superbly well. Thrown into a fast-moving, event-driven traversal of the novel's plot, human actors probably cannot succeed in being faithful to Flaubert's characters, who so often move but do not advance.

How then can a film be true to the novel? Before attempting his own adaptation of *Madame Bovary*, Claude Chabrol waited until he was sixty—an old man, by Lord Henry's estimate, although one still desiring to be faithful, and to respect "à la lettre l'indication du texte." Even his detractors praise Chabrol for being "scrupulously accurate, both in his attention to the novel's details and in his recreation of nineteenth-century France."[15]

Obsessed with the novel, Chabrol had persuaded himself that it was impossible to make into a film. He lacked the nerve, he says, until he worked with Isabelle Huppert—in whom he found his "ideal incarnation" of Emma. Chabrol and his ideal performer seem agreed to avoid not only exaggerated expression, but often any expression at all. They appear to have taken their cue from the many observers in the novel—husband, lovers, the guests at the wedding on the morning after—who stare into Emma's face and can read nothing. Admirers of Huppert's many screen performances recognize her often muted expressiveness as an artistic choice: it serves as a foil for a power in reserve, which flashes forth without restraint at moments like the reading of Rodolphe's farewell letter. In an interview about her creation of the role, Huppert suggests that her watchful Emma resulted from a responsiveness to "impression" rather than a striving for actorly "expression," and a taking into account of impressions registered in her own subconscious or unconscious as well as that of the character. Huppert relates this, for example, to her performance at the Vaubyessard ball, a seven-minute scene throughout which her character takes in everything visible and audible that surrounds her, while her attentive face approaches an almost zero degree of expressive signification. "It's the most beautiful day of my life," she tells Charles as they prepare to leave, "the most beautiful day of my life"—yet her face and voice project the most minimal of actorly "texts" for us to read. Compare Valentine Tessier's self-consciously theatricalized performance of pleasure, which alternates with a franker contempt for Charles, in Jean Renoir's four-minute ball scene—or the riot of histrionic self-disclosure that crosses the face of Jennifer Jones in Minnelli's dizzying realization. Huppert's very inscrutability seems to me the most interesting feature of the "Chabrolian Realism" that Stam analyzes.[16] But it creates a problem for an adapter who seeks fidelity to a novel that reports freely and frequently on its central character's interior life.

For its first fifteen minutes Chabrol's film dramatizes, in the manner of the 1975 BBC miniseries adapted by Giles Cooper, and even embarks from the same scene (the setting of Rouault's leg).[17] Suddenly, however, an off-screen voice invades the acoustic space of a dramatic scene between Charles and Emma. The film's subtitles translate the voice as follows:

> As their life together became more intimate, a growing detachment distanced her from him. Charles's conversation was as flat as pavement. His borrowed ideas trudged past in colorless procession, without emotion, laughter or dreams.[18]

We have arrived at the kind of resistant moment in the film's narration that Bluestone describes: the representation of habitual behavior and circular time. In a script composed of inexact quotations—dramatic dialogue worked out of narration and story material—the disembodied male voice utters two consecutive sentences of exact quotation, from Flaubert's narration in the beginning of part 1, chapter 7. Who is this speaker, this authoritative voice from nowhere, who seems to have been watching along with us?

In her study of voice-over narration, *Invisible Storytellers*, Sarah Kozloff talks about our unwillingness to accept a voice-over latecomer—a "tardy speaker"—"as the teller of a film that has already been unfolding for quite a while." But she does not describe my experience watching Chabrol's film. On the contrary, I quickly yield to my desire for the knowledge he seems to have, and I begin to rely on him rather unquestioningly. This late-arriving voice, certainly, is not the film's narrator in any total sense. Whether we follow Tom Gunning in calling the film's total discourse act the enunciation of a "narrator," or David Bordwell in speaking of a non-"anthropomorphic" act of "narration," we know that a film is "told" by the entire ensemble or process of the film's narrative effects. Within this ensemble of effects, as Bordwell insists, "personified narrators are invariably swallowed up." Chabrol's film offers no better example than the moment from part 2, chapter 13, when Emma reads Rodolphe's farewell letter. As she climbs the stairs leading to the attic, we see the shadow of Emma staring at the unfolded letter. A sharp attack of music announces her reaction, as the reality of what Rodolphe has written begins to sink in.[19] Music seldom performs a narrating function in the film, and never as blatantly as it does here. But we recognize that the narrating voice in no way produces the music; both music and narrating voice, supplying different kinds of information, belong to the arsenal of visible and audible effects that compose what Bordwell calls the film's "narration."

Yet the voice in Chabrol's film comes from somewhere. "Off-screen sound," Noel Burch observes, "*always* brings off-screen space into play." Kozloff agrees: "the addition of extradiegetic sound forces the viewer to realize that the story is itself framed by other space and other time, that the 'world' pictured on the screen is enveloped by another world." This "narrating place" contains and manipulates the "story place"; it is what I would call a scene of discourse, which contains a scene (more accurately, multiple scenes) of story. Chabrol's film might be inviting us to imagine Flaubert himself, circa 1856, since the voice of actor François Périer speaks only text from the novel. Or perhaps the film projects a more contemporary *reader* of the novel, whose imaginary space is a "mindscreen" filled with the dramatic scenes we also see.[20] But the authority of this voice arises, for me at least, from the recognition that it *repeats* the novel, as no character voice in the scene of story does.

Consider the film's representation of part 2, chapter 11, in which Hippolyte loses his leg. Chabrol's long scene (a full ten minutes, in a film that is barely over two hours and twenty minutes) is unusually attentive to details in the text, such as the redness of the box and the barometer crashing to the floor. But it is especially careful to fill the projection screen of Isabelle Huppert's barely moving face with Flaubert's descriptions of the character's interior life, voiced from off-screen:

> She repented, as of a crime, her past virtue. . . . The memory of her lover came back to her with a dizzying pull . . . ; and Charles seemed as remote from her life, as eternally absent, as impossible and annihilated, as if he were near death, and in his last agony before her eyes.[21]

The narration achieves what Kozloff calls "anchoring," a term she borrows from Barthes's 1964 essay "Rhetoric of the Image." Barthes describes how narrative captions in magazine advertising, for example, project meaning onto "polysemous" and potentially ambiguous visuals. The text "has a *repressive* value" in relation to the visual; it helps me, as Barthes suggests, "to combat the terror of uncertain signs."[22] And narration in Chabrol's film "anchors" the visual image in precisely this way. Our chief access to a character's interior life is the language of the novel, produced by the voice of this other witness. Without this device, the film's Emma expresses no memory, no dreams, no desires—at least no certain ones.

Kozloff suggests that the "power" of voice-over—filled with "pretensions to truth"—typically enjoys an "immunity to criticism." It inspires trust, and answers questions that even the most compelling pictures do not. The speaker watches with us, but knows more. Since the voice in Chabrol's film repeats the authority of Flaubert's text, it even has the "repressive" power to contradict other evidence. Late in the novel, following the bailiff's inventory of the house in Yonville, Emma goes to Léon for money. Chabrol compresses the dialogue from part 3, chapter 7. "Try," Emma begs Léon, "I'll love you so." When he protests that he does not know where to look, she brazenly suggests, "Your office!" The camera then holds on Huppert's almost motionless face for thirteen seconds, before cutting back to Léon, as he awkwardly pretends to come up with a solution: "How stupid I am. My friend Morel's back. His father's rich."[23] When I play scenes from Chabrol's film for my students, I show them a doctored version of this one. Most of them have read the novel for the first time, and their memory of this scene is imperfect. My deviously manipulated clip removes both the narrator's voice and the subtitled translation. What we see is Emma's blank face, for thirteen long seconds of silence, before the reverse shot establishes Léon and the dialogue continues. I ask my students, "What on earth is she thinking?" Her face is one of Barthes's "uncertain signs," and my professorial demand that the class supply a signified seems to inspire the "terror" Barthes describes.

Then I play the scene as Chabrol completed it, with the English subtitle added. The voice of François Périer informs us, first of all, that the eyes we watch are "burning" with an "infernal audacity." If we have seen a milder quality radiating from Huppert's face (as I do) we can now correct our impression. Emma's eyelids, we hear, are "drawing together" (they are not) in a manner "lascivious and encouraging" (this too is far from clear, although Huppert blinks a few times). Then, as we continue to stare at her face, we must take on faith the novel's report that "the young man felt himself weakening beneath the calm determination of this woman who was inciting him to crime." Typically the voice-over simply fills out the visual image; in Stam's amusing phrase, it "comes to the rescue whenever visual translation seems impossible."[24] But here— in small yet distinct ways—it contradicts the image. One wonders if the owner of the off-screen voice even bothers to read the text of cinematic images, or merely turns his eyes away to read the authoritative text of Flaubert's prose.

Where have I experienced this clash before? At the Musée des Automates: there is a bright blue sky, shining behind a nighttime scene, and the text commands us to see stars and waves of darkness. Chabrol's voice-over anchors the spectacle in the same dissonant way—and despite my usual gratitude for the information that the voice provides, I catch myself here falling through the gap between two texts.

The mere repetition of Flaubert's text, in other words, is no guarantee of fidelity to that text. Reading aloud the entire book on the soundtrack would not change things. A *complete* repetition of Flaubert's novel—every word of it, which even in a recitation as brisk as Chabrol's narrator supplies would produce a running time of at least fifteen hours—would not give us "the book." The reason for this is that competing texts, like the text of Huppert's face (however "cool" and "bloodless" critics like Stam find it), are enormously interesting, and never more so than when they stage a rebellion against Flaubert's authority.[25] At moments like the one drawn from part 3, chapter 7, I stand in the gap between two signifying systems, and am faced with a choice—since, clearly, Huppert's Emma is doing something different than the voice suggests, and might be *thinking* something different.

The lesson I took away from multiple viewings of Chabrol's "faithful" film, as I began to contemplate staging *Madame Bovary* yet again, was an anticipation of Hutcheon's assertion: even the performance that repeats the source does not replicate it. If textual anchoring has a repressive effect, as Barthes suggests, the interpretation of a performing body can push back, and even stage a rebellion. In a film or stage adaptation, the gaps that open among multiple signifying systems are probably inevitable, and sometimes very wide. Potentially the gaps produce creative spaces for the adaptation's audience: spaces where, as Iser suggests, "communication begins."

Chamber-Theatrical

A gap opens right away when a film or play casts an actor—*any* actor—in a well-known role. Huppert jokes with her interviewer that Emma Bovary "is deeply anchored in a collective imagination," and thereby lacks an appearance of her own. She belongs to everybody, and could be anybody: "blonde, brunette, redhead. This time, she will be redhead!"[26]

What should Emma Bovary look like? The thirty-eight-year-old Huppert, whose age is hard to guess from her onscreen appearance? The forty-one-year-old Valentine Tessier? The twenty-nine-year-old Jennifer Jones? The thirty-two-year-old Frances O'Connor, fresh from *Mansfield Park* when, in 2000, she became one of television's several Emmas? The thirty-year-old Francesca Annis, so recently Roman Polanski's Lady Macbeth when she played Emma in 1975? Or should Emma look like the dark-haired, dark-eyed woman on the cover of my Gallimard paperback? People who knew Delphine Delamare said she looked just like the young woman in a painting by Joseph-Désiré Court, which René Dusmenil reproduces in his volume of Flaubertian "iconographic documents." Which is correct? Dominick LaCapra reflects on the way in which Emma's eyes seem to change color, for example, as the light changes in Flaubert's novel. While "we do not know precisely what she does look like," he concludes, "we are tempted to say that, presented with any picture of her, we would exclaim, 'That's not quite it.'" To the professor of intellectual history, the not-quite-it-ness of Emma makes her "a magnificent figure for the interplay between determinacy and indeterminacy" in Flaubert's text.[27]

When I first staged *Madame Bovary*, in the summer of 1987, I had recently read LaCapra's study of the novel, and was inspired to keep the image of Emma in play. I cast eight actresses, who rotated through the roles of Emma and narrator over the course of three evenings. An announcement in the program jokingly reassured the audience, "When in doubt, remember: Emma is the one in the white sweater." I tried this again with four actresses in New York the following year, but the device occasioned the reviewer's chief complaint.[28] So for the 2006 production, I "mainstreamed" the script to feature one actress in the title role, and on a very few occasions gave her a double. A second actress became an alienated image of the younger self she remembered, whom Emma could study in action—as she sought answers, for example, to the question of *why*, dear God, she ever got married.

But one thing remained from my reading of LaCapra, two decades earlier. Here I first encountered the suggestion that Emma's death performs an allegorical function. The novel's disgust with the "conquering bourgeoisie" might arise from the failure of meaningful social reform in the revolutionary activity of 1848, which began not long before Delphine Delamare's death. If we can say that the world of *Madame Bovary* presents the bourgeois "condition" before 1848—"the condition of those who thought basely and stupidly"—we can say as well that the author framed his portrait on the reassertion of this condition during the 1850s. LaCapra comments: "The revolution of 1848 might almost be termed *l'absent* of *Madame Bovary*—the event that never takes place in it. . . . Emma's suicide might be seen as a surrogate."[29] A fancy intellectual theory—but intriguing enough to suggest even more elaborate comparisons between Flaubert's 1848 and other failed revolutions, like May 1968 in Paris, or the disappointed promise of social revolution arising from America's decade of assassinations, Vietnam protests, and "summer of love."

I was staging a play with narrators, and unlike Chabrol's voice-over actor, my team of narrators would keep their bodies. They needed a true theatrical scene, a time and a place: a materialization of the "other" world of "off-screen space" that Kozloff and Burch imagine. In all three productions, I motivated the repetition of text by making my narrators *readers* of Flaubert's famous book. The narrators became young American women, in college not long after 1968, engaged in a translation exercise for class. They have been handed the novel in French, and proceed to reimagine it in English. These reader-translators (in a very American scene of discourse) imagine, and describe into existence, the onstage character bodies (in a foreign scene of story) that we in the audience see and hear. The novel has not been updated. According to the

Madame Bovary (Northwestern, 2006): the narrator reads the bodies of Emma and Charles (still from video by Gary Ashwal).

words the actors speak, events still take place in the France of the 1830s and 1840s. But the narrators imagine it all in modern dress, like modern-dress Shakespeare. The *mise-en-scène* cloaks Flaubert's events in the modernity of the Eisenhower, Kennedy, and Johnson administrations, the modernity that falls somewhere between Rosemary Clooney and Janis Joplin.

Parts of the adaptation employ the chamber theater method developed by my former teacher Robert Breen, which stages the "interior dialogues" between narrating voice and character consciousness implicit in much novelistic narration. An onstage narrator starts sentences that her characters complete, sometimes while speaking of themselves in the third person, and we in the audience have to adjust our ears to something that does not sound exactly like conventional dramatic dialogue. Early in the first act, Charles arrives at Rouault's farm to set his broken leg. A narrator, holding a French-language copy of the novel, engages in a translation exercise that summons forth a second text composed of actors' bodies.

> NARRATOR Monsieur Rouault's wife had been dead for two years. His daughter helped him run the house.

[EMMA approaches to meet CHARLES; they go to ROUAULT's bedside.]

NARRATOR [Reading from the novel.] "Une jeune femme, en robe de mérinos bleu" . . . [Turning to watch EMMA, as ROUAULT groans.] A young woman received Monsieur Bovary at the door. The fracture was a simple one.

CHARLES [Aside to NARRATOR, with relief.] Without any complications. [Begins to prepare and bandage the splint.]

NARRATOR Charles couldn't have wished for anything easier. Recalling his teachers' bedside manner, he cheered up the patient with little jokes.

ROUAULT [To EMMA, as CHARLES makes a joke.] Alors, plus vite! Plus vite!

EMMA [Searching for her sewing kit.] Je ne peux pas trouver mon étui.

NARRATOR [Directing CHARLES's attention to EMMA.] As his daughter sewed bandages, she kept pricking her fingers and raising them to her lips to suck them.

CHARLES [Aside to NARRATOR.] Her hands weren't pretty. A little rough around the knuckles, maybe.

NARRATOR The best thing about her was the eyes. [Reading, while EMMA directs her gaze at CHARLES.] Her look came at you frankly with . . . [Studying EMMA.] . . . a candid boldness.[30]

In scenes like this, my narrator repeatedly turns back to the authoritative text—her copy of the novel—to check a detail. The narration she speaks frequently "anchors" the image of the characters, in the way Kozloff describes. But her characters, once set in motion, race on ahead of her—and often she is forced to choose between the book and that other text, the text of bodies in space. Unlike Chabrol's voice-over narrator, she chooses to read the bodies. In the resulting interaction, she even molds and shapes the scene—bodies, objects, moods, and tempos—to help her focal characters attend to the details that they need to notice. LaCapra's Bakhtin-inflected reading of the novel suggests that, as silent readers, we experience narrator-character dialogues (rather than interior monologues) when reading passages like the one from part

1, chapter 2, on which the above-cited passage from my 2006 script is based. LaCapra observes:

> The narrator intervenes or intrudes more actively to direct attention to details that contradict Charles's perception and that take the privilege of describing Emma away from him. Indeed the narrator (almost like an impatient schoolmaster) seems to say in *sub rosa* fashion: "Forget about her hands, you oaf! Look at her eyes. That's where her true beauty lies."[31]

The narrator as impatient schoolmaster: my narrators in 2006 are doubled figures, students themselves, subjected to discipline, as well as their characters' "masters" and disciplinarians. They help to maintain an atmosphere of the classroom and the practice room that pervades the entire staging.

The production begins by showing us two forms of dreadful, deadening repetition. The first is piano practice. Emma does not yet possess the fluency of a public performer. At an absurdly slow tempo, she starts, stops, and starts again an "easy piece," the statement of the theme in the Andante grazioso of Mozart's A major sonata, K. 331. The second is the language lesson. As Emma abandons her practice in frustration and disgust, a classroom forms onstage, and young Charles prepares to enter the scene of his first humiliation. The dissonant setting for Flaubert's opening paragraphs is one that the narrator might remember from her own American childhood; here she engages in a dialogue with one of the long-suffering students, who briefly shares the narrating function. The French teacher drops a needle on a phonograph, and we hear a language-instruction record from a 1958, *Learn French in Record Time*: "Hello. This is Dr. Savant, your French professor. I am going to help you learn French in a new and easy and enjoyable manner. Now, open your book to page eleven. . . ."[32] Young Charles nervously stands apart from the other students, who wearily repeat the lessons coming from the phonograph.

TEACHER Répétez!

STUDENT 1 We began to recite our lessons.

[Recorded language lesson: "Qui est ce petit garçon?"]

STUDENTS [Mumbling.] Qui est ce petit garçon?

[Recorded language lesson: "J'ai mangé du fromage."]

STUDENTS J'ai mangé du fromage.

STUDENT 1 The new kid was all ears, like he was listening to a sermon.

[Recorded language lesson: "Où est mon chapeau?"]

STUDENTS Où est mon chapeau?

Like recorded music heard over and over on the radio—fifties pop and sixties rock, as well as classical—the recorded language lesson belongs to the cultural memory of the production's narrators, and makes its way into the soundscape of the world that these narrators imagine.

Using devices of repetition as the characters' ground of experience, from childhood to adulthood, I developed variations of a "mechanical scene" for staging passages in the novel. The following mechanical scene adapts the end of part 2, chapter 9. It shows an early stage in Emma's affair with Rodolphe, and stresses the repetitive nature of the characters' adult behavior.

[CHARLES forms a "horse" downstage with two chairs. Upstage, RODOLPHE stretches out on his bed. When CHARLES mounts the "horse," EMMA rushes up to RODOLPHE and surprises him, literally behind CHARLES's back. As she rises from RODOLPHE's bed and returns downstage, CHARLES dismounts, as if returning home at the end of the day; he sees her, speaks, and waves. Then he mounts the "horse" again: a new day begins. This action grows more rapid as it repeats.]

CHARLES [Waving goodbye to his wife, as he leaves in the morning.] Ma femme!

NARRATOR One morning when Charles left before dawn, Emma was seized with the fantastic notion of seeing Rodolphe right away.

EMMA She could get to Rodolphe's chateau quickly,

NARRATOR stay an hour,

EMMA and be back before anyone would notice.

NARRATOR She was weak with desire. Day was breaking. . . . There was her lover's house . . . the walls seemed to open for her as she approached . . . the door . . . the latch. At the end of a bedroom she saw a man asleep.

[At the NARRATOR's signal, a golden glow of light illuminates RODOLPHE's bed.]

RODOLPHE [As EMMA utters a cry.] It's you—you, here! How on earth did you get here? Your dress, it's wet . . .

EMMA I love you.

NARRATOR [Signalling the light off, as EMMA moves away from RODOLPHE.] It was a big success—so she tried it again.

[Recorded language lesson: "Veuillez répéter: un, deux, trois."]

CHARLES [Beginning the repeated sequence.] Ma femme!

NARRATOR Whenever Charles left early, she crept down the steps leading to the river, across the cow plank . . . the chateau . . . the door . . . the latch . . . the sleeping man. [Signalling light on.] She always arrived out of breath, her cheeks rosy, her whole body giving off a fragrance of sap, green grass, fresh air. Entering his bedroom,

RODOLPHE she was like a morning in spring . . .

EMMA I love you.

NARRATOR The yellow curtains let in a muted, golden glow. [Signaling light off, as EMMA moves away.]

[Recorded language lesson: "Veuillez répéter: onze, douze, treize."]

CHARLES [Beginning the repeated sequence.] Ma femme!

NARRATOR [Signaling light on.] Emma would grope her way across the room, the dew still clinging to her hair like a halo of topaz.

EMMA I love you.

NARRATOR It always took them a good quarter of an hour to say good-bye. [Signaling light off, as EMMA moves away.]

[Recorded language lesson: "Veuillez répéter: quatre-vingt-un, quatre-vingt-dix, quatre-vingt-onze."]

CHARLES [Beginning the repeated sequence.] Ma femme!

NARRATOR [Signaling light on, as EMMA reaches the bed.] Emma always wept—she never wanted to go. [Signaling light off, as EMMA moves away.]

[Recorded language lesson: "Cent, mille."]

CHARLES [Beginning the repeated sequence.] Ma femme!

NARRATOR [Signaling light on.] One day she arrived unexpectedly.

EMMA I love you.

NARRATOR [Signaling light off, as RODOLPHE stands and frowns.] Something wasn't right.

EMMA What's the matter? Are you sick? Tell me . . .

NARRATOR So he told her, gravely,

RODOLPHE that her visits were getting a little . . . imprudent. She was compromising herself.

NARRATOR [As EMMA begins to run her pattern more slowly and cautiously.] Little by little, she began to share Rodolphe's fears.

CHARLES [Beginning the repeated sequence.] Ma femme!

By laminating a repetitive action onto the edited text of the novel, the scene underscores the speed with which even adultery loses a feeling of eventfulness and falls into routine. Only a chapter later, Flaubert's narrator informs us that "by the end of six months," Rodolphe and Emma "were, with each other, like a married couple tranquilly nourishing a domestic flame."[33]

As intended, such mechanical scenes provoked audience laughter—never more so than late in the production. In Flaubert's novel, the opening of part 3, chapter 5, employs the *imparfait* ("she would do this," "they would say this") to condense into one rich description the many Thursday meetings that form the first phase of Emma's affair with Léon. In 2006, my narrators performed a two-minute reduction of these half-dozen pages while they watched the lovers go through their day together in Rouen. But the Emma and Léon actors performed a repeated action, in counterpoint to the narrators' description of one typical Thursday. Navigating the stage in this scene required a bit of athletic prowess. Two steep, eleven-riser staircases connected either side of the main stage floor to a high platform, which here represented the hotel room where the lovers would meet. It was possible, then, for Emma and Léon to pass on the street, ascend to the high platform by different staircases, embrace passionately ("Quelle étreinte!"), sink to the bed, stand, bid

Madame Bovary (Northwestern, 2006): Emma and Léon race to the hotel room, while the narrators watch (still from video by Gary Ashwal).

goodbye for a week ("À jeudi! . . . à jeudi!"), and descend to the street, once again by different staircases.[34] To the audience's surprise and delight, the accelerating lovers—one moving clockwise and the other counter-clockwise—mechanically completed this circuit five times during the two brief minutes of narration.

The scene achieved something onstage that I had been thinking about since visiting the Musée des Automates in Ry, eight years earlier. I wondered if live actors could do something similar, in a way that audiences would enjoy from night to night—and indeed they could. Yet the effect of this experiment was crucially different than the spectacle of motorized puppets. For what the Northwestern audiences in 2006 enjoyed was not sheer repetition, but the force of something cumulative—a display of athletic virtuosity, in which the runners must complete their lap, hit their mark, in order to deliver their lines on cue. Bert O. States suggests that when we watch a play in the theater, we do not view the actors simply as representations or significations of characters in a fictional world. We attend to them simultaneously as phenomena in our own world: human beings engaged in the performance of something demanding (like the skillful *imitation* of automata) and subject to the same laws of physics that govern our own bodies. States calls the "significative" and the "phenomenal" the two "keys of perception" that constitute our "binocular vision" and govern how we read the performing body.[35] If our significative eye sees the mechanical behavior of characters, our phenomenal eye sees two hard-working actors executing a piece of choreography that grows more difficult with each circuit. To my great surprise, the phenomenal spectacle of human actors striving to hit their mark added something poignant—a viewer's nervous awareness perhaps that, being human, they might fail—to the harshly reductive comedy that had delighted me in Ry.

The reassertion of human striving and human frailty in my staging experiment reminded me that my goal was never to put the Musée des Automates onstage, as a kind of *ballet mécanique* or virtuoso prank at the novel's expense. Rather, I was interested in staging the struggle of an individual against what Chambers calls the "law of repetition" to which everything in the novel seems subject. This struggle is most evident in, but not restricted to, the character of Emma. The human drama that has drawn me back to the novel for two decades is a hybrid one, neither pure tragedy nor pure comedy—and certainly not the farce of people who behave like machines, but nothing more. It is, rather, a drama in which our perceptions of the characters constantly oscillate between identification and detachment, through "modulations of irony and empathy" that strike LaCapra as some of the novel's most distinctive technical achievements. Again and again, we witness the spectacle of our strongest desires failing to lead us beyond our most automatic habits—the spectacle, for example, of the fullness of the heart overflowing into the emptiest and stalest of metaphors. At times "when we wish to conjure pity from the stars" with our words, the sound we make is more like the noise of "a cracked cauldron on which we knock out tunes for dancing-bears"—or so the narrator observes, when the language that expresses Emma's overpowering anguish sounds to Rodolph, in his "critical superiority," like the same "stuff" that he has heard "so many times" from so many other mistresses.[36] Charles is never more heartbreaking than in a scene that simultaneously renders him ridiculous. When he utters the one "grand phrase" of his lifetime, "C'est la faute de la fatalité!" ("Fate is to blame!"), he is blissfully unaware of expressing his profoundest, most original insight through repetition of one of the novel's hardest-worked clichés.[37] Emma's great yearning for eventfulness—the "chance d'un événement" that she imagines disrupting even the flattest of lives—sparks her rebellion against an existence filled with identical days. When, late in the novel, her desperate situation looms before her "like an abyss" ("telle qu'un abîme"), she runs toward it "in a rapture of heroism" that is "almost joyful." The leap into the abyss will destroy her, but at least it will be an event—"something truly done," to borrow Hedda Gabler's phrase. She seeks to escape the "chain of repetitions" that her relationship with the men in her life has come to represent. But at the moment of her most singular achievement the novel makes her the target of some of its harshest irony. The blind man arrives, as a parody of the phantom "other man" Emma has sought, and forms another link in the chain. Eventfulness sinks into repetition. Even Emma gets the joke: she dies laughing "an atrocious, frantic, desperate laugh."[38]

In heraldry, *mise en abyme* names a style of repetition: at the center or heart of a shield, the designer places a small replica of the larger image. We find movement into the abyss in any reflexive device, such as a play within a play, that duplicates in reduced or stylized form the art work that embeds it.[39] We find it as well in more commonplace, commercial imagery: on the Land O'Lakes butter box, for example, an Indian maiden holds a box with a picture of an Indian maiden holding a box with a picture, and the image recedes into infinity. For Emma, the desired meaning of the leap into the abyss is eventful: the annihilation of self that can happen, in death, only once. Viewed differently, of course, placement or movement *en abyme* rejoins Emma to an infinite repetition. Such movement is an ironic refutation of the transport of heroism that drives her to the pharmacist's shop, and sends her home almost serenely with the illusory feeling of a duty accomplished. The long scene of Emma's death sets off from a fantasy of heroic and purposeful activity, and concludes with laughter provoked by a horrifying image that threatens to repeat throughout eternity. As this transformation unfolds, the narration pulls back from engagement with Emma's inner feelings, and describes her agony with growing ironic detachment. The tone is uncertain, indeterminate, and potentially comic (although in a cruel and grotesque way). This accounts, perhaps, for why the death has never seemed very compelling in any of the realizations for film or television that I have seen: the "tragic" stagings before the camera have lacked the inflection of the narrator's ironic consciousness.[40] In my experience of reading the novel, the death revisits a tension that appears more obviously in earlier scenes, such as the description of Emma and Rodolphe's affair in part 2, chapter 9 that inspired the mechanical scene I describe above. It is a tension between the reaching out toward significant, singular action and the undertow of recurrence.

In seeking ways to stage repetition, I hoped to create an abstract gestural counterpoint to the conventional dramatic realism in which some of the dialogue scenes would be played: a kind of behavioral imperfect tense, which would alternate with and contrast the performance of one-time-only events in the overall stage composition. At one extreme, we see the characters' unique, completed actions in a relatively unmediated way, as they would appear to other residents of the dramatic world. At the other extreme, we see their actions through the distorting perception of an ironic narrator: as stylized repetitions into which the characters continually slide, without being fully conscious of doing so.

The 2006 adaptation pushed this physical stylization further than my earlier stagings. If such choreographed repetition distorted the text, it "faithfully" reproduced an aspect of my thinking about the text—the latest chapter in my own story of reading—in the way that my casting of eight Emmas in 1987 reproduced my thinking at that time. A commonplace of recent theory is the insistence that adaptation takes place not in a vacuum, where the source text is available in a closed and hypothetically pure state, but in a "vast and variegated" cultural context that brings an old book in contact with an abundance of texts—from scholarly assessments to toy-theater spectacles to popular songs—that its author never foresaw. Ultimately, for Hutcheon, "adaptation is how stories evolve and mutate to fit new times and different places." Whatever my desire for the presence of the thing itself, *Madame Bovary* began for me as a text in translation, and my experience as an adapter has merely continued the telling of its story in other words. I cannot simply repeat my source, even if I quote it extensively (as my three-evening version did most elaborately); Chabrol's unrealized desire to remain faithful to the letter of the text helped me to see this. At most I can achieve what Hutcheon, echoing her theory of parody, calls "repetition with difference." The difference arises from the interpretive gaps that readers fill, the spaces where communication begins. It arises as well from the shifting scenes of reception in which great works "are enriched with new meanings," as they "outgrow what they were in the epoch of their creation." So it seemed to Bakhtin, late in his career, as he contemplated literature's life across what he called "great time."[41] And so it seems to me, as I begin my third decade of adapting *Madame Bovary*.

Endnotes

1. Wall, *Flaubert* 241–42; Flaubert qtd. in Troyat 183.
2. Bruckner C21.
3. Leitch 1; Naremore, "Introduction" 15; Ray 44; Stam, "Beyond" 74–75; see Stam, *Literature* 144–90.
4. Wilde 46; Leitch 14; Iser qtd. in Leitch 18; Dovey qtd. in Leitch 18–19.
5. Hutcheon xiv, 6–7, 9, 84; see 111; see also Edwards, "Adaptation."
6. Hutcheon xiii.
7. Vérard, *Ry* 16, 19–20; Vérard, *Epilogue* 18–20.
8. For a fuller discussion of Bovary tourism in Ry, see Edwards, "Mechanical."
9. Wall, *Madame* 3. At the Galerie Bovary museum, of course, the tourist reads this in French: "Nous étions à l'étude, quand le Proviseur entra, suivi d'un *nouveau* habillé en bourgeois. . . ." See Flaubert 21.
10. Wall, *Madame* 263.
11. Wall, *Madame* 156–57 (part 2, ch. 10).
12. Wall, *Madame* 106 (part 2, ch. 6), 278 (part 3, ch. 7), 60–61 (part 1, ch. 9); Tanner 301.
13. Vargas Llosa 172; Chambers 176; Tanner 268.
14. Stam, *Literature* 173; Bluestone 202.
15. Chabrol qtd. in Boddaert 103; Donaldson-Evans 28; see Stam, *Literature* 176–77.
16. Chabrol qtd. in Boddaert 25; Huppert qtd. in Boddaert 141–44; Chabrol 15–24:15; Renoir 26:15–30:45; Minnelli 34:15–43:00; see Stam, *Literature* 175–82.
17. See Bennett 0:35–6:38.
18. Chabrol 15:30–16:00. The narrator speaks the following: "à mesure que se serrait davantage l'intimité de leur vie, un détachement intérieur se faisait qui la déliait de lui. La conversation de Charles était plate comme un trottoir de rue, et les idées de tout le monde y défilaient, dans leur costume ordinarie, sans exciter d'émotion, de rire ou de rêverie." See Flaubert 70.
19. Kozloff 77; Gunning 22–25; Bordwell 61–62; Chabrol 1:28:30–1:30:30.
20. Burch qtd. in Kozloff 77; Kozloff 77, 57. By adding "scene" to narratology's "discourse" and "story," I suggest that onstage narration in a play creates its own dramatic scene, which embeds and frames the scenes of represented action; concerning the discourse/story distinction, see, for example, Chatman 19. I borrow the term "mindscreen" from Kawin.
21. Wall, *Madame* 172; Chabrol 1:20:00–1:20:30. The film's English subtitle abbreviates the text that Chabrol's narrator speaks: "Elle se repentait, comme d'un crime, de sa vertu passée. . . . Le souvenir de son amant revenait à elle avec des attractions vertigineuses; elle y jetait son âme, . . . et Charles lui semblait aussi détachée de sa vie, aussi absent pour toujours, aussi impossible et anéanti, que s'il allait mourir et qu'il eût agonisé sous ses yeux." See Flaubert 247–48.
22. Barthes 28–29; see Kozloff 14–15.
23. Kozloff 96; Chabrol 2:00:15–2:01:00.
24. Wall, *Madame* 278; Stam, *Literature* 177.
25. Stam describes Huppert's performance as "relatively cool" and "somewhat bloodless" before it "comes alive as the film proceeds"; see *Literature* 178–79.

26. Huppert qtd. in Boddaert 130.

27. Dumesnil 52, 229; LaCapra 156–57.

28. The "trick" of "quartering" Emma "works surprisingly well" for much of the script, but ultimately "makes the death scene ridiculous"; see Bruckner C21.

29. LaCapra 67, 201.

30. See Breen; all passages from the Northwestern production quote my unpublished script as revised on 12 Feb. 2006.

31. LaCapra 156.

32. Institute side 1.

33. Wall, *Madame* 158.

34. See Flaubert 345, 347.

35. States 8, 14; see 19–47. On the sporting arena as a model for the actor-audience relationship in the theater, see for example Brecht 6–7.

36. Chambers 175; LaCapra 135; Wall, *Madame* 177 (part 2, ch. 12).

37. Wall, *Madame* 326; Flaubert 445 (part 3, ch. 11). Charles addresses his "grand mot" to Rodolphe, who has used the high-sounding "fate"—"a word that always makes an impression"—in a cynically calculated way, both in wooing Emma and in leaving her; see Wall, *Madame* 136 (part 2, ch. 8), 188 (part 2, ch. 13).

38. Flaubert 96 (part 1, ch. 9), 403 (part 3, ch. 8); Wall, *Madame* 293; Ibsen 770; Chambers 182; Wall, *Madame* 305 (part 3, ch. 8).

39. See Dällenbach 7–113.

40. Stam suggests that Chabrol "deploys something close" to such ironic inflection in the death scene, by "moving us in and out of various subjectivities"; see *Literature* 178.

41. Hutcheon 142, 176; Bakhtin 4.

Works Cited

Bakhtin, M. M. "Response to a Question from the *Novy Mir* Editorial Staff." Trans. Vern W. McGee. *Speech Genres and Other Late Essays.* Ed. Caryl Emerson and Michael Holquist. Austin: University of Texas Press, 1986. 1–9.

Barthes, Roland. "Rhetoric of the Image." *The Responsibility of Forms: Critical Essays on Music, Art, and Representation.* Trans. Richard Howard. New York: Hill and Wang, 1985. 21–40.

Bennett, Rodney, dir. *Madame Bovary.* 1975. DVD. Time-Life, 2003.

Bluestone, George. *Novels into Film.* Baltimore: Johns Hopkins University Press, 1957.

Boddaert, François, et al., eds. *Autour d'Emma: Madame Bovary, un film de Claude Chabrol.* Paris: Hatier, 1991.

Bordwell, David. *Narration in the Fiction Film.* Madison: University of Wisconsin Press, 1985.

Brecht, Bertolt. "Emphasis on Sport." *Brecht on Theatre: The Development of an Aesthetic.* Ed. and trans. John Willett. New York: Hill and Wang, 1964. 6–9.

Breen, Robert S. *Chamber Theatre.* Englewood Cliffs: Prentice-Hall, 1978.

Bruckner, D. J. R. "A Look at Emma Bovary." Rev. of *Madame Bovary*, perf. Alchemy Theater Co. *New York Times* 22 Sept. 1988, late ed.: C21.

Chabrol, Claude, dir. *Madame Bovary.* 1991. DVD. MGM, 2002.

Chambers, Ross. *The Writing of Melancholy: Modes of Opposition in Early French Modernism.* Trans. Mary Seidman Trouille. Chicago: University of Chicago Press, 1993.

Chatman, Seymour. *Story and Discourse: Narrative Structure in Fiction and Film.* Ithaca: Cornell University Press, 1978.

Dällenbach, Lucien. *The Mirror in the Text.* Trans. Jeremy Whiteley and Emma Hughes. Chicago: University of Chicago Press, 1989.

Donaldson-Evans, Mary. "A Medium of Exchange: The *Madame Bovary* Film." *Dix-Neuf* 4 (2005): 21–34.

Dumesnil, René. *Flaubert: documents iconographiques.* Vésenaz: Pierre Cailler, 1948.

Edwards, Paul. "Adaptation: Two Theories." Rev. of *A Theory of Adaptation* by Linda Hutcheon and *Adaptation and Appropriation* by Julie Sanders. *Text and Performance Quarterly* 27.4 (2007): 369–77.

Edwards, Paul. "The Mechanical Bride of Yonville-l'Abbaye (Batteries Not Included): Remapping the Canonical Landmark." *Opening Acts: Performance in/as Communication and Cultural Studies.* Ed. Judith Hamera. Thousand Oaks: Sage, 2006. 199–238.

Flaubert, Gustave. *Madame Bovary: moeurs de province.* 1857. Paris: Folio-Gallimard, 1972.

Gunning, Tom. *D. W. Griffith and the Origins of American Narrative Film: The Early Years at Biograph.* Urbana: University of Illinois Press, 1994.

Hutcheon, Linda. *A Theory of Adaptation.* New York: Routledge, 2006.

Ibsen, Henrik. *Hedda Gabler.* Trans. Rolf Fjelde. *The Complete Major Prose Plays.* New York: Plume-NAL, 1978. 689–778.

Institute for Language Study. *Learn French in Record Time.* LP. Columbia, 1958.

Kawin, Bruce F. *Mindscreen: Bergman, Godard, and First-Person Film.* Princeton: Princeton University Press, 1978.

Kozloff, Sarah. *Invisible Storytellers: Voice-Over Narration in American Fiction Film.* Berkeley: University of California Press, 1988.

LaCapra, Dominick. *Madame Bovary on Trial*. Ithaca: Cornell University Press, 1982.

Leitch, Thomas. *Film Adaptation and Its Discontents: From Gone with the Wind to The Passion of the Christ*. Baltimore: Johns Hopkins University Press, 2007.

Minnelli, Vincente, dir. *Madame Bovary*. 1949. DVD. Warner Bros., 2007.

Naremore, James, ed. *Film Adaptation*. New Brunswick: Rutgers University Press, 2000.

Naremore, James. "Introduction: Film and the Reign of Adaptation." Naremore, *Film* 1–16.

Ray, Robert B. "The Field of 'Literature and Film.'" Naremore, *Film* 38–53.

Renoir, Jean, dir. *Madame Bovary*. 1934. VHS. Hen's Tooth Video, 1989.

Stam, Robert. "Beyond Fidelity: The Dialogics of Adaptation." Naremore, *Film* 54–76.

Stam, Robert. *Literature through Film: Realism, Magic, and the Art of Adaptation*. Malden: Blackwell, 2005.

States, Bert O. *Great Reckonings in Little Rooms: On the Phenomenology of Theater*. Berkeley: University of California Press, 1985.

Tanner, Tony. *Adultery in the Novel: Contract and Transgression*. Baltimore: Johns Hopkins University Press, 1979.

Troyat, Henri. *Flaubert*. Trans. Joan Pinkham. New York: Viking, 1992.

Vargas Llosa, Mario. *The Perpetual Orgy: Flaubert and Madame Bovary*. Trans. Helen Lane. New York: Farrar, 1986.

Vérard, René. *Epilogue de "l'affaire Bovary": la victoire de Ry*. Rouen: éditions Maugard, 1959.

Vérard, René. *Ry, pays de Madame Bovary*. Ry: Galerie Bovary Musée des Automates, 1983.

Wall, Geoffrey, trans. *Madame Bovary: Provincial Lives*. By Gustave Flaubert. London: Penguin, 2003.

Wall, Geoffrey. *Flaubert: A Life*. New York: Farrar, 2001.

Wilde, Oscar. *The Picture of Dorian Gray*. 1891. New York: Signet, 1962.

David Catlin

Curiouser and Curiouser: Reflections from Twenty Years in the Lookingglass (Theatre), or ~~Stealing~~ Borrowing from the Best

Process

The Creation of an Ensemble

"Falling!" Schwimmer's young directorial voice is simultaneously force-ful and nurturing as his fellow student—Andy White—braces for a fall backwards from atop a table into the outstretched arms of the cast of student actors. "Falling." In a moment of quiet, personal terror, Andy rocks back on to his heels—his center of gravity passing the point of righting himself—and tips back into the void behind him. Falling, his eyes clench closed, his stomach jumps, and his arms proudly try not to reach back for something, anything to catch on to. He plummets back-ward, slowly—*would the fall never come to an end?* Will the hard as-bestos-tiled floor crack his skull? Shouldn't they have caught him by now? Andy plunges at 32.2 feet per second per second toward his cast mates into a newborn trust that will be challenged and nurtured over this elongated rehearsal process. Unknown to any of us then, this is the beginning of a trust that will profoundly deepen in an as yet unfath-omable twenty-year future together. Finally, a netting mattress of ten hands and forearms arrests Andy's downward momentum, returns him to terra firma, and stands him up on shaking legs, his pate and trust unbroken.

We are on the campus of Northwestern University in Evanston, Illinois in the early fall of 1986, rehearsing for a February production of *Alice in Wonderland*. David Schwimmer is directing, using some of his own bar mitzvah money to bankroll this self-produced student production. The cast of six includes future Lookingglass ensemble members Andy White, Larry DiStasi, myself, and Joy Gregory, who played Alice. The script was originally adapted by Andre Gregory and the Manhattan Project. Andre Gregory (no relation to Joy Gregory) was a peer of theater visionary Jerzy Grotowski and appeared in the title role of the film *My Dinner with Andre* and as John the Baptist in *The Last Temptation of Christ*. Under Andre Gregory's direction, another group of six students (NYU) immersed themselves in a long improvisational rehearsal process that began in 1968 and culminated in production in 1970. Some seventeen years later, Schwimmer sought to emulate that groundbreaking production—he had a copy of Richard Avedon's book *Alice In Wonderland: The Forming of a Company and the Making of a Play*. The book details in text and exquisite photography what their adaptation/rehearsal process and final creation had been.

While our peers worked on the latest Christopher Durang or John Guare play, we buried ourselves in whatever rehearsal space we could sneak into during the fall and winter quarters. (In 1986, Northwestern had both an excellent scene shop and theater complex, but a dearth of rehearsal rooms.) Our first task was to develop an ensemble. Using Viola Spolin exercises—or derivatives of Viola Spolin exercises—we fell from tables, took turns being lifted by the group, walked blindfolded, sat blindfolded, ran blindfolded, spent hours and hours creating wordless worlds of nonsense and emotion in what was purely thrilling to experience as a young performer and surely tedious for anyone to watch. Elements important to ensemble are trust, group awareness, and group decision.

Establishing Trust

Trust exercises are designed to build confidence within the group, allowing performers to stretch themselves further than they otherwise would. In the game *Buzz*, a performer creates a repeatable sound and gesture that the group immediately imitates until another performer is selected to create a new repeatable sound and gesture. Members of the group are encouraged to make sounds and gestures that are goofy—the more ridiculous the better. Knowing that you can make an outlandish proposal and that the group will immediately support you by repeating that outlandish proposal builds trust.

During a *Trust Walk*, a performer is blindfolded and guided by the sound of another's voice. The blindfolded individual is stripped of their primary source of sensory information—their sight—which often reveals a latent fear and vulnerability. A willingness to rely on someone else to keep us from bumping into a wall or stepping off the edge of the stage without putting our hands out to fend off the unseen danger requires courage and trust. Variations of this exercise include the incorporation of chairs or adjusting the speed of movement of the blindfolded individual.

There is a trust exercise where the group lifts an individual above their heads, spinning that person around, flipping them over, and "floating" them around the room. We are all accustomed to being on our feet, to find our balance and foundation. Literally having your footing taken away by a group, giving all your weight to that group, can be unsettling or scary. Eventually a euphoric feeling of buoyancy replaces that uneasiness as the group provides an experience that seems to defy gravity. This activity also shrinks the boundaries of personal space, accelerating a physical, nonsexual intimacy that is vital in the creation of physical theater.

An important rule of improvisation is "Yes and . . ."—the idea being that no matter how absurd my proposal is, all will support it and so affirm my idea. This allows for transformation to occur—a pair of tongs can "become" a crab claw, a person can "become" a duck or a playing card. With transformation and group affirmation, the audience's willing suspension of disbelief becomes that much easier. In the game *Rocket Ship*, the cast is given two minutes to build a rocket ship. Once the ship was built we would improvise some kind of adventure or journey and a nonsensical narrative was created. This activity might take hours as the actors give in/submit themselves to playing. No actual words are permitted (though occasionally nonsense language is allowed). Just as *Trust Walk* removes the primary source of perception, *Rocket Ship* (and other similar silent activities) removes our primary tools for communication and demands a nonverbal (primal, preverbal) physical communication. Similar wordless improvisations were more specific to the *Alice* stories.

Group Awareness

In the creation of a play it is very easy to concentrate on one's own behavior. So much of acting can be an internalized experience. Am I funny? Do they like me? Am I a good actor? The game *Donkey* demands that people work in groups of three to create various physical and verbal images—Rabbit, Palm Tree, Angel. The group stands in a circle, and the person who is "it" travels randomly inside the circle pointing at individuals, naming the image (again, for instance, Rabbit, Palm Tree, Angel) and counting to three. That individual and the two people on either side have three seconds to create Rabbit or Palm Tree. *Donkey* and games like it develop focus on group creation.

An exercise called *Mobile Body Sculpture* allows the group to collaboratively (and without words) create a series of physical tableaux. In one version of this exercise, a single actor would enter the center of the circle and strike some kind of arrested pose. Another actor enters and finds a way to build on that image in a manner that is physically connected to the first actor. Another actor enters and connects to the image and so on and so on. As the sculpture is being built, the actors are encouraged to support the positions of their fellow actors or to make choices that enhance or challenge the images. Once all the actors are in, a beat is established where the sculpture moves on three counts and freezes on the fourth, creating the frozen sculpture. Themes or ideas—war, love, children, the surface of the sun—may be called out by the outside leader for the group to respond to as it morphs from one statue to another. The group is encouraged to challenge each other physically, finding places to lift someone or stand on another. A physical understanding of the group's strengths, flexibility, and physical control emerges.

Group Decision: Nobody Lead, Nobody Follow

Many of our exercises are geared toward getting the group to respond as one. We have an exercise we call the *Chord*. The actors stand in a circle facing in and breathe simultaneously. The breathing eventually begins to change and a new sound emerges—a hum, a percussive beat, rounded notes. The goal is that no one person consciously takes the lead or merely waits for some one else to make a proposal. This demands a heightened state of listening with the whole body and a preparedness to respond immediately.

We also use a *mirror* exercise, which has multiple variations. *Mirroring* is precisely copying the movement of the person in front of you so that whoever is leading is undetectable to an observer. Mirroring can be done in pairs, with designated "a" and "b" participants who switch leaders/followers on an outside verbal cue and progress to switching leadership on a silent internal agreement between "a" and "b." Mirroring can also be done in a large circle with nobody leading and nobody following. Again, a heightened state of group awareness is necessary and innate leadership or subordinate behavior must be relinquished. Additionally, these exercises require a deliberate, wordless physicality, which in turn enhances individual physical grace.

What began to develop after weeks and months of these games and activities—games and activities that sometimes clearly connected to the Lewis Carrroll stories and sometimes did not—what began to develop was this intimate sense of trust between the young actors. We knew that we could fall backwards and someone would catch us. We knew that we could be intensely vulnerable with one another. There also developed a heightened physical and emotional awareness of each other—an awareness that was more common to long married couples or championship sports teams. We anticipated each other's movements and intentions, we began to know each other's fears and limits as well as our strengths and weaknesses. Wordless communication developed and our peripheral vision became enhanced. The group acted as one, the strength of the whole became greater than the sum of its parts.

Play

All of these activities and exercises develop both the ensemble and a sense of "play" within the ensemble. Watching children at play, one notes the inventive qualities of imagination and creation; the ability to transform themselves and ordinary objects into whatever the story wants; and (when playing well with others) an ability to feed off each other's creative impulses. The physical manifestation of this is often expressed just behind the performer's eyes—a twinkling indication of other worlds, boundless possibility, and fathomless soul. You can see it in all great performers, whether they are acting in a tragedy (Deanna Dunegan in *August Osage County*) or a comedy (Charlie Chaplin) or even in sports (Michael Jordan shooting the ball at the buzzer).

Performance

By the time February arrived we'd rehearsed so long that we forgot we were going to perform the show for an audience. I remember the first time we ran it in front of people. We were in one of the purloined re-

Alice in Wonderland at the Edinburgh Fringe Festival August 1987. Photo: George Catlin

hearsal rooms. The cast for *The Mee-Ow Show* (an annual student comedy show) had performances the same night we did, so we arranged for them to watch a rehearsal run. Some ninety minutes after we started—as Alice awoke from her dream with a start—the *Mee-Ow* cast was suddenly hooting and hollering, applauding wildly. So immersed were we in the story—and had been for so many months—that the applause seemed foreign—not exactly unwelcome—but neither did it seem connected to what we had done (save for the fact that they were looking at us). That purity of focus—to be entirely consumed by something—is truly rare.

We opened *Alice* later that week on Friday, 13 February 1987—a day that would be very lucky for us—for four performances at Northwestern University's Jones Residential College. The show emphasized a "poor-theater" aesthetic; Andre Gregory was a colleague of Jerzy Grotowski, who authored *Towards a Poor Theatre*, which proposed that all theater requires is an actor and an audience. The set and props were simple—a table and six bentwood chairs; a package of dinner rolls and a tub of cream cheese for the Mad Hatter's tea party; some old umbrellas to create a forest of trees; and a roll of photographer's paper (the kind they use for backdrops) to create a paper curtain. Our costumes were purchased from an Army-Navy surplus store and the cast was encouraged to embellish the baggy olive-green pants that functioned as a base costume with character-specific nuances. Alice wore a traditional Alice costume—white dress, lacey apron, and striped socks. Alan Goldwasser, who played Lewis Carroll, was terrible at sewing and opted to hot-glue his costume together. This choice proved imprudent given the challenging physicality of the show—pieces of Alan's costume would pop off throughout each performance. Larry DiStasi attached vinyl tubing to the side of his pant legs. His vision was that the other actors would blow milk into the tubing to create some kind of throbbing insect veins or arteries as he physically transformed himself into the Caterpillar.

Like the Andre Gregory version, ours was a very physical telling of the *Alice* tale—the actors' bodies transformed, as needed, into different characters, animals, and objects. The show began with us all huddled in a tangle of bodies behind the paper curtain, breathing as one to create the fearsome tale of the Jabberwock with its "jaws that bite and claws that catch." A single lighting instrument silhouetted our bodies as we enacted the famous poem. When the Jabberwock was slain and the poem came to its climax, we burst through the paper, tearing it, and so began Alice's fall down the rabbit-hole—an almost-acrobatic, frenzied, and dynamic movement sequence choreographed to kinesthetically evoke the sensation of falling. Four of us created a single mushroom upon which Larry's Caterpillar sat cross-legged and smoking a hookah. The mad tea party was played on, underneath, and around the table that, at one point, was flipped violently, sending the Dormouse (also played by DiStasi) flying. A scary moment occurred early in the rehearsal process—before our group awareness had matured—that had us huddled around Larry's writhing body, his spine seemingly snapped by an unfortunate landing on the uprighted table's edge. As Humpty Dumpty, I smashed a real egg into my face and fell from atop a teetering pile of bentwood chairs that were stacked on top of the table. We transformed into mice and crabs and dodos and ducks and pigs and a frog-footman. And when Alice waved good-bye to the White Knight (Andy White), the frenzied fall down the rabbit-hole was reenacted in exact reverse order.

Given the show's enthusiastic reception on campus, we decided to take the production to the Edinburgh Fringe Festival in August of 1987. We set about raising money for it. Alas, Schwimmer's bar mitzvah savings had all been spent on the Northwestern University production. Dean Zarefsky, of Northwestern's School of Speech, agreed to put up half the money if we could raise the other half.*

After a white limo delivered us to O'Hare—Schwimmer didn't want to risk us all traveling to the airport separately—we took off to Heathrow and waited in London for the long train ride to Edinburgh, Scotland. We lodged together in the basement of a bed and breakfast, sleeping four to a room.

The Mee-Ow cast from Northwestern was also there and staying in the rooms upstairs. After a cooked breakfast we'd make our twenty-minute walk to the Chaplaincy Center where we performed at noon. During the Edinburgh Fringe Festival, any sizeable room or hall becomes a venue for theater and performance—each space often hosting a half a dozen different shows every day, starting in the late morning and running well past midnight. We were concerned that people would mistake our version of Alice as a piece of children's theater, so our press release stressed that it was a physical version that grown-ups would enjoy. The Daily Scotsman called it an "adult-version" of Alice in Wonderland in its one-line blurb. A lot of people showed up in trench coats.

To further compete for festival audiences amidst the hundreds of other productions, we street performed at the foot of Edinburgh Castle. We'd do scenes from the play or stand frozen as Schwimmer would "sculpt" us into statues. Crowds would gather and stare at the odd American college kids. Some would take the promotional flyers that Schwimmer would place in our stock-still hands.

Walking home one night after a couple pints of Guinness—the Mee-Ow cast referred to them as "teriyaki milkshakes" owing to their brown syrupy texture—we decided to start a theater company. We loved the ensemble way of working. We loved the intense elongated rehearsal process. We loved the muscular physicality of this style of performance. And we loved working on a play that came from a literary source—that was, at its center, a great story. We loved the playfulness, the cleverness, the nonsense and the purpose of it. Schwimmer believed that the Alice

*Richard E.T. White, then Artistic Director at Wisdom Bridge, caught a performance and started booking us into elementary schools as part of their outreach program. Joyce Sloan allowed us to use Second City's ETC space to host a fundraising event and Ed Debevic's provided some of the food—Larry and Schwimmer were roller-skating waiters there, and I made hamburger patties in the back. With additional support from family and friends and generous people such as Former Ambassador to Great Britain John J. Louis and Hope Ableson, we raised enough funds match Dean Zarefsky's challenge.

stories were, in effect, loving gifts from Charles Dodgson (who wrote under the pseudonym of Lewis Carroll) to the real Alice (Alice Liddell), a child friend. Everything about the play, the adaptation, the underlying literary source, the physicality, the poor theater aesthetic seemed to invite us to push the boundaries of traditional theater. Gregory's work was nearly twenty years old by that point, but our production still felt like an awakening, a first step toward a new kind of theater unlike anything we had experienced before.

> HUMPTY. What if you had two eyes on the side of your head and your mouth up above?
> ALICE. That wouldn't look very nice.
> HUMPTY. Wait until you've tried . . .

Charles Dodgson—via Andre Gregory and Richard Avedon—seemed to challenge us to reach beyond the status quo; to take familiar elements of performance—acrobatics, dance, film/video, ritual, music, storytelling—and combine them in new ways.

The Lookingglass Theatre Company's board of directors recently challenged the ensemble to identify our core values. We came up with an initial list of eleven or twelve and wanted to further distill those to three or four essential values. Ben Cameron, formerly head of the Theatre Communications Group, suggested the metaphor of weaving. It is difficult to see the pattern when you are sitting at the loom making the work. But if you look back at what you've done, relevant patterns become clearer. Looking from a distance, we saw that much of the Ensemble's work had elements of *collaboration, invention,* and *transformation.* These Lookingglass core values pervade every part of our company both onstage and beyond—from boardroom and administrative office to the work we do in classrooms in the public school system. Those core values are essential to the storytelling and were established in that first production of *Alice* in 1987.

After returning home from Edinburgh, we spent the fall selecting members to start the company. The original eight members—Eva Barr, Thom Cox, Larry DiStasi, Joy Gregory, David Kersnar, David Schwimmer, Andy White, and myself—assembled in our first meeting on February 13, 1988—exactly one year after the opening of *Alice* on campus, to formally found the company. Schwimmer, the son of two lawyers, brought a six-page agenda with bullet points like "Mission Statement," "Company Name," and "Late —Penalties—a dollar-a-minute?" and "First Show?" We set about discussing what kind of theater we wanted to make.

Inspiration and Influences

Early in our history, there was a desire to "steal" from as many kinds of performance as we saw, read about, or even in some cases, merely heard about. We sought to build on the innovation of others. We were initially inspired by Andre Gregory and the Manhattan Project, but also by others like Grotowski and the Open Theatre. Before graduating, Schwimmer directed a production of Jean-Claude Van Italie's *The Serpent*, originally created with the Open Theatre.

Northwestern University

At the time, the Northwestern theater freshman took introductory courses in theater, performance, and communication. Acting classes began in the sophomore year and for the most part a student would study with the same acting teacher and class until he or she graduated. There was a general progression of curriculum, focused on the classics, starting with the Greeks followed by Shakespeare, Moliere, Ibsen, Shaw, and eventually moving into more contemporary material—Pinter, Albee, Orton. All of the founding members were in the Theatre Program in the School of Speech and many of us were in David Downs's acting class. David and other members of the theater faculty—Bud Beyer and Ann Woodworth—had studied with Alvina Krause, who is credited with founding Northwestern's Theater Department. Her background in oral interpretation had great influence on the theater and acting curriculum at Northwestern.

World of the Play

As students in David Downs's class we were taught to identify and examine the "world of the play." That is, if I am acting in a French farce, I might study ballet to indicate the lightness of my spine or even the deft delivery of lines. Or I might look at the paintings of Rene Magritte to inform a sense of whimsy or subversion. The deliberate pointillist brushwork of Georges Seurat and its precise placement of paint might suggest a similarly deliberate and precise landing of ideas and phrases. If the story is Russian, I might listen to balalaika music or Tchaikovsky to inform how I walk or the cadence of my speech or how the emotions of my character might crescendo. One might even note the French influence on

Russian culture and how both a lightness of mood and heaviness of the soul can coexist within a character. By studying the world of the play (and the world that the playwright was living in) a *style* of performance emerges that allows the text to work—that is, to create the intended response with the audience. Northwestern's acting program has a liberal arts orientation (rather than the singular theater training focus of a conservatory), and students are required to take courses outside their major. This broad approach to learning reinforced the message we were studying in acting class—that to be students of theater, we had to be students of life.

Style is "how" the story is told, and this early exploration of style has had an impact on the Ensemble's fascination with how we tell stories. More than one critic of our work has suggested that Lookingglass focuses on style over substance. My opinion is that the substance of our work is not always found on the immediate surface, but is deeply psychological and is often found contained within the metaphor.

The Actor as Director

Often an acting program offers a practical curriculum that emphasizes getting the actor to work. David Downs's class was more focused on getting the play to work than the actor. Downs challenged us to think like a director—to identify what it is that the playwright is ultimately getting to—i. e., the substance of the story. What is the story about? What do we want our audiences to feel or do when the play is over? Why does this play need to be told? As actors, every choice we make for our character should build toward that end goal. That was a very freeing idea: to remove the focus from the self and locate it on the story. That shift in thinking had a profound effect on us, creating story-centric artists. I think the focus away from the self, combined with three years working together in an acting class, allowed us to more easily embrace the ensemble ethic.

Adapting Literature

The concept of performing non-traditional text as theater—books, letters, myths, fairytales—is inviting in many ways. Foremost, perhaps is that the underlying sources are among literature's great and enduring tales from throughout history and around the world. Many of these stories have survived hundreds and thousands of years. For a story to endure indicates an inherent universal truth that has ensured each story's preservation. There is likely to be contained within the story or myth

Lauren Hirte as Alice. Photo: Michael Brosilow.

some reasoning or revelation that illuminates the human experience. The act of reading can be an individual exploration of what it is to be human. Theater provides a similar, but communal version of this experience. Both a book and a play demand that the reader and audience actively imagine details—visual and aural details that a static visual form, such as film, might provide.

From an actor's perspective, the ability to portray a role that perhaps no one has ever performed before is deeply engaging—there is no actual, definitive performance hanging over the actor's head. Yet an actor must also compete with the million different versions of those characters that have been cast in the imaginations of generations of readers. A book also contains a wealth of character description not commonly found in a traditional play. These characters have been created by the world's master storytellers—Homer, Dostoyevsky, Dickens.

The challenge for the adapter can also be great—to capture the essence, to distill hundreds of pages into a single evening (or even a series of evenings) without sacrificing the soul of the novel or other text. Often beloved characters need to be killed off or collapsed into other characters. An adapter is more beholden to dramatic tension to keep the audience engaged. With a book, the reader may set it down and return later, in some cases years later. Books are also completely unencumbered of geographical and chronological shifts—flashbacks and shifts in location can happen between sentences and are not slowed by scene shifts and costume changes.

When starting the company, the idea of adapting literature was appealing for many reasons. We didn't have to pay a playwright. We could reach back to stories in the public domain and adapt them ourselves. We were emboldened to do so by the faculty of Northwestern's Performance Studies Department. Frank Galati taught a class called Presentational Aesthetics, in which student directors were encouraged to adapt any text—short stories, poems, astrology readings, letters, anything—into a five to ten minute piece to be performed and discussed in class. Galati's professional adaptation of John Steinbeck's *The Grapes of Wrath* inspired many of our artists to tackle large sweeping epic pieces of literature. Paul Edwards taught a summer performance class called Summer Fiction, in which students would stage and perform different works of fiction every week or two. Paul's larger adaptations of stories by Flaubert and F. Scott Fitzgerald provided further examples of distilling literature's great stories into theatrical events. Dwight Conquergood had a class that required students to create solo performances based on the biographies of living or dead individuals.

Stealing from the Circus and the World of Dance

As we were founding the company, Pilobolus toured Chicago with their unique dance-theater performance. Pilobolus's style is muscular and acrobatic; creating a series of impossible images. By impossible, I mean that we watch the groupings of dancers become something that no longer seems human or humanly possible; images that are not quite comprehensible. These images cascade one after the other in a way that is elusive—each one hard to hold onto because the next arresting combination of bodies pushes the last one out of the brain. The physicality kinesthetically draws the audience to the edge of their seats. The audience inhales without exhaling, hoarding its own breath in dizziness. We thought if we could create a similar kind of expressive physicality, yet with a distinct storyline, we could create a truly extraordinary and distinctive theater experience.

Cirque du Soleil also came to Chicago in its early days of tent touring. Gone were the animal acts, allowing the audience to focus on the impossible gravity-defying human feats of daring. Gone also were the iconic white-faced, red-nose clowns, more likely to induce fear or ennui than laughter. In their place, fantastical characters with dark edges made us laugh and amazed us with their multi-disciplinary skills as they walked on rolling globes, played guitar, and flew through the air on trapeze. The calliope gave way to electronically supported live music, sung or played in modern wordless compositions. The now iconic blue and yellow tent provided a return to a more intimate experience than the massive indoor arenas American commercial circuses used to present their shows. Cirque du Soleil escalated the level of theatricality in its overwhelming use of spectacle and introduced a wisp of narrative and a visual cohesion to the acts. Just as we were passionate about redefining the theatrical experience, here was an example of a company redefining the circus industry and creating a new tradition of circus art. Again, audiences found themselves breathless, at the edge of their seats watching the impossible, experiencing the defiance of danger and gravity.

We go to the theater to encounter the impossible, to experience the defiance of danger and gravity in a communal environment. The "impossible" might be witnessing an actor transform into a completely different person. Or the impossible might be the willing suspension of disbelief that allows an audience to "see" details in a set that aren't there. The danger and gravity are psychological and emotional. We watch characters wrestle with the demons of jealousy, unrequited love, betrayal, alcoholism, racism. Comedy has inherent danger—the fear of telling a joke that no one laughs at, dying on stage, or the fear of not getting a joke or laughing at something that others find serious. The use of circus arts in our work adds a real sense of the impossible, genuine danger, and the literal defiance of gravity.

Peer Influences

At the same time, the New Criminals, led by John Cusack and Jeremy Piven, were creating work that was a collision of rock-and-roll and Commedia dell'Arte technique. We did workshops with members of their company and incorporated what we gleaned—heightened emotional states, white-face, passing the focus—into Schwimmer's staging of *The Jungle* and other shows. Mark Messing and Cin Salach created Loofah Method that combined dance, poetry, film, computer-generated music, and TV trays into unique low-tech performances. Redmoon Theater creates both large- and small-scale object work that can be site-specific or designed for traditional theater venues.

European Influences

In the 1990s, the Chicago International Theatre Festival brought some of the world's exciting performance companies to Chicago and provided low-price vouchers to Chicago's theater community. The audacious visual spectacle of the Netherland's Dogtroop made an impact on the work that John Musial creates for Lookingglass. A climactic moment from Musial's *The Great Fire* saw an enormous wall of shelves come crashing to the stage floor and was reminiscent of the visual onstage destruction of Dogtroop's performance at the Skyline Stage on Navy Pier. The whimsy of *Le Cirque Imaginaire*—featuring a very young James Thierray and his parents—created images that would haunt us and be referenced in our staging of Steven Berkoff's adaptation of Kafka's *The Metamorphosis*. At one point James scooted between the four tall peg stilts that his father was using to traverse the stage in a lumbering, giraffe-like fashion. In *Metamorphosis*, Larry DiStasi (as Gregor Samsa) moved cockroach-like, two peg stilts and two crutches creating spindly insect legs, as Heidi Stillman (Gregor's sister) scooted beneath her brother. Canada's Carbon 14 created *Le Dortoir*, a mostly wordless dreamscape set inside a dormitory, and this influenced many of our movement sequences, including work created for *The Master and Mar-*

garita. Other influences include Karen Finley, Pina Bauch, Bread and Puppet, and Jelly Eye Drum Theatre.

Ensemble Inspirations

Chicago is among the nation's leading centers for ensemble theater. The ensemble work of Steppenwolf, Remains, Body Politic, Organic, Wisdom Bridge, and Compass Players blazed a path for companies such as Lookingglass and others to follow. In the case of Steppenwolf and Remains, these ensembles acted as mentors for our younger company. Nationally, the Bloomsburg Theatre Ensemble (Northwestern grads who followed Alvina Krause to a small town of 12,000 in central Pennsylvania to found an ensemble company), Theatre de la Jeune Lune (Minneapolis), Mabou Mines, and the Wooster Group were all important to us. Each of these companies gave us ideas about how to model our organization, administratively and how we interacted as artists. John Malkovich reportedly was asked what he thought the key to Steppenwolf's success was. He answered that it had to do with respect—the ensemble members respected each other even when they did not always get along.

Lookingglass Mission Statement

We spent many evenings after our various day jobs debating over the wording of our mission statement. We opted to let the language be more elaborate, more poetic, to reflect our love of literature, to set us apart from other theater companies and to indicate that we were interested in making profound experiences. We wanted to make theater exciting for all and particularly to compete for the attention of our own MTV generation, who seemed to be distracted from going to the theater by experiences prepackaged with visual and aural information—music videos, movies, and video games. We wanted the theater we made to be different from anything you'd seen before and committed ourselves to learning new methods of performance. We wanted to push the envelope of theater experience. We also wanted our work to be affordable and to be the kind of work that all could enjoy.

"Oh my, how curious everything is!"—Alice
    Lewis Carroll's *Through the Looking Glass and What Alice Found There*

When Alice walked through the looking glass, she walked into a world beyond imagination. She walked into a world more involving and intoxicating than any movie or circus, more thrilling than a high-speed chase, more frightening than a child's nightmare, and more beautiful than a thunderstorm on a hot summer night. She awoke with a new sense of herself in the world and her own power within it.

Reflected in Lewis Carroll's achievement is the mission of the Lookingglass Theatre Company. Through theater, which invites, even demands, interaction with its audience, our goal is to fire the imagination with love, to celebrate the human capacity to taste and smell, weep and laugh, create and destroy, and wake up where we first fell—changed, charged, and empowered.

The Lookingglass Theatre Company combines a physical and improvisational rehearsal process centered on ensemble with training in theater, dance, music, and the circus arts. We seek to redefine the limits of theatrical experience and to make theater exhilarating, inspirational, and accessible to all.

Playgoing is often a cerebral experience; ideas are received through the brain. Some plays are emotional journeys that are experienced through the heart. We wanted our audiences to experience our work from the gut—the sensation when your breath is taken away and your stomach drops. At our most idealistic, we hoped that a person would leave the theater feeling a bit woozy in the stomach; that on the way home perhaps or lying in bed, the effects would travel upward to the heart and shake up the soul up a bit; and maybe the next day over coffee or stepping out into the first morning light, the previous night's theater experience would finally percolate up to the brain, fire up some new synapses, and leave a person feeling and thinking differently about the world he or she lives in.

Over the last twenty years, we've thought of changing our mission statement, refining it—but in the end we find that we still profoundly believe in it, so much so that the ensemble remains deeply engaged in the company in a way that I believe is rare for organizations over twenty years old.

Naming the Company

After toying with names such as Ironwood Ensemble, Open Hand Theatre Company, Liquid Mountain, Underground Theatre Conspiracy, and Theatre-A-Go-Go, we eventually agreed on the Looking Glass

Theatre Project. We liked the reference to Lewis Carroll and the accompanying associations of madness, clever language, highly theatrical characters, and a transformative journey/adventure. We also liked the idea of a looking glass for its metaphoric connotations: as a mirror—for theater to reflect life—and as a magnifying glass—to examine an idea or issue. We loved the indication of process that the word "project"confers—that something is being made rather than merely presented. Ironically, we later embraced a typo in a press release that accidentally changed our company name to Lookingglass Theatre Company.

For our first professional production—as the Looking Glass Theatre Project—we had two goals: create our own adaptation of Lewis Carroll's *Alice* stories and take the Chicago theater scene by storm. Following the example of Andre Gregory and the Manhattan Project, we set about a long improvisational rehearsal process to stage *Through the Looking-Glass, and What Alice Found There*. David Kersnar, founding co-artistic director, directed and was in charge of the first *Alice* adaptation. Again, we rehearsed for months and months prior to production. Again, the aesthetic was poor theater, although this time the budget afforded a $35 strobe light, sheets of foam for the floor, and a used parachute from the Army-Navy Surplus. We hired a dance instructor to teach us movement and a gymnastics coach to begin working on tumbling and rudimentary acrobatics.

The Mary Zimmerman Approach

Not long after starting the company, we saw a student production of the *Odyssey* directed by Northwestern University grad student Mary Zimmerman. The production was staged in two parts and took well over four hours. The performance was completely transformative, and inventive, a multidisciplinary blending of text, movement, and film—not unlike the work we were seeking to make. What was different was the lyrical physicality, the use of gesture, formal staging, and the layering of text within the soundscape—all a welcome contrast to our raw muscularity. We convinced Zimmerman to stage the professional world premiere with Lookingglass. Mary Zimmerman soon joined the company as an ensemble member, and a unique Lookingglass aesthetic began to emerge.

Much of what I have learned about adaptation, I have learned from observing Mary Zimmerman or from being an actor within her creative process. What is perhaps most unique about Zimmerman's rehearsal method is that there is no script on the first day of rehearsal. Occasionally there might be a single scene or a song written, but often nothing—certainly nothing tangible for an actor to begin committing to memory or making choices about. What does exist on that first day is her relationship to the source material. This relationship usually—depending on the underlying text—has been accumulating in her since her childhood, when as a precocious young reader she consumed many of these ancient stories. At some point later in life they return to consume her again, often on a subconscious or just-below-conscious plane. Some personal issue that is working itself out summons the story, and she pitches it to the company. The pitch is often very expressive of what the audience's experience might be—filled with visual suggestions of what she envisions happening. But what is often most persuading to the group is how passionately she is taken by it all—even if that passion, or rather the source of that passion, is only tacitly understood. When the proposal is voted in she begins truly immersing herself in the story, devouring various translations of the stories. While preparing for *Argonautika*, she reported having to limit how much she could read at night for fear that the material would keep her awake throughout the night. Though no scene writing is happening at this point, she is beginning to see how certain scenes will be—there will be a centaur, harpy puppets, a launch sequence where the ship's sails are hoisted and the heroes embark on their epic adventure. She begins to see certain actors playing particular parts, and she begins intense conversations with designers to plan the various production elements.

Given the constraints of time and physics, the set must be designed and in process of being constructed prior to the first day of rehearsal and consequently prior to a script being written. This dictates several important things. The designer cannot turn to a script for traditional cues. The designer must have more thorough communication with Mary and a deeper understanding of the source material. It also dictates that the design should have some scenic flexibility to accommodate what is discovered in the rehearsal process. The script can also therefore respond to the design.

Costumes, props, and lighting must also be responsive to the production's shorter creation process—though Mary has many ideas about what she knows she wants from those departments in advance of rehearsals starting.

She might also have some casting ideas already in place—this actor will play Hercules or Sheherazade or Odysseus. But other actors might not have a single line or part until weeks into the process, which can be unnerving the first time you work with Mary. Because the ink is still wet when the actor does get his or her pages, and because there is not a lot of time to tinker and explore, the actor must make strong initial choices and therefore not overthink the character. This also allows Mary's writing to respond to the specific strengths and weaknesses of her cast, many of whom she has worked with before.

In a traditional process the playwright's script might be sacrosanct. All the director's effort is to make the written word work on the stage. Indeed, play scripts are sometimes worthy of that reverence. In the Zimmerman process the script is fluid. The script responds to what she is responding to within the story, the design, the cast, and even a little bit to the realities of time and space: I need this costume change to happen here so I'll create a brief moment between the two rival kings. She is at once immensely collaborative—the show develops around and because of the work of her team of artists—and at the same time almost dictatorial. She has an unyielding and clear vision of the show vital to the show's artistic success. The words she chooses come from the underlying author, the translator, herself, and occasionally her cast. This allows for her work to convey its ancient, communal truth while speaking to its audience with a very immediate voice.

Lookingglass Alice—A Return to Wonderland

The opening of our theater in the Water Tower Water Works on Friday, June 13, 2003 (another lucky day) marked an important new chapter in our company's history. After fifteen years of being nomadic—twenty-two different venues in that span of time—we finally had a permanent home. My fellow ensemble member, and then artistic director, Laura Eason, thought it appropriate for us to return to where we first fell, to the Alice stories that had launched, inspired, and provided the name for our company. Given that I had been part of the original cast from both of the earlier productions, Laura asked me to propose a new version of this seminal source material.

Finding a Personal Connection (or Way in) to the Work

Central to all our proposal processes is the question, "Why does this story need to be told?" Schwimmer had often talked about these Alice stories as a loving gift from Charles Dodgson to the real life Alice, Alice Liddell.

At the time Laura asked me to work on this I had just become a father for the first time. Before my daughter was born, I had always strangely presumed that my real relationship with my daughter would start when she was three or four. I had taught drama through Looking-glass and at the Actor's Gymnasium in Evanston, and I seemed to jibe best with the post-toddler set.

I soon realized how profoundly connected I *was* to my daughter from the moment of her birth and before, how the mastering of each stage of her life was met with simultaneous celebration and a surprising sense of mourning. When she was able to sit up on her own I was, of course, thrilled. But I also realized that gone too was that helpless babe that desperately needed me to hold her for everything. When she began to crawl, I realized I would never know again that little creature who relied on me to carry her across the room. When she was two she wanted to be a princess. At six she talks like Hannah Montana or Sharpay from *High School Musical*. And her three-year-old sister can't wait to be six. Even then, when my first daughter was only two, I was gripped with this dread that she was rocketing through life and that life was rocketing by me. I began to empathize with how Dodgson felt to see his beloved friend Alice growing up and out of her childhood. Or perhaps more accurately, the wonder-child disappearing.

My adaptation became a way of telling my daughter to slow down, not to grow up so fast. I thought that given Carroll's love of childhood, I could find something in every scene that might help my daughter hold on to what is great about being young.

The Big Idea

This led to the "big idea" or thematic guide to shape the structure of the adaptation. In *Through the Looking-Glass, and What Alice Found There*, Alice steps through a mirror above the fireplace mantle. She soon discovers that she is on a chessboard surrounded by giant chess pieces. Carroll constructed the story so that Alice (as pawn) moves across the board to become a queen, meeting various characters along the way.

I began to see the Alice story as a journey about growing up and becoming a queen. Having a daughter who wanted to become a princess gave me an immediate and personal way in to the adaptation: each square would represent a stage in life on the way to becoming an adult. As I immersed myself in the many terrific stories and adventures from the two books, I thought about what life stages each story might represent. With only eight squares on the chessboard, this meant that I had an inherent limit as to *how many* stories to include and a thematic guide/big idea to determine *which* stories to use.

In thinking about growing up, I thought a lot about the self. And given the prevalent theme of mirrors, I thought of Charles Cooley's "looking glass self." The idea being that how we think of ourselves is influenced by how we perceive others to think of us. In early versions of the script, I had two Alices, an older and younger Alice who would exist simultaneously, one living the journey and one reflecting on her adventure. However, I began to like the idea that the actress playing Alice was the only woman in the cast. It would give the play a dominant male energy to perhaps reflect the unbalanced power created by the age difference between the seven-year-old Alice Liddell and the adult Charles Dodgson. It was a disturbing balance that could overwhelm Alice, but also give her something to overcome. This casting choice also connected all the characters Alice meets more directly to Dodgson. There was also something fun and appropriately deviant about men playing many of the female characters. So I decided to use Dodgson as the reflection. This allowed the opportunity to explore the psychological impact that Dodgson and the real Alice had on each other.

ALICE. Mr. Dodgson?

DODGSON. (over microphone) Y-y-y-yes, Alice?

ALICE. Where are you, Mr. Dodgson?

DODGSON. I am here. Alw-w-ways here.

ALICE. No, you went away.

DODGSON. I n-n-never went away. You did.

ALICE. But, I'm here.

DODGSON. Yes. I see you.

ALICE. Where is here?

DODGSON. Where you are. I am there. I am here.

I was further struck by Carroll's observation that we often think of the mirror as an exact copy of ourselves but that it is actually opposite.

ALICE & DODGSON. Curiouser! Inside a looking glass, I'm supposed to see . . . Myself. No, my self. Then which hand am I holding up?

ALICE & DODGSON. My—

ALICE. Left.

DODGSON. My Right.

ALICE & DODGSON. Curiouser and curiouser!

Design Process

Dan Ostling, who frequently collaborates with Mary Zimmerman, created the set. He had the idea that we should start the play visually acknowledging people's expectations of what they would see and then explode those expectations. We toyed with trying to have the furniture actually fly out over the audience. We turned to John Tenniel's iconic illustrations for the Alice stories. We decided to start with the idea of the looking glass itself. We split the theater into two halves with two separate audience entrances. Audiences entering on one side would see a Victorian fireplace, large armchair, a mantle clock, and a large mirror above all against a giant curtain of black fabric. In the mirror the audience could see the other half of the audience who had entered into a mirror image of what they were seeing. For the most part people believed that there actually was a mirror reflecting the back of the mantle clock that they were looking at, rather than the actual back of a different mantle clock that the other audience was seeing the front of.

When the play starts, one side of the audience sees Alice sitting in a Victorian armchair talking to her cat and hears the voice of Dodgson, a voice that seems to exist in her memory. The audience on the other side sees Dodgson sitting in a Victorian armchair and hears the voice of Alice that seems to haunt his memory. When the clock strikes thirteen they stand and discover each other in the mirror. When they both touch the mirror there is a loud shattering sound, a blinding light, and the curtain of black fabric comes crashing to the ground—our explosion— revealing the other audience, the other world, that we are very much in a theater. The voice of the stage manager is heard:

SARA. (V/O from the booth) Strike furniture please. Standby Lights 9 & Sound 65. Stand by, White Rabbit. Try not to miss this cue. We are standing by, Mr. Dodgson.

DODGSON. Thank you.

ALICE. Where are we, Mr. Dodgson?

DODGSON. Through the looking glass.

ALICE. On the other side then?

DODGSON. On the other side.

The set is cleared by stagehands, and the White Rabbit as Dodgson prepares to send Alice down the rabbit hole.

ALICE. White Rabbit! Where did he go, Mr. Dodgson?

DODGSON. He's headed d-d-down this rabbit hole.

ALICE. Down the rabbit hole? What do you suppose it's like, falling down a rabbit hole?

DODGSON. Something like the moon tugging at your apron strings.

ALICE. Like being off balance, then?

DODGSON. Like being adrift in a sea of tears.

A blue wave of fabric crashes across the stage.

ALICE. A sea of tears? How wonderfully sad.

DODGSON. Or like being in love.

ALICE. In love? Like a grown-up?

DODGSON. Oh, no grown-ups are so seldom off balance and that's why I shouldn't recommend that.

ALICE. Yes, but Queens are ever so full of poise and grace and, and . . . balance. And, I should so like to be a queen.

DODGSON. And so you shall. Off you go then, down the rabbit-hole with you.

Alice then falls down the rabbit hole, which is a round steel hoop called a Lyra. The lyra is attached to a winch at a single point allowing it to spin and be hoisted in the air. Our choreographer Sylvia Hernandez created a routine to express the long floating fall that Carroll describes.

Would the fall never come to an end?

As Alice floats down the rabbit hole in the air above the stage, thirty-foot-long pieces of blue fabric are manipulated to create the *sea of tears* on the floor. For me this is a reference to the watery amniotic sac where we spend the beginning of our life. We built into the soundscape the sound of a fetal heartbeat. Falling down the rabbit hole is the journey down the birth canal. She lands with a thump and her adventure is finally born and her trip begins.

The baby that turns into a pig (from the Pig & Pepper chapter in *Alice's Adventures in Wonderland*) represented our infanthood (and was later cut when the show clocked in at two hours and twenty minutes). The Cheshire Cat is that first strange and scary friend:

> CHESHIRE CAT. Keep the squares in front of you. One square at a time, as the lady says. You will travel from one square to the next and on again to the next. Square after square until you reach the end. The first square belongs to the Queen. The second square is where you begin. Square after square until the eighth and final square—and then you will become a queen. Along the way, you'll meet the other pieces of this game—your knight, your queen and myself. Among others.

The first square is occupied by the Red Queen who in our play is an amalgamation of the Queen of Hearts (*Wonderland*) and the Red Queen (*Looking-Glass*). She is parental and represents all things rational—order, rules, and etiquette.

> RED QUEEN. One step at a time. From A to B to C and so on. Take away the rule and what remains? Chaos. Upon entering the ballroom, as upon entering unto society, a young woman, of reason and comportment, shall so endeavor to bear about her all manner of manner, and must reject those improprieties deemed low and vulgar, such as and including specifically, unnecessary expressions of pleasure and whimsy. A young woman must curb any impulses which might result in idle laughter or such similar activities that might cause one to scoff at the rules which govern civilization and that have allowed for the betterment of mankind in its progress from Barbarism and Chaos.
>
> Tempt not Cataclysm and Catastrophe with aforementioned whimsy.

The Red Queen is also enormous. The top of her head is thirteen feet above the stage floor. We wanted to create a size perspective between the Red Queen and Alice similar to that of a newborn and its parent. Across the stage in the eighth square, Alice sees the White Queen. She is elderly and represents all that is irrational (love, nonsense . . .).

ALICE. Am I addressing the White Queen?

WHITE QUEEN. If you call that addressing—It's not my notion of the thing at all. I call it unwinding.

ALICE. I didn't unwind the yarn.

WHITE QUEEN. You didn't yet, but you soon shall. And once it's all unwound it will all surely wind up in the end, no doubt. The tales always do.

ALICE. But why should I be responsible for something I haven't done yet?

WHITE QUEEN. But surely you shall do it, and so why shouldn't you be responsible?

Pawn to Queen's Third / The Toddler Phase

Alice meets the Caterpillar in the third square. The caterpillar, like a toddler, is all legs and questions—"Who are you?" I thought of an inchworm measuring its world—collecting and cataloguing information.

CATERPILLAR. Whatwhatwhatwhatwhatwhatwhatwhat?

ALICE. Excuse me . . .

CATERPILLAR. Whywhywhywho are *you*?

ALICE. Who are you?

CATERPILLAR. Who are you?

ALICE. Who am I?

CATERPILLAR. Who are you?

ALICE. Oh, Caterpillar, I—I hardly know, just at present—at least I know who I *was* when I got up this morning, but I think I must have been changed several times since then.

CATERPILLAR. Whenwhenwhywhy . . . what?

ALICE. I can't explain myself, because I'm not myself, you see.

Three men play the caterpillar to give it many legs and voices. The costumes are inspired by toddler pajamas—initially they were like Dr. Denton's flannel, one-piece footed pajamas. But that choice proved too hot for the actor's intense physical movements, so they were redesigned to be like two-piece cotton Gap toddler pajamas that my daughter was wearing at the time.

The shirts and pants are a pale (inchworm) green with dark green stripes to evoke the ribbing on a caterpillar's belly.

Pawn to Queen's Fourth / Our First (Non-parental) Teacher

Alice meets the White Knight, who is both heroic and absurd. He is forever inventing things, much of it nonsense, challenging Alice to think beyond the rational, ordered world of the Red Queen. He introduces concepts of identity and existence:

> WHITE KNIGHT. It's the Red King asleep and snoring! What do you suppose he's dreaming about?
>
> ALICE. Nobody can guess that.
>
> WHITE KNIGHT. He dreams about *you*. And if he left off dreaming, where do you suppose you'd be?
>
> ALICE. Where I am now, of course.
>
> WHITE KNIGHT. Not you! You'd be nowhere. Why, you're only a sort of thing in his dream! If that there king was to wake, you'd go out—bang!—just like a candle!

Pawn to Queen's Fifth / Preadolescence

Alice has her first encounter with schoolboys, Tweedledee and Tweedledum. I remember in fourth and fifth grades that every day some one would be "called-out," meaning they were challenged to be in a fight after school. Usually these middle school melees never materialized because the challenge was inadvertently (or sometimes intentionally) forgotten. In the book the Tweedles are fighting over a broken rattle.

> Tweedledum and Tweedledee agreed to have a battle,
>   For Tweedledum, said Tweedledee, had had spoiled his nice
> new rattle.

In our version they are "fighting" for Alice's attention. In our initial version the two actors created a series of escalating pantomimes vying for her favor—picking a bouquet of flowers, winning an enormous carnival bear, calling a trained dove to land on her finger. This escalates to a pushing and shoving match before Alice interrupts to introduce herself. In the current version of the show, the actors are especially gifted dancers, and one member of the cast is able to beat-box, so we changed the pantomimes into a dance-off.

Carroll describes Alice's initial encounter as:

And suddenly they were dancing.

Phil Smith, from the ensemble, had the idea that it would be fun if at some point in the play a raucous dance party just seemed to start. It made sense to put it there. I remember my own awkward sixth grade dance with all the attendant fear and anxiety—pale faces and eyes pie-shaped like deer caught in high beams. Will someone dance with me? Will they think I'm handsome or pretty? Sylvia Hernandez DiStasi choreographed a sequence of school-days dance moves—running man, robot, roger rabbit—that progressed into a three-person tango and eventually had Alice flipping out of their arms, asking them

> ALICE. Do you think I'm pretty?
> TWEEDLES. Ahhhhhhhhhhhhhh! (*they exit*)

Pawn to Queen's Sixth / Teen

From an early age we are fascinated by the unknown world of the grown-up party. My daughters spend hours having tea parties, trying on adult-like conversations. I remember being clad in flannel pajamas, listening at the banister to the laughing voices of my parents and their bridge club. Or I was sitting at the top of the stairs on New Year's Eve as champagne and Harvey Wallbangers and ice cream bombs were consumed below. I remember being fourteen and hearing about the college parties my brothers went to. I couldn't wait to experience all that firsthand. We selected the Mad Hatter's tea party to represent a teen's first taste of adulthood.

Pawn to Queen's Seventh / Young Adulthood

Alice meets Humpty Dumpty in our seventh square—the last square before she becomes a queen. She must survive the grief we all endure at the inevitable loss of a loved one.

Pawn to Queen's Eighth / The Pawn Becomes a Queen

To mark her achievement there is a grand, frenzied ball—in our production Sylvia choreographed a routine we called *bungee-juggling* where Alice (on bungee cords) is juggled amidst several brightly colored giant exercise balls. Giant balloons of complementary colors are thrown into the audience. The effect is dizzying, distorting, and celebratory—we aren't use to seeing balls this size being juggled. At the climax of the routine Alice performs a *fast-spin* on the bungee cords creating a blur of color. She lands as the sounds of the party fade away and she is crowned a Queen.

Previews

During the preview process for the initial run, we tried various endings. Previews are a vital stage in our process for creating new work. Given the physical demands of this kind of work, rehearsals during previews are also needed to make adjustments for injuries. The day after each preview, we generally have about five hours of rehearsal to make cuts and changes to the show. The long rehearsal on Tuesday and the Wednesday afternoon during the second week of previews allows for significant changes to occur. For instance, our very first run of Alice clocked in at two hours and twenty-one minutes. By the end of that second week of previews the show ran one hour and thirty-six minutes.

Lookingglass Alice *opened February 13, 2005, eighteen years to the day after we opened* Alice in Wonderland *at Northwestern University on February 13, 1987. In 2007,* Lookingglass Alice *traveled to the McCarter in Princeton, the New Victory in New York City, the Arden in Philadelphia, and back to Lookingglass in the summers of 2007 and 2008. There have been 292 performances of* Lookingglass Alice. *In the Fall of 2008, Lookingglass Theatre Company staged its fiftieth world premiere, an adaptation of Fyodor Dostoyevsky's* The Brothers Karamazov, *written and directed by Lookingglass ensemble member Heidi Stillman.*

If you wish to inquire about performing Lookingglass Alice *or to obtain a copy of the script, please contact Brea Hayes (bhayes@lookingglass theatre.org).*

Anna D. Shapiro

The Discipline of Directing

Recently, I directed a new play called *August: Osage County*. The first iteration was performed at Steppenwolf Theatre, the theater that had commissioned, developed, and workshopped the play over the course of two years. Tracy Letts, the playwright, had asked me to direct the play before the first draft was even completed, so I had been with the project from the outset. The sprawling, three-act, three-plus hour production was challenging to direct, but not oppressively so, and I enjoyed the process a great deal. Of course, I thought it would live ever so briefly in real life, as most plays do, and then disappear into the ether and leave me with my own fond memories.

August: Osage County won the 2007 Pulitzer Prize for Drama as well as the Drama Desk, Outer Critics Circle, and Tony awards for best play, and I myself received those awards for direction. In late 2008, we left for London and the National Theatre, and in the summer of 2009 begins the national tour. And I am wondering, as I always do, what it all means.

There have been several instances in the past few years that have demanded from me an ordered recollection of my professional life—why I started directing, why I started teaching, how I do both, and why I continue to pursue either. These assignments have always been exciting to me, the answers coming easily but not without thought as they helped me understand my day, whether that be the one spent in the rehearsal room or the one spent in the classroom. I have, on one hand, a very practical relationship to directing. I understand it in its most basic formula: *a sequence of assignments that result in a controlled and repeatable event that always looks like it's happening for the first and only time.* On the other hand, directing is a deeply personal experience as it allows me to create environments that, for me, are rife with meaning. I am endlessly fascinated by the relationship between my interests in those environments and those of the rest of the world—where do I meet my fellow man? Where do we diverge? And these questions have always led me to teaching.

I believe it is the role of a teacher, especially a teacher of artists, to create an environment that encourages students to investigate, develop, and articulate their own points of view. They must learn how to *find* the stories that have meaning for them as well as tell them. Certainly a successful directing teacher creates opportunities for students to develop a comprehensive understanding of the sequence of events in rehearsal, the craft of the actor, the visual vocabulary that includes the theatrical impact of images, and text analysis, but they also have to have in place a system designed to support the internal process of becoming a *thinker.* Because as much as directing is a collaborative act, it is also equally solitary, and the demystification of that part of the process is critical to the success of any directing professor. And these two conversations, that of the director and the teacher of directing, have been going on simultaneously in my life for ten years. As I grow older and the world around me grows darker, the questions around these issues have taken on more complexity, and as a result, so has their place in my own soul. I am a different artist today than I was even five years ago, and I am re-engaged in the question of the value of this work and the ethics of educating artists to continue its practice.

The event that *August* has become has served as a catalyst for much of this thinking. Although I have great fondness for the production—I believe Tracy Letts has written a deeply engaging and entertaining play—it is not the kind of work that has occupied my interest over the past six or seven years. The primary characteristics of that work have included a very direct engagement in the sociopolitical dynamics of our time.

August: Osage County at best triangulates its relationship to our current condition through the metaphor of family. If the history of American Realism has been its evolving portrayal of the failure of the patriarchy as made manifest in the kitchens and living rooms of O'Neill, Williams, and Miller, then Tracy Letts has certainly joined their company with his lacerating account of the demise of that same patriarchy. There is much value in this commentary surely, but it is at times made toothless by its comparative gentleness. Certainly people may yell and throw things, but they hurl their insults at one another and never at the system that has created their condition. In fact, the idea that they themselves may be victims of a terminally ill societal structure (not just family) is only glancingly addressed. The work sits very comfortably within the culture, not questioning but observing, not tearing down but lamenting.

These qualities in *August* have become challenging only because the play simply won't go away. That I was content to engage in the work when I thought it would only live for a moment is what was confounding and certainly bore examination. My most fertile artistic relationship of the past seven years has been with the playwright Bruce Norris, for whom I have directed four premieres (*The Infidel, Purple Heart, The Pain and the Itch, The Unmentionables*). The most recent of these include productions in Chicago (Steppenwolf Theatre), New Haven (Yale Repertory Theatre), and Off-Broadway (Playwrights Horizons). Bruce Norris's work, and so by extension my own, is more directly engaged in the dissection of the life of the petite bourgeoisie in America at this moment. Bruce's work uses to its advantage the (unfortunate, of course) homogeneity of the audience and asks them very directly to answer for the actions of the characters they are observing. The work is sharp and indicting but it is also, to me, deeply moving. The conversation is so alive and so of the time that it becomes oddly personal. It is these plays that have given me my adult artistic life, and I have participated in them as if they were my own. And because I trust Bruce Norris's point of view, I have needed to engage in very little self-examination when we begin a project. I realize that this comfort, combined with my experience of the comparative smallness of theatre as a cultural event, had made me intellectually lazy. As a result I was not (and sadly, am not) able to fully embrace the most successful production of which I have ever been a part.

As a teacher, this has been a challenging moment. At Northwestern, we demand of our students a thorough and complex interrogation of their interests and a fully articulated point of view on chosen projects. I have learned over the last several years that in order to teach this process at a graduate level, a program must have certain codified structures for learning and yet must always make room for the shifting personalities and experience-levels contained in each incoming class. In my first three years of restructuring the program, I made minor changes each year to the 450 Advanced Directing Seminar series, the cornerstone class for all first-year directors. These changes were primarily in readings and in-class material (as it seemed to me that different groups of graduate students would have different needs and interests regarding texts)—in other words, no real substantive changes. In the past three years, however, I have overhauled the series completely, changing not just the materials but the *thinking*.

Early on, the courses were overly prescriptive and did not allow for different ways to think about a project. Currently, the courses in the series include a very specific explanation of the goals of each assignment while offering very little recommendation in how those goals need to be accomplished. Ironically, this change in the series was born out of observing my students battling the same challenges I have been engaged in over *August*. What I saw in the students was that they had very little understanding of why they were choosing the plays they were choosing and, as a result, they were unable to successfully lead a project effectively. What we needed to offer them was a system of self-examination that helped them to *see* and then helped them to *share*. The biggest hurdle for them, oddly, had been time. Imagine the impatience of youth coupled with almost-zero job opportunity in a medium that exists for only a moment, and you have a good idea of the challenges facing young theater artists. Our students are actually victimized by a culture that not only rarely values what they do, it *rarely even lets them do it*. And so because there are so few opportunities, they move into a permanent gratitude and that gratitude makes artists careless. For me, it was the (perceived) temporal nature of the event (*August*) that had made me careless, for I had all the time in the world. So, at school and within ourselves, we have to construct a new culture, one that values expression and dignifies the artist's process as well as the artist's role in society. And to elevate my own understanding of my responsibility as an artist and as a teacher of artists, I must continue to develop a curriculum that better reflects that demand for our students—creation as responsibility versus as luxury.

Academic Goals

We have made huge strides in the M.F.A. program in the past several years. Our practical coursework, which partners directors and designers on a myriad of different projects throughout three years, is one of the strongest in the country. Core curriculum is taught by teams of directing and design faculty, most of whom have current and ongoing professional relationships with one another. A professional director lives most of his or her collaborative creative life with designers and yet most schools have an actor/director cohort structure that does not support this real-world model. Northwestern's continued commitment to educating artists within the practical realities of what will be their professional life is what makes it one of the most attractive and exciting programs in which to teach. The university and the School of Communication have supported the goals for growth and development which include (but are not limited to) full enrollment of three students per year, new faculty positions/hires in both directing and design, a new 200–level course series in directing that is taught by candidates in their third year, expanded relationships with our Performance Studies Department, Radio, TV, and Film, and the university at large, and expanded relationships with local and national artists.

This year, the directing program will begin construction of two dedicated black-box classrooms that will allow us to fully explore our practical coursework as well as give much needed space back to the Theatre Department as a whole. It is a very heady time for us because with this aspect of our program thriving, we have the opportunity to turn our attention to imagining an equally exciting and challenging academic curriculum that reflects Northwestern's commitment to a well-rounded liberal arts education, as well as addresses the complex questions regarding the role of culture in society and the role of performance in culture.

My goals for the Directing Program include the creation of a new rubric for theoretical coursework for the M.F.A. Currently, our academic requirements for the degree are amorphous—the history coursework changes each year and depends on the current interests of the history, literature, criticism, and theory faculty. This is certainly an exciting part of student life and I am grateful for the HLCT contribution, but the result of this structure is that we, as a program, are not guiding the experience of our students with any real consciousness. As a result we are not only less able to track a critical aspect of our students' development, but we are passing up the opportunity to educate them in the specific intellectual demands of their field. Next year we will begin a search for a contemporary theater scholar whose focus is directing and authorship. We will work together, along with interested members of the Theatre Department faculty, to develop coursework that asks our students to investigate and understand the historical role of the storyteller in community, the evolution of that role and its function not only within Western culture but throughout the world. I have particular interest in developing a course in the role of storytelling in countries in conflict, how drama has been used both historically and currently to address oppression, war, genocide, and revolution.

At Virginia Tech in the aftermath of their tragedy, the university instituted a mandatory volunteer program for both faculty and students. I grew up in Evanston, and I am struck yet again as a member of the faculty by the great good fortune we all enjoy in our lives at Northwestern. It is my hope to develop a similar program in the Theatre Department and look for support to take it campus-wide to serve the Chicagoland area. As we ask our students to understand both historically and theoretically their own responsibilities as artists in their communities, they must understand first the communities to which they belong. To that end, I would also like to expand upon our current internship program.

Historically our internships have been designed around the student's interests as they relate to project development. For example, a student working on *The Bacchae* traveled to Greece; another working on writing new coursework in directing observed several different directors in different parts of this country. While these trips have been valuable and have certainly enhanced the life-experience of the traveler, I am unconvinced that they have deeply served the *student*. In other words, it has been difficult for me to see a cohesive relationship between this opportunity and our goals for our developing artists. My hope is for the international internships to now coincide more directly with the new coursework in helping to identify, for each individual, a more comprehensive understanding of *their place in the world*. The internship would become a time of true observation—to be able to experience first-hand not just how others tell stories but why others tell stories. Because our students are so challenged by this question in themselves—the "why" of their choices—any opportunity we give them to investigate, contemplate, and interrogate this critical question is invaluable to their development. We do our students a great disservice when we continue the Western practice of educating our artists in isolation from the rest of the world.

I am also working with Martha Lavey, the artistic director of Steppenwolf Theatre in Chicago, to develop a relationship that would bring our third-year directors' final projects to Steppenwolf for performance. Certainly, this idea grows from a shared interest in the cultivating of young artists but it is also far more complex than that. We both have moments where our roles, she as curator and I as educator, put us in contact with the vast divide between ourselves and the young people in whom we have an interest. Put quite simply, their taste is sometimes just baffling. During the first two years of a graduate student's life at Northwestern, this gap is never limiting for them—I rarely say no to a project simply because I don't like it (or, as they would say, don't get it) and we end up having wonderful and heated discourse about the work throughout. (Obviously this can be a helpful teaching tool—certainly there is nothing more informative for a student than having to define themselves *against* their professor.) The challenge arrives in their third year, when the project they are choosing has to be programmed into the season at TIC, our university theater with a subscription base mostly from the North Shore. At this point, the students have to expand (or contract) their interests to include something palatable for that community—a community that is, although supportive, certainly not their own. For Martha Lavey there is a similar problem, in that she has programming demands, but more to the point for Steppenwolf, she doesn't have a forum constructed to feature young voices that doesn't carry huge financial risk. The object in bringing the projects to Steppenwolf is twofold: our students get to continue investigating their true interests while taking on the responsibility of producing at a major institution, and Steppenwolf is able to offer programming to an underserved audience they wish to cultivate. Far more exciting is that this trajectory asks the student to continue to engage practically in the central theoretical challenges of the program: you are now joining the world conversation. What do you have to say?

So, now that I have so grandly entered the world conversation, what do I want to say? It is impossible now for me to consider my directing career separately from my teaching. Recently, I was offered the artistic directorship of a major institution associated with a major university, where I would have also received an appointment. The process was valuable for several reasons, not the least of which is that it revealed to me that my life as an educator is critical to me and that I must make that life at a university committed to innovation in arts practice. For me, Northwestern is that place. I understand very clearly the larger value of my work with young people—the nurturing of the next generation of theater artists—and I search now for that same clarity in my own personal work as a director.

Recently I went to see the latest Tom Stoppard play on Broadway, *Rock & Roll*. I had been so looking forward to it—I am a huge fan of Mr. Stoppard, and I believe him to be, for the most part, a most astute chronicler of the human endeavor. I thought, perhaps, that the play would enlighten me. Teach me. I was sadly mistaken. Very quickly I found the play boorish and prickly and even worse, condescending about ideas too important to be so trivialized, like oppression and revolution. I found the whole thing intensely bourgeois and disconnected, and I felt something I think many people feel when they go to the theater: disdain. What on earth did this have to do with anyone's actual *life*? Why should I *care*? And so I did something I never do. I left.

The play was running just across the street from *August: Osage County*, and I wandered in to our theater to watch the end of the second act before heading home. And while I stood in the back, something happened inside of me. I let the audience's experience, so different from the one I had just had across the street, enter my consciousness. And they were enchanted. Enthralled, even. And for that moment I stopped thinking about what it was for me as the director, what it lacked in political insight or intellectual nuance or how it didn't match the narrative I had written for myself, and took in what it meant *for them*. There are no stars in *August*, no one you would recognize from film or television, and I realized that this allows the audience to believe that what they are watching *is really happening*. And they see, I suppose, themselves. *August* is, in the end, simply about the people who are left behind. And in that, too, I think they see themselves. How brave of them, I thought.

I am a director because I believe in my own impulses and my own point of view, and that belief encourages me to tell stories that will move, provoke, and change people. But I became a director because I wanted to be a part of the world. And it pains me that I live in a country that seems with every passing day to want nothing more than to destroy it. And so I recognize that it is my job to find and create the work that will make me proud to be an artist when I suspect I should be a warrior. And I will continue to search for that work in artists and projects I trust as well as in places and people of whom I am less sure. Because maybe that is why we are telling stories in this country. Maybe that is why. To try to pull together, by whatever means necessary, an ever-fracturing community in order to remind us of what we share, even if that is just that we are being left behind. Perhaps if we can see that clearly and we can teach our young people how to act up not just to their responsibility but to their potential, we will live to fight another day.

Bruce Norris

On the Utter Uselessness of Theater, and Why We Should All Learn to Relax About It

Fellow creators of theater, here's a story: My father lives in Houston, Texas. He is eighty-two years old, a religious, conservative man who lives by himself (being divorced from his second wife), and once a week he drives himself to his local HEB grocery store where he buys seven Lean Cuisine entrees, his dinners for the upcoming week. He stacks these entrees (safe to assume the *same* seven entrees each week) in a corner of his otherwise empty frost-free refrigerator freezer, and at six P.M. every evening he takes the topmost box from the stack without stopping to consider which entree he has chosen, places it in his microwave, heats it, and dutifully ingests it without regard to flavor, aroma, essentially unaware of what it is he is eating. It is edible, it is nutritious, and for my father, that is sufficient. Anything else would amount to self-indulgence, which, of course, is sinful. As he says to me when I visit, "I don't *live* to *eat*, I *eat* to *live*." Because God has given him life, and his life is merely a preparation for the far *greater* and more rewarding existence that is to follow in some blessed realm, where, one assumes, he will have access to an unlimited supply of Lean Cuisine entrees.

We Americans are the cultural descendants of Puritans, of people who turned against the perceived decadence of the Church of England (?!!) and who came to this continent to lead humble lives of purity and morality and self-denial, and whose numbers broke off into various sects:

Shakers, Quakers, Calvinists, and so forth, and my father simply continues, in his own way, this American tradition. For him a meal is a matter of survival, not pleasure—just as the Shakers might have spurned a comfy sofa in favor of a hard wooden chair. Too much *pleasure*, too much regard for the material world, distracts us from the *purposeful* nature of existence. And putting aside for the moment Puritanism's schizophrenic sibling in American psychology—the rapacious acquisitiveness born of free-market economics—it is nearly impossible for us to divest our selves of our obsession—a kind of *national* obsession—with *purpose*. Best seller? *The Purpose-Driven Life*.

And the obsession transcends politics. The last ten years have divided this country straight down the middle on one issue after another, but we can all agree on this: we take our positions very seriously, because we each know them to be *right*, and the rightness of our intentions fills us with a sense of *purpose*. Everything we do is blessed with these incantations. Liberal: I use this brand of dishwashing liquid *because it's better for the environment*. Conservative: I drive this gigantic car *because it protects my kids*. The examples are endless, but the consistent element on both left and the right is the conviction that our behaviors aren't *random*. We even sing the *national anthem* before a fucking football game, as if it were some kind of service to the county to sit your ass in a bleacher seat and cram a bucket of nachos into your head.

Of course, this thinking is particularly embarrassing when it finds expression among those of us on the left. We educated lefties look at an America contaminated by racism and false religiosity and conspicuous consumption—*see those disgusting Republicans in their SUVs driving to their tasteless mega-churches*. And, to demonstrate our superiority we go on vacations to Buddhist monasteries where we eat bowls of gruel and sleep on a stone floor, contemplating the future of Tibet, or on eco-vacations to Belize to endure lectures about the importance of the rain forest and come home covered in mosquito bites and virtue. We lefties—unless we are unabashed hypocrites—feel an enormous sense of shame about all of our privilege. Yet, finding few practical outlets through which to expiate that shame, we put it to all sorts of hilarious—yet *purposeful*—causes, convinced of our righteousness. It's somewhat less hilarious when the right—our administration of the last eight years—is equally persuaded of its own righteousness, and we wind up invading a country and torturing its citizens.

The problem with all of this for me is this: I work in the theater. And that troubles me because it seems that nothing I could do for a living—almost nothing—could conceivably have less of a *purpose*. We who participate in the creation of theater tend to be, by and large, fairly lefty in our politics, as do all—for lack of a better word—*artists*. And art may be many things, but the one thing art almost certainly *isn't*—and don't let anybody tell you otherwise—art isn't *useful*.

If you're at all like me, your original encounter with theater probably went something like this: You were an average child, maybe undistinguished academically, not so great at sports, and one day either by accident or by choice, you went to see a *play*. Maybe you'd been dragged to some miserable student matinee at some admirable regional theater, maybe it was a musical, maybe children's theater—the point is, you wound up watching this thing and for *you*—unlike the other children in attendance—for whatever reason, it *appealed* to you. For me, it was the *sets*. How did they *do* that? The stage revolved! Where did that castle go? It disappeared into thin air! And in a state of youthful enchantment, I decided I had to participate, and one thing led to another, and I took some acting lessons, and in one performance of *The Sound of Music* . . . I got a *laugh* . . . And that continues to be what I do—in a rarefied way—to this day. I write *plays* that are met with varying degrees of success, and I still act, occasionally. And I'm incredibly lucky because I've been able to do something I enjoy and still manage—sometimes barely manage—to make a living.

But somewhere along the way—not *somewhere*, I know where: college—I was asked the question *why* this was what I had chosen to do. I was being asked to identify the *purpose* of my decision to involve myself with theater. There had to be a *why*. I had a particular teacher who predicted that, for each of us, there would come a moment in the middle of our theatrical careers, either halfway up a ladder hanging lights, or sitting backstage waiting to go on as an understudy, where we would find ourselves questioning why we had chosen to do what we do, and that it would behoove us to be prepared for that inevitable moment with an answer. That teacher then died of AIDS.

And so I began to formulate all sorts of theories in anticipation of that moment. I would spend my life creating theater, I thought, but it wouldn't be for foolish reasons. Not for my *ego*. Not to *get laid*. Not because I'm a fundamentally lazy person and theater has easy hours. Not for any of the obvious reasons which had motivated me in the first place. I would reorient my thinking to focus on the *good* theater creates. Of course, I had to reconcile myself to the fact that this would most likely make me *poor*—and I didn't grow up *poor*. We belonged to a country club with a golf course! But *theater* people are, generally, fairly *poor*, relative to other college-educated types. And—as is the case for every other impoverished American demographic—if I couldn't be *rich*, I thought, then at least I could be *virtuous*. Virtue is the traditional consolation of the unsuccessful. So that if I happened to find myself eating Cup O'Noodles five nights a week I could at least tell myself it didn't matter, because I'd be doing the *virtuous* work of theater. I'd be *proud* to be eating Cup O'Noodles!

And then I was an actor for a long time. I was even fairly successful, by the standards of the business. I did plays in New York and Chicago for measly sums of money, but of course, the size of the paycheck was irrelevant because these were "important" plays in "prestigious" theaters. And I got the occasional TV or film job to pay the bills. But I always told myself, well, I'm just temporarily here in sleazy, capitalist L.A. for the *money*, and as soon as I've made some of it I'll go back to Chicago and work in that un-air-conditioned storefront theater for free because that's the *important* work. Unlike the unambiguously horrible *crap* produced in the profit-making-complexes of Hollywood or Broadway. I wouldn't be seduced by *money and pleasure*. I would do the *good work*.

Strangely like . . . my father. And all of this arrogance was made immeasurably easier because—I should add—I was living off of a *trust fund* set up by the same man. But after I hit age thirty and that trust fund was all spent, it was up to me to explain to myself, *rigorously* explain what exactly I thought I was doing. And I hung onto some kind of vague feeling that, if I wasn't going to make a shitload of money—like the other children I had gone to school with—that I would someday be rewarded in some *other* way. But what way? In an afterlife? In Theater Heaven? To which I would gain entrance by doing a whole lot of Brecht and Chekhov? And what would this heaven look like? An awards ceremony? Would I be stuck for eternity with insufferable theater people? Would we all sit around watching Brecht? Tony Kushner on alternate Fridays? And do I even *like* Brecht? Or *Tony Kushner?* I became very troubled about *why* I seemed to have made choices that led me—by this point, in my *mid-thirties*—to still be worried about where my next meal was coming from. I was *convinced* that there was some reward to be had at the end of it all. But if there is no theater heaven, then why the fuck was I doing all of these plays? What, teleologically speaking, did it all *accomplish?* And what if it accomplished absolutely *nothing?* I guess that would make me . . . sort of an *idiot.*

Now, unlike my father, I'm not a religious person. I don't have an authoritative text to turn to for answers. I'm just an atheist. And let's not get into all that—the *why* of it. Either you have what it takes to be a "believer" or you don't, and I *don't* . . . And, I know. Maybe you think, "*oh, I don't believe in 'god' in the usual sense.*" You'll tell me, with great originality, that you see God as a kind of unconscious collective human impulse toward compassion or enlightenment and suggest that I could substitute secular rationalizations for a secular salvation: the Good of the Planet, the Good of Community, the Good of Humankind—just pick one and use it to construct some belief system that you can rigidly adhere to. Or wait. Even better: Have a couple of kids. Have two or three kids and then you'll have a built-in justification for your life: you'll *have* to grow up and learn to participate in the adult economy, otherwise your children will *starve* and they'll never go to *the right schools* and they will hate you forever. So you'd better hurry up and either get some children or some religion or some political motivation because, if you *don't*, you'll start to think that your life doesn't have a *purpose*, and you can't live like that. Anything but that.

So, the older I got, I started thinking that maybe what I should do is involve myself with the kind of theater that directly *helps* the world. Plays like *The Exonerated* and *The Laramie Project*: issue-driven plays that address contemporary problems and give us real political *meat* to chew on while we're having drinks in the lobby afterward. But then . . . why did so many of those plays make me feel so bored? Weren't they simply regurgitating the preexisting beliefs of the audience and confirming their sense of virtue? Is there even such a *thing* as political theater in the United States? And how would we define it? Would political theater cause a person to go out and change what they actually *do*? And was there ever a *play* that accomplished such a thing?

(I knew a man who periodically traveled to Laos to create theater for the Hmong people. He staged a play in a Hmong village all about the great water spirit that lives in the sewer and how the spirit punishes those who drink from the sewer by making them sick. And in the play, the villagers learn to defecate in latrines instead of in their own drinking water. Now *that's* an evening of theater.)

But I didn't *want* to go to Laos and live in a hut. I didn't actually want to help anyone. I started to realize somewhere along the way, that I didn't actually *give a shit* about other people. All I wanted was to sit in an air-conditioned theater and put on costumes and have people applaud for me and then go out to a nice meal afterwards. I wanted to act

out psychologically against my parents and, like a spoiled child of priv-
ilege, rub my family's collective faces in the dirt. And worst of all, in my
mid-thirties, as my relationship fell apart due to my own rotten misbe-
havior, I realized I wasn't even a force for good in my own *personal* life.
I was discovering that, on balance, my life—by any reasonable stan-
dard—was creating more *harm* than good.

So, what the fuck *was* I doing theater for? If the project of creating
"political" theater was dull at best and logically impossible at worst (in
the United States, anyway) then at least the theater that I helped to cre-
ate should have a message of *hope* because *hope* is good, right? We have
to *hope*. And if a play makes us *hope* really hard that things will get bet-
ter in the world or that human nature will improve . . . maybe . . . some-
how . . . ? Or, at least a play could, you know, illuminate the human
condition? Or inspire poetry in our souls? Or something? At the bare
minimum, it should *at least* do the one thing all plays are required to do:
provide the cleansing *catharsis* that derives from an audience's identifi-
cation with a compelling "protagonist" right? We should *like* the char-
acters, *root* for them. We all know this. And how do we know it? Well,
because Aristotle *told* us so. But then . . . who the fuck was Aristotle
anyway? I'll tell you who. A *critic*. Some opinionated little jackass who
pranced around Athens telling everybody what kind of plays people
were supposed to like, and then he wrote down his *opinions*, and we still
take them seriously.

(A brief thought about critics: Most careers are self-selecting. You
don't choose to join the police force if you don't already possess—to
some extent—a taste for law and order, maybe even for cracking skulls.
So what would make a person choose to become . . . a *critic*? Doesn't it
seem a safe assumption that those who choose this particular line of
work might, more often than not, be working through some preexisting
need to condemn the work of others? Doesn't the very choice to be a
critic, like the choice to be, say, a proctologist, raise questions about the
motivations of the practitioner?)

(Another thought about critics: People love to go on about the
"good" theater critics. The ones who've supposedly done so much to
promote "good" theater. And they always mention the same handful of
self-anointed tastemakers: Kenneth Tynan, Brooks Atkinson, John
Lahr; and we all remember the handful of careers that these guys helped
foster, but we never seem to remember that for every Joe Orton or
Harold Pinter that got a leg up, there's a hundred careers kicked into the
gutter by these same guardians of culture.)

As film and television and the Internet have entirely superseded the theater as cheap and reliable sources of dramatic *pleasure*, the rest of us, lagging behind, have created something known as "serious theater," and we've desperately tried to replace the *pleasure* once derived from attending the theater with something akin to *virtue*. We tell ourselves and others that attending theater is more virtuous in nature than attending the latest summer blockbuster or playing the latest video game. We claim that our theater is *deeper*, that it ponders the intricacies of the human experience, raising it above more pedestrian kinds of entertainment. Which of course all *sounds* good, but is it actually *good* for us to go to an open-air theater in some park and watch yet another production of *Hamlet*? Does it *change* us? Make us *better people*? How, specifically? Give examples. And how would such an improvement be measured? Would it make a difference if the production is . . . set in Zimbabwe? Addressing the current political crisis there? Would that somehow make theater-going an act of *virtue*? I don't think so. And, the truth is, I don't think Shakespeare ever *cared* about *doing good* in the world, or *uplifting* people, or creating *hope*. Nor, I think, did Samuel Beckett, or Aeschylus, or Neil Simon for that matter. I don't think they really *gave* a shit. Sure, some playwrights did: Ibsen, Shaw, Brecht, Arthur Miller—they wanted to shake things up a little, which I admire. But then, you don't exactly pack your picnic basket to go and watch *Ibsen in the Park*. You don't see Arthur Miller *festivals* springing up all over the place. Virtue just doesn't sell that many tickets. Oh, it sells a few. But virtue is not a sustainable reason for attending the theater. The reason is supposed to be the *pleasure* it provides. And when it ceases to be pleasing we cease to consume it. You can't blame people for turning away from theater when it becomes the entertainment equivalent of cod-liver oil.

(And, forgive the cheap shot, but do we really think that *any* art has the power to *transform* people? It's a bit simplistic, but do we really think that the rotten crimes of human nature occur because of insufficient exposure to *art*? Hitler read plenty of books. He liked to *paint*! So did John Wayne Gacy! Jeffrey Dahmer, Osama Bin Laden, Andrea Yates, Dick Cheney . . . ? Do we really think the problem with any of these people is that they never saw a really good production of *Hamlet*? Isn't it more likely that the formation of our natures *precedes* our encounters with art and that we come away from those encounters largely unchanged?)

Now, here's the part that's perverse: *I've* written plays, some of which could be called *satire*. And satire is a type of *purposeful* writing that tries to turn a harsh light on some of the unflattering aspects of our behavior. So, in a sense, I'm the principal culprit of exactly the sort of posturing I'm trying to condemn. I'm arguing against *myself*. But do I really want the future of American theater to resemble, as closely as possible, *The Lion King*? No. I *hate* the fucking *Lion King*. Puppets and talking animals and Elton John's atrocious music. And meanwhile, I sit in my drafty little apartment writing plays—tendentious, crabby, little screeds—none of which could ever survive in a commercial marketplace. I rely on audiences with a masochistic need to deprive themselves of easy pleasure and who will pay me to do just that. So, wouldn't I be the first casualty of the success of my argument? I can't survive without an audience's steadfast belief that the theater they enjoy has a *purpose*. Otherwise, I'd go broke. And, that, eventually, is where my thoughts on this subject always lead—back to *money*.

I work (*have* worked) at "regional" theaters. Theaters which, for better or worse, were created through public covenants, starting in the fifties and sixties, with the intention of bringing "culture" to communities remote from the theatrical smorgasbord of New York. These theaters are, by definition, "not-for-profit." At least, it says so on their tax returns. And in New York, I work at the same types of theaters—they're just smaller, with dirtier dressing rooms and more elderly audiences. Now, a couple of dubious notions underlie the existence of these institutions. One is the notion that dramatic theater, like the ballet or the symphony or the museum or the botanical garden—is a vital cultural necessity, which without taxpayer and private support might vanish from existence to be replaced by theme parks and NASCAR stadiums—and where oh where would we be then? Libertarians are free to discuss the merits of this notion as they see fit. But for our purposes, let's call this the "Theater As Public Trust" argument: we must support live theater Because It Is a Civic Good. The other notion that justifies the existence of these places is this: that, without an alternative to the money-driven schemes of the commercial theater, alternative voices—such as mine—would disappear. Forget me—what about Sarah Ruhl or David Greenspan or Suzan-Lori Parks or Adam Bock or Wallace Shawn—writers whose work I truly enjoy. Where would they be? What would they do? I think we all know: temp work.

A not-for-profit theater provides a haven for those innovative writers (or are we just untalented?) whose voices are currently—perhaps forever—unintelligible to the great dull mass of consumers. They provide us with shelter until such time as we can either stand on our own or sell out to Disney. We'll call this the "Theater As Halfway-House" argument. And, by deploying these two arguments in their favor, not-for-profit theaters receive public largesse and private donations (or, should we say, *tax dodges*) from philanthropists (or, should we say, *millionaires*) in order to survive. And because neither of these arguments can be proved or disproved, because they have to simply be taken on faith, theaters spend a great deal of time and energy nurturing this faith-based image of themselves. They create student-outreach programs and workshops for young writers and auxiliaries and boards-of-directors and have post-show discussions where Important Questions Are Asked and they generally strive to validate their tax-exempt status. Which is all well and good, but . . . doesn't it start to feel a little bit like that *other* tax-exempt place where people gather? Like *church*? And, nothing against church but—let's face it: church is fucking *boring*. We secular types turned to the theater to *get away* from church. Theater is *dirty* and *funny* and *irreverent*. *Anti*-reverent. Save the reverence for Sunday morning. Theater is for *Saturday night*.

(By the way—what's up with all of these post-show discussions? What possible purpose could they serve other than—1. to flatter an audience with the illusion that the creators give a shit about their opinions and thus encourage them to renew their season subscriptions, or—2. the same function as a Hollywood focus group; namely, a marketing tool to help writers, directors, and producers streamline the "product" so as to move more units? But why would this be necessary at *non-profit institutions*? Or maybe—3. to *foster dialogue between the artist and the community*? But when you go to a museum and you're looking at a shark in formaldehyde, they don't hand you Damien Hirst's cell-phone number and let you talk it over with him. When you buy a novel it doesn't come with the author's e-mail address. So why should we theater people be subjected to such a fucked-up thing? Just asking.)

But, naturally, institutions want to *grow*. The boards of directors of these theaters are always stocked with captains of industry or investment bankers, people whose lives have been dedicated to the amassing of wealth and prestige and position and who, gosh-darn it, just see *growth* as an imperative; people who come from the world of *for-profit* (what other world is there?) and who tend to see a lack of *growth* as a disservice to shareholders. And, in the case of a theater, the shareholders are *the audience*, right? We have to *grow* the audience. That is the *purpose* of our theater. Otherwise our theater . . . will *die*. And it's not hard to convince the creative people either. Hey—bigger offices, nicer dressing rooms, better salaries for the actors—what's not to like? But, we'll need to organize a capital campaign to raise money for the new facility, and, if you could, we'd also like a brief mission statement, no more than three pages, outlining exactly why this theater is such an *irreplaceable civic necessity.*

There's money to be had in positioning yourself as a public utility. Like PBS, whose existence depends on maintaining its audience's belief in its rarefied status, the theaters we work in depend on the same kind of evangelism. I just received an e-mail from the literary manager of a theater that has commissioned me to write a play. He is applying for a grant—(a.k.a. *money*)—based on the content of the plays he's currently paying authors to write. The plays should in some way *justify* the grant. The problem is, as I've said, theater is inherently *unjustifiable.* Try it. Justify *Waiting for Godot.* Explain to me how it has improved the world in two concise paragraphs. And don't get me wrong—I like *Waiting for Godot.* I really do. But I can't tell you what is good or useful or comforting or uplifting (ha!) about it. Now, I could easily tell you what is good or useful about air conditioning or penicillin or bicycles or maybe even computers. But . . . *Waiting for Godot?* For the life of me, I can't tell you why it's any better or worse, any more or less deserving of public support than, say, *Mamma Mia!* (currently in theaters). Is *Waiting for Godot* a superior work of art to *Mamma Mia!?* I honestly don't know. Now, to be fair, I haven't *seen Mamma Mia!* But I haven't avoided seeing *Mamma Mia!* because it's not *good.* I haven't seen it because it's not to my *taste,* whereas *Waiting for Godot* is. And all *that* makes me . . . is a *snob.* I'm a snob. And I wish I wasn't. My life would probably be a lot easier if I could enjoy *Mamma Mia!* I'd probably be *richer.* I'd probably be *happier.* But I can't be. I'm stuck with my own taste, because my taste is part of an identity that I constructed—pathetically—to elevate myself above the bullies and overachievers that tormented me in Junior High school. My snobbery is a *failing.* And it's one thing to *be* a snob, but quite another to *advocate* snobbery. That's what *critics* do. And for me to start believing that my snobbery is some objective measure of the value of any work of art is to delude myself. Art *has* no value. As I've said before about the value of theater: to claim that theater is *good* for the world is like claiming that ornaments are good for a Christmas tree; they make the tree *prettier,* of course, but it's still just a dead tree.

One more story, and then I'll stop: a few years ago I adopted a pet gerbil. An albino gerbil, female. She died last year, but in her memory I'd like to mention this: after she'd lived in her plastic habitat in my apartment for a few months, I began to notice that my gerbil had a routine. She'd sleep most of the day, then about four-thirty she'd begin her daily tasks. These involved grooming, eating, running on her wheel, grooming again, followed by a nap, more running, eating, and sleep. And as I watched her day after day, going about this apparently *vital* daily routine, I started to have the horrible awareness that I was doing the exact same thing. Like her, I lived in a little box and had my own daily routine involving grooming and eating—sometimes I even go to a gym and run on a human-sized exercise wheel. And while I'm fully aware that my routine is every bit as arbitrary and meaningless as my gerbil's, I'm extremely upset whenever that routine is disrupted. And it seems to me that we all get caught in similar routines of *belief* and that giving up our beliefs is as hard for us as it would be for my gerbil to give up running on her wheel, may she rest in peace. A wheel to nowhere was her *purpose* in life, and *my* little need—to create theater—just goes around and around and around.

All of this is a rambling way of saying that perhaps the pursuit of virtuous purpose is incompatible with the act of making theater. That, in spite of all its seductive beauty, theater is, quite possibly, an entirely *useless* artifact. And I think we sometimes need to remember that we're in the business of creating luxury items and useless baubles of necessity to no one. And that we're doing it for our own selfish pleasure. The pleasure I derive from creating theater is selfish. And it's completely *subjective*, so I can't even really *share* it. It's just what I'm *into*. It's my *kink*. And that . . . is entirely as it should be.

So if you're writing a play, or directing one, or acting in one, and you want me to buy a ticket . . . Please, just don't tell me it's *good* for me. Don't tell me you're doing it to help me or to uplift my heart or to show me the right way to behave. And don't tell me it's good for the *world*, either. And if it makes you feel better about yourself to stage the play in an abandoned warehouse and to assemble a cast of homeless people to raise awareness about economic violence—go right ahead. I'm sure you could get a big grant from the city to underwrite it.

But don't expect me to come. Okay, I'll come. I probably know someone in the cast. But don't expect me to enjoy it.

Laura Eason

"Written by ____ Adapted from ____" Adaptation and the Voice of the Playwright

Building a House of Your Own

Imagine you have just inherited a gigantic mansion. It was built more than a century ago with the most luxurious materials of the time. It is a unique place full of character, beauty, charm, and inspiration. The kitchen needs work and the upstairs layout is a little awkward, but, all in all, there is a great deal to love.

Now, say your newly acquired mansion has to be removed from its current location. The only land belonging to you is a little plot down by the stream where the mansion will never fit. So, you decide to save what you can by building a new, smaller house using salvaged materials from the mansion. To make a plan, you ask, "How much do I want the new house to look like the old? What do I want to keep? What do I want to let go of? What new materials will I need? How can I preserve what I love about the mansion but still make the new house distinctly my own?"

This metaphor for adaptation is imperfect (maybe it should be turning the house into an airplane to more clearly underline the difficulty of turning a novel into a play?) but it will suffice.

The metaphor is helpful, first, because it gets at a general assumption about adaptation; that as an adapter, you merely edit the original text down to something playable in two or so hours in the theater. In my experience, good adaptation always involves some degree of invention in at least one, if not all, of the elements—story, plot, character, dialogue, setting, description, and conception of the piece for a three-dimensional theatrical space. Good adaptation, although clearly connected and deeply indebted to the original text, should be able to stand alone from the source material, and in an ideal world, its story and intentions would be taken on its own terms.

Secondly, most people understand that it isn't any easier to build a house with salvaged materials than it is to build something totally new. However, many people think that an adaptation is easier to write than an original play. As the author of eight full-length original plays and eight full-length adaptations, I state emphatically that writing an adaptation is at least as difficult as writing an original script.

Finally, there is the notion that adaptors lack a *voice*, the thing we are told we are looking to find as a playwright, because with adaptation you are often trying to match the voice of the author of the source material. So, the question seems to linger, "what kind of writer are you if your voice can be subsumed?" The truth is adaptation is a constant conversation between the voice of the playwright and the voice of the author of the work being adapted as the playwright decides what "materials" to keep, how to use them and what of his or her own voice to add to the construction. The ways in which an adaptor chooses to mirror or not to mirror the voice of the source material is a major choice of the adaptation process and one that should be viewed as a choice. And in situations where a seamlessness of voice is desired, I would challenge anyone to prove that convincingly capturing the voice of, say, Charles Dickens, Dorothy Parker, or Don DeLillo does not require great skill.

Finding the Big Idea

My adaptation work has been a combination of commissions that were brought to me and projects I have found on my own. Whatever way I come to a project, I first read the text a couple of times. From that reading and rereading, *the story that I want to tell begins to emerge*. This may seem surprising, but it is usually the case that the story you choose to tell as an adaptor is somewhat different than the story told in the source material. For example, I chose to adapt the Jules Verne classic *Around the World in Eighty Days* for Lookingglass Theatre in 2008, but the story I wanted to tell as an adaptor included new and different story elements.

This might be viewed as radical, but it is essential to good adaptation. Novels have a different structure than plays and typically tackle many themes and include a multitude of characters and ideas, more than a stage play can comfortably accommodate in an evening of theater. Of course, some adaptations are several evenings long, but even those rely upon limiting choices at their center.

For me, the story or the "big idea" is the most important thing that helps chart the course of my adaptations. I do not use the terms *story* and *plot* interchangeably. *Plot* encompasses the action and events that happen, and the *story*, the "big idea," is the meaning or motivations behind the action, why characters do what they do. In *Around the World in Eighty Days*, for example, the *plot* would be that Phileas Fogg makes a bet to travel the world in eighty days. The *story* or *big idea* that I came to for the adaptation is that Phileas does go on a seemingly whimsical journey, but he is actually a lonely man searching for what is missing in his life, something he himself doesn't realize until he has returned home and found the love of his life. The idea of Fogg's loneliness as a motivator for both the journey and for what happens to him along the way is not clearly confirmed in Verne's text, although elements of it are there. Knowing the big idea helps to illuminate and clarify what characters and plot elements will be important in the adaptation and exposes what gaps or inconsistencies there may be between the source material and that big idea of the adaptation.

A few years ago, I was approached by Ed Sobel, Steppenwolf Theatre Company's Director of New Play Development, about doing an adaptation of Mark Twain's *Adventures of Huckleberry Finn* for Steppenwolf Theatre's young adult program that he would direct. The play would be conceived for a primarily high-school-aged audience and, because students would see the show during their school day, the play could be no longer than an hour and a half. I was excited to engage in this way with this most classic of American novels and quickly agreed to the project, knowing, though, that I had to really focus the story to fit within the given parameters of the adaptation.

After reading the novel several times, which I had never done in school, and talking with Ed about his and Steppenwolf's interest in developing a stage adaptation, a clear big idea emerged: the development of young, runaway Huck's morality through his relationship with the escaped slave Jim. What I chose to keep from the original novel, then, were Huck's adventures that were most closely tied to Jim and Huck's evolving morality. This meant leaving out or greatly condensing action where Jim was largely out of the picture, a surprisingly large amount of the book. This meant not including many of Huck's marvelous, hilarious adventures, full of rich and rewarding social satire, but such is the case with adaptation. You have to work within whatever confines there might be and, generally, make hard choices.

I knew any choice I made in relation to the most significant and beloved of American novels would be controversial. In an attempt to clarify my adaptation concept, I gave the play a different title than the novel, calling it simply *Huck Finn*. I hoped this would emphasize that my play was an essentialized version of the novel, focusing more on Huck's character and his relationship with Jim than on his adventures.

To explore more specifically my process of adaptation and the way choices have played out in some of my productions, I would like to explore in more depth two very different adaptations: Jules Verne's *Around the World in Eighty Days* that was commissioned and produced by Lookingglass Theatre in Chicago in 2008, and a collection of short stories called *The Coast of Chicago* by Stuart Dybek, commissioned and produced by Walkabout Theater, also in Chicago. These two adaptations offer several nice contrasts: one is a text I chose to adapt, the other was brought to me; one is a novel, the other a collection of short stories; one is a translation, one was written in English; in one I eliminated the narrative voice, in the other the narrative voice was maintained and became a framing element for the piece; one has an author who is long-dead, the other author is alive and well and living in Chicago; one is a classic text from the nineteenth century often encountered by people in their childhood, the other is a less well known text, with stories written in the last twenty years; one was developed with long-time collaborators, the other was developed with people I had never worked with before; and, finally, one of the adaptations I directed, the other I did not.

Adapting *Around the World in Eighty Days* into *Around the World in 80 Days*

I decided to adapt *Around the World in Eighty Days* very specifically for my own theater company, Lookingglass Theatre of Chicago, where I am one of twenty-two multi-skilled ensemble members who are writers, directors, actors, and designers. Although Lookingglass's work varies, we most often do adaptations of classic stories, frequently epic in scale, that are told in a highly theatrical, strongly visual and/or physical way. Some of the novels/stories/myths that Lookingglass members have adapted include: *Hard Times* by Charles Dickens, adapted by Heidi Stillman; Ovid's *Metamorphoses* adapted by Mary Zimmerman; and an adaptation of Lewis Carroll's *Alice's Adventures in Wonderland* and *Through the Looking Glass*, called *Lookingglass Alice*, by David Catlin. Because we often tell stories with images communicating as much as the text, our adaptors often direct their own pieces, as was the case for the works mentioned above and for my production of *Around the World in 80 Days*.

I had been looking for a classic text to adapt for Lookingglass for some time and was taken by *Around the World's* epic story. It had adventure and humor and plenty of room for the company's signature theatricality that is easily accommodated in our relatively new flexible theater space in Chicago's Water Tower Water Works. I quickly finished a first draft. A reading with the Lookingglass Ensemble of this initial pass, which was still quite close in both plot and story to the novel, revealed that I didn't have nearly enough of my own point of view/voice in the piece yet, nor had I locked in on the "why" of my story strongly enough.

It has become clear to me over time that part of my process is a first draft that stays too close to the original material. Part of the reason for this is reverence, since I usually love the literary work in the first place to want to adapt it. There is also a feeling of deference to the authors, especially when they are celebrated literary figures. One can't help but ask, "Who the hell am I to change the words of Mark Twain?" For me, this reverential first draft that lacks enough of my own voice and perspective is inevitable. Once it is done, however, and is universally acknowledged as lacking, as it always is, I can begin to let go of the original work and craft subsequent drafts with my "why," my "big idea," as the guiding light, inventing plot elements, dialogue, and characters as the story demands.

Moving into the second draft of *Around the World in 80 Days*, my big idea for the play became clear very quickly. The transformation of Fogg as a character is not deeply explored in the original text. He falls in love by the end of the novel, but the transformation of his character and evidence of what he might have learned during his journey is unclear. Making the play clearly about Fogg's loneliness and rigidity giving way to a realization of the importance of curiosity and how life can only be fully lived when approached with a curious mind and an open heart was a big idea I could deeply believe and invest in. This worked with the novel but also reflected my vision for the play. Hints of Fogg's transformation are in the text, but my play would make this big idea the foundation on which everything else was built.

The other thing that shaped my big idea was thinking of the play living in its moment. The advantage of writing something new for the theatre, even when it is based on an old text, is the opportunity to directly relate to the moment we are living in—historically, politically, philosophically. During any given play's development at Lookingglass we always ask, "why must this story be told" to explore how the story will be relevant to a modern audience. The same was true for *Around the World*. What would the play say, politically and/or philosophically, to an audience in May 2008 in Chicago?

In the world of the novel, Phileas Fogg lives during the time of the British Empire and takes his wealth for granted and England's domination of the world in stride. He offers little to no criticism of England's mission to conquer the world and remake it in its own image. Nor does he have any insight into his own life choices and how they support the worldview of his nation. I started writing the play during the third year of the Iraq war. A protagonist representing a country that blindly believes in exporting its own way of life, even at the cost of destroying the people and culture of the conquered land, felt very relevant to America in 2008. Most places on earth have been touched by some aspect of American culture, with many places changed forever, having lost local traditions in food, customs, and ways of life, to the "American way." American goods are exported or replicated in restaurants and shops all over the world. American culture saturates any land where there is electricity. For all its greatness, America's exportation of its way of life and has had and will continue to have tragic implications in other cultures as, of course, did the British Empire. Although there may be those who would balk at a comparison between American's export of our culture and the conquests of the British Empire, there are many similarities. This seemed fertile land for the adaptation to dig around in. Although my goal was to make a family-friendly piece that was a great night in the theatre, I wanted my story to also speak to these larger issues in a subtle but persuasive way.

After getting clear on the big idea, one of the biggest decisions always comes to the forefront: should the narrative voice be kept or not? The text of *Around the World in Eighty Days* that I adapted was a translation of the original work that dates back to the late 1890s. Although Verne's work is in the public domain, modern translations are not. I chose this older translation to avoid rights issues but more importantly because I preferred the more formal, sometimes archaic language that seemed in keeping with the formality of the characters and the time period of the action, 1872. And Verne's narrative voice, even in a dated translation, although very fun and witty, didn't feel essential to my story. Many of the descriptions of the foreign locations traveled through, passages that fill the narrative with interest and delight, could be put in the mouths of characters. Important plot elements described by the narrative could become action, and essential character details described in the novel could be embodied by the actors playing those characters.

Usually the structure of a novel, as opposed to short stories or other source material, more closely follows the structure of a play. When adapting a novel there may be less invention in structure and plot than there is when adapting something other than a novel. This was true for *Around the World in 80 Days*. My adaptation was to generally follow the plot of the novel. Of course, there were simplifications, inventions, and rearrangements, but my voice manifests itself most strongly in this adaptation in the characters and their development, not in changes to the plot.

For writers in the theater our version of "show, don't tell" manifests in trying to avoid extended exposition in scenes. Dramatists try to quickly get across important aspects of situation and character through behavior and minimal expositional dialogue and, if it is used, narration. Telling instead of showing is a real trap for adaptation, because so often you are taking source material with narrative that tells you what is happening or who the characters are and that must be activated in a theatrical context, which can be challenging. This was certainly the case with *Around the World in 80 Days*.

"Show, don't tell" came into play for me very early in the conception of the adaptation in relation to the introduction of our protagonist, Phileas Fogg. The novel starts with an incredibly elaborate, three and a half-page description of Fogg. In detail, this lengthy description establishes where Fogg lives, that he is "an enigmatical personage, about whom little was known, except that he was a polished man of the world . . . he had no public employment . . . belonged, in fact, to none of the numerous societies which swarm in the English capital . . ." and that he was "a member of the Reform Club, and that was all." It makes clear that Fogg is wealthy, but no one knows how he made his fortune, that he was "the least communicative of men. He talked very little, and

©Sean Williams (www.seanwill.com)

seemed all the more mysterious for his taciturn manner. His daily habits were quite open to observation; but whatever he did was so exactly the same thing that he had always done before, that the wits of the curious were fairly puzzled. . . . no one seemed to know the world more familiarly" but no one could ever remember him ever going anywhere. "His sole pastimes were reading the papers and playing whist . . . but his winnings never went into his purse, being reserved as a fund for his charities . . . he was not known to have either wife or children" nor "relatives or near friends . . . He lived alone in his house in Saville Row, whither none penetrated." The extended description goes on to include more details of his settled and regular manner and the fact that his nature required his sole domestic help "to be almost superhumanly prompt and regular." And that he had, "On this very 2nd of October, dismissed James Forster, because that luckless youth had brought him shaving-water at eighty-four degrees Fahrenheit instead of eighty-six."

The question came, then, how to *show* Fogg in all his regularity and routine and also get across my story of his loneliness and isolation all in three minutes or less without it being overly expositional?

My answer was this: I devised the beginning of the play to be a three-minute movement sequence set to music that I called *A Day in the*

Life. It attempted to establish everything described above about Fogg in an active way and let the audience in on what they needed to know about Fogg as we began the story. This is how the script describes the sequence.

> *Lights up.*
>
> A Day in the Life
>
> Day 1: Morning in London, Monday September 30th, 1872.
>
> *Out of bed rises Phileas Fogg, handsome, around 40, a man so precise that to say his life runs like clockwork is no exaggeration.*
>
> *In a movement sequence we see Fogg, in a very regimented routine:*
> —Wake up
> —Stretch and touch his toes
> —Put on his suit coat
> —Have tea and toast delivered by his valet James
> —Get his hat and walking cane from James
> —Bid "Good-day" to James
> —Exit his home
> —Arrive on the street
> —Approach a beggar woman who asks him "Alms for the poor?"
> —Give money to the beggar woman, emptying a little purse into her hand
> —Walk down the road
> —Bid "Good-day" to a flower seller.
> —Take a flower from the flower seller for his lapel.
> —Nod and walk on as she says "Good-day Mr. Fogg."
> —Arrive at the Reform club
> —Play whist with one other gentleman
> —Win at whist
> —Collect his winnings into a little purse
> —Bid "Good-evening" to the gentleman who bid him the same
> —Begin his walk home
> —Bid "Good-evening" to the flower seller who bids him the same
> —Arrive at home
> —Give his coat, hat and cane to his valet James
> —Bid "Good-night" to James after he bids him the same
> —Sigh
> —Go to sleep
>
> *A moment of silence.*

From my earliest conception, I had imagined that Fogg getting out of bed would be staged with him emerging from a trap in the floor. What I didn't realize until our final dress rehearsal was how much the large, open trap (created by our set designers Jacqueline and Richard Penrod) that Fogg stands over before descending into it to go to "bed" would look like a grave. This image greatly helped to heighten Fogg's isolation and loneliness. To deepen it further, the actor playing Fogg, Philip R. Smith, added a deep sadness to Fogg's sigh, and we added an extra beat of Fogg standing and looking into the bed/grave. This allowed time for his state of mind to register with the audience.

After the sequence was completed, it repeated again. Although the townspeople around him were slightly different, Fogg's every action was exactly the same. During the second sequence, a few townspeople tell us a little more about Fogg. The action continued under the dialogue:

STREET-SWEEP: So, that's Mr. Phileas Fogg, is it?

FLOWER SELLER: Cuts quite a figure, eh?

STREET-SWEEP: Must be a wealthy man.

FLOWER SELLER: Undoubtedly. But no one knows how he made his fortune and, from what I hear, he's the last one to ask.

STREET-SWEEP: Generous?

FLOWER SELLER: Not lavish but when money is needed for a noble or useful cause, he seems to supply it quietly.

STREET-SWEEP: On the town much, is he?

FLOWER SELLER: No, keeps to himself, hasn't any family or friends beyond his whist partners at the club. But a fine fellow is Mr. Fogg!

When the second sequence finished, there was a moment of silence and the repetition began for a third time.

A moment of silence.

Day 3: Morning in London, Wednesday October 2nd, 1872.

The day in the life pattern begins to repeat.

In movement sequence, we see Fogg once again:
—Wake up
—Stretch and touch his toes

—Put on his suit coat

—Have tea and toast delivered by his valet James

At the moment Fogg's lips touch the tea everything comes to a screeching halt.

FOGG: James—the temperature of the tea. It is not at the required 97 degrees.

JAMES: Terribly sorry, sir. I expect that's it for me, then. Shall I place an advertisement for a new man before I go, sir?

FOGG: (Calmly, quickly) If you would.

Movement sequence continues as we see Fogg:
—Get his hat and walking cane
—Bid "Good Luck" to James
—Nod as James says "Good-bye" and exits in resignation
—Exit his home

The story continues from there. But the sequence showed all we needed to know to set up Fogg. The sequence also made the audience feel constricted by the repetition, so that the third time through, the audience began to feel a little stuck in a rut, too. That way, when the adventure finally began, the audience had a palpable, experiential sense of the repetitive pattern being broken, not only an intellectual one.

In relation to the other main characters, there were significant amplifications and/or changes that I made that helped to pull through the themes of my story. First, Fogg's Valet, Passepartout, comes to Fogg after a life in the circus, seeking a more settled existence. To emphasize Fogg's disinterest and separation from the world, I created in the text an ongoing, playful battle between Passepartout's natural curiosity and his proclaimed desire to settle down, amplifying both Passepartout's curiosity about the world and the intensity of his fight to conquer his interest. This strongly motivated his actions and provided some comedy as well. At the end of the play, we saw that Passepartout's curiosity had rubbed off on Fogg when, in an invented moment that is a callback to the opening scene with James, Passepartout serves a cup of tea to Fogg.

Passepartout pours Mrs. Aouda and Fogg each a cup of tea and begins to exit as Fogg takes a sip.

FOGG: (Stunned) Passepartout, this is not my regular tea.

PASSEPARTOUT: No, sir. I brought it back from Japan. I thought you might like it.

FOGG: Yes, well. (Realizing) It is good, I must say . . .

The acceptance of the unfamiliar tea is a small gesture, but for Fogg it is profound.

The most significant character change was manifest in Mrs. Aouda, the well-educated Indian widow whom Fogg and Passepartout rescue from certain death during a ritual Suttee (an archaic tradition where widows were burned to death on the funeral pyre of their husbands). For me, Mrs. Aouda is a victim of her time. Verne paints her as a beautiful and kind creature but gives her almost no inner life. And although Verne states clearly that Mrs. Aouda "received a thoroughly English upbringing" and from her command of the English language, English "manners and her schooling, could have been taken for a European" she says almost nothing, only having twelve or so lines of dialogue before she, surprisingly, proposes to Mr. Fogg. He doesn't explore her pain over leaving her homeland or what she experiences when seeing and interacting with unfamiliar cultures and peoples on the journey. Her unexplored story had potential. Through expanding and deepening her character, I realized I could explore many of the social, political, and philosophical questions I wanted to raise in the adaptation.

In the novel, when we first meet Mrs. Aouda during the procession of the Suttee, she is basically unconscious from drugs given to sedate her. After Fogg and Passepartout rescue her from the funeral pyre, they carry her lifeless-seeming body to the train with them. As she sleeps off the effects of the drugs, Verne quotes a lengthy passage from the poet-king, Yusuf Adil, possibly invented by Verne, celebrating the charms of a queen of Ahmadnagar describing her "shining tresses" and "white and delicate cheeks." When Mrs. Aouda finally awoke, she . . .

profusely thanked her deliverers, rather with tears than words; her fine eyes interpreted her gratitude better than her lips. Then, as her thoughts strayed back to the scene of the sacrifice, and recalled the dangers which still menaced her, she shuddered with terror. Phileas Fogg understood what was passing in Aouda's mind, and offered, in order to reassure her, to escort her to Hong Kong, where she might remain safely until the affair died down —an offer which she eagerly and gratefully accepted.

First meeting Mrs. Aouda as an unconscious rescue victim and then as a teary, grateful supplicant wasn't a strong entrance and wouldn't introduce a heroine worthy of our interest in 2008. Instead, I made Mrs. Aouda awake and alert, immediately and throughout, concerned but self-possessed. When Fogg offers to escort her out of India to safety, Aouda looks away. The invented scene continues . . .

> FOGG: I regret if my offer has in any way displeased you.
>
> MRS. AOUDA: No, I am humbled by your generosity. I am glad to live and graciously accept your offer, Mr. Fogg. But you see . . . I had come to accept my death, no matter how bitterly I regretted it. And now, to be alive and forced to leave the home I love and all the many treasures in it? To never have my feet touch the soil of my country again . . . ? To never to hear the singing voices of my sisters or see the morning light on their children's faces as they grow up in our garden in Bombay . . . ? You see, Mr. Fogg, even with your generous offer, I cannot yet look forward to the world beyond the one I have known —for it soon will be lost to me forever.
>
> FOGG: I see. Well, we will discuss everything when you've had more time to recover.
>
> MRS. AOUDA: Thank you, Mr. Fogg.
>
> *Mrs. Aouda finally turns her eyes to Fogg. They hold eyes for a moment longer than expected.*
>
> FOGG: Any Englishman would have done the same.

In this invention, I gave voice to the complicated reality of Mrs. Aouda having to leave her native land even though it meant saving her life. I also added the final line of Fogg's. "Any Englishman would have done the same" to express his inability, at this point in the story, to engage emotionally with Mrs. Aouda. His brisk, proper, almost dismissive response to her heartfelt words often received a laugh of recognition from the audience at his limitations in the moment.

It was important to me that all of my invented dialogue seamlessly blended with Verne's and that the quality of language in the adaptation felt consistent. To this end, I wrote all original dialogue with an "old-fashioned" syntax and tone so that my dialogue and Verne's would be indistinguishable.

Thematically in the play, Mrs. Aouda is both pushing Fogg out of the comfort of his routine and expanding his vision of the world. Both force him to be uncharacteristically spontaneous and become, in a sense, off-balance. For Mrs. Aouda, Fogg is a man of total confidence in the ability of things to work themselves out, and she finds this inspiring. As Fogg's distant and disinterested façade begins to belie the kind and generous nature underneath, she, surprisingly, begins to fall for him just as he begins to fall for her. I wanted to express these ideas first theatrically and then textually.

From before even finishing the first draft, I had an image of Fogg and Aouda sitting at a table out on the deck of the *Rangoon*, the first ship they ride together, silently sipping tea. I imaged, though, that the tabletop would tip somehow and the cups would slide back and forth. I wanted it to be an unexpected, unavoidably playful and off-kilter sequence between them. I named it the Tea Dance. Here is how it is in the script:

> TEA DANCE:
> Music plays as Fogg and Aouda sit at a table drinking tea on the deck of the *Rangoon*. The boat tips and their teacups slide off the table variously. They catch them and this become a playful dance as they sip a sip, put down their teacups, lose their teacups, catch the other's teacup, hand it back and begin again. This cycles through three times and is ended when the teacups are cleared.

In the Lookingglass production, the tabletop was hinged and the actor playing Fogg controlled the movement of the table. The sequence was expertly choreographed by the play's movement director, Tracy Walsh, and executed brilliantly by the actors. The result was playful and charming. It showed the growing relationship of Fogg and Aouda as well as the spontaneity and slightly off-balance quality Fogg has around her.

The scene that follows the Tea Dance is almost totally invented but pulls some location description from Verne's narrative. It continues to explore Fogg and Aouda's developing relationship and the eye-opening perspective, as well as humor, she provides for him.

> MRS. AOUDA: The waves are still quite strong. Last night, I thought I was to be forcibly thrown from my cabin! Did you sleep at all, Mr. Fogg?
>
> FOGG: I slept quite well.

MRS. AOUDA: But we've slowed down so considerably, and I know you must board a ship in Hong Kong no later than November fifth!

FOGG: I see that Passepartout has filled you in on the details of our journey.

MRS. AOUDA: Now that I know, I am even more indebted to you.

FOGG: Nothing to be indebted for until I have left you safely with your cousin. As soon as we arrive, I will seek him out. Everything will be arranged with mathematical precision.

MRS. AOUDA: (*After a moment, looking around*) The scenery is lovely, is it not? I sailed this route once with my father. We are near the straits of Malacca.

FOGG: Indeed. The straits link China, India, and the Near East.

MRS. AOUDA: It is so beautiful —the mountain on one side, the forest of Bamboo on the other. Did you know that legend says it was discovered four hundred years ago by a brave Hindu Prince? Supposedly, he named the city after a Malaka tree that had given him shelter during a storm.

FOGG: Malacca is at the center of the maritime trade in this region and was an inevitable and logical result of its geography, regardless of who discovered it.

MRS. AOUDA: (*Smiling at Fogg*) I suppose it was. Although I think I like the other story better, don't you?

FOGG: I do enjoy your perspective.

MRS. AOUDA: And I yours.

FOGG: It is certainly . . . novel. (*Realizing the time*) For today, I must bid you adieu. Whist awaits. But tomorrow . . . shall we visit at the same hour we begin today?

MRS. AOUDA: Yes, that should work out . . . with mathematical precision.

Mrs. Aouda's desire to be autonomous in spite of the dependency she finds herself in is not something Verne was overly concerned about, but was something that I found important. In the novel, when the group arrives in Hong Kong, Mrs. Aouda learns that the cousin she sought to stay with no longer lives there but has moved to Holland. The scene in the novel, just after Fogg has broken the news to her, goes like this:

> Aouda at first said nothing. She passed her hand across her forehead, and reflected a few moments. Then, in her sweet, soft voice, she said: "What ought I to do, Mr. Fogg?"
>
> "It is very simple," responded the gentleman. "Come to Europe."
>
> "But I cannot take advantage—"
>
> "You do not take advantage, nor does your presence in the least harm my project."

That is the end of the conversation. Fogg has Passepartout book three cabins on their next boat and that is that. In the play, Mrs. Aouda more strongly asserts her independence and Fogg is clearly knocked off balance by that.

FOGG: Mrs. Aouda, I have news of your cousin.

MRS. AOUDA: Yes? Did you find him?

MR. FOGG: No. He made an immense fortune here but quit this country two years ago. He now lives and works in Holland.

MRS. AOUDA: Well . . . I wonder what I am to do now?

FOGG: Quite simple. Come with us to London and, from there, I will secure your safe passage to Holland.

MRS. AOUDA: I thank you, Mr. Fogg, but no. You have already done too much for me. I am not your responsibility. I am my own.

FOGG: (With difficulty, maybe for the first time in his life) Yes, but . . . I cannot . . . rather, how will you . . . I mean, perhaps you would care to . . .

MRS. AOUDA: (Stunned by his stumbling) Mr. Fogg . . . ?

FOGG: (Recovered) As you have never been to Europe before and do not know your way, it simply seems the most logical course of action that you join us.

MRS. AOUDA: (Teasing a little) Oh, well, if it is the most logical course of action, I suppose that it's best.

FOGG: (*Oblivious to teasing*) Very well, then.

MRS. AOUDA: (*Sad Fogg doesn't get teasing*) Very well.

In the novel, Fogg buys Mrs. Aouda "the necessary purchases for the long voyage before them. It was all very well for an Englishman like Mr. Fogg to make the tour of the world with a carpet-bag; a lady could not be expected to travel comfortably under such conditions." Fogg acquits his task "with characteristic serenity, and invariably replied to the remonstrances of his fair companion, who was confused by his patience and generosity: "It is in the interest of my journey—a part of my programme."

In the play, the purchases came out of a more practical impulse for Fogg, and Aouda's "remonstrances" were more strongly stated. The scene in the play went like this:

FOGG: Since we are bound for colder climes, I think it necessary we purchase you some traveling clothes.

MRS. AOUDA: I suppose it is. But I shall keep track of your expenditures on me, Mr. Fogg, and someday I will repay, if not your kindness, at least your pocket.

FOGG: I will have Passepartout engage an additional cabin aboard the Carnatic when he goes to have the passports stamped.

Mrs. Aouda nods in thanks and turns to look out at the view.

The scene continues inspired by some Verne text from a slightly different point in the novel. I took narrative observation and changed it into an exchange between the characters continuing to reinforce Aouda's effect on Fogg's view of the world. Verne's text reads:

Passepartout wandered, with his hands in his pockets, towards the Victoria port . . . he found a confused mass of ships of all nations: English, French, American, and Dutch, men-of-war and trading vessels, Japanese and Chinese junks, sempas, tankas, and flower-boats, which formed so many floating parterres.

The scene reads like this:

MRS. AOUDA: Have you seen the Canton River before? It is so different than what I imagined. There seem to be ships here from all nations.

FOGG: Yes, trading vessels, junks, sempas, tankas . . .

MRS. AOUDA: And, look, the flower-boats —like so many floating gardens.

FOGG: Yes, I suppose that is what they look like. Floating gardens. Hmm.

In the second act, as the group makes their way across the American plains by train, I thought it was a perfect opportunity for Aouda to address British colonialism. The scene folds in some of Verne's description of the landscape but both Mrs. Aouda and Fogg's dialogue is invented as she speaks to him, frankly and critically, about British imperialism.

FOGG: (*Looking out the train window*) From ocean to ocean, they say. In the past, the journey from San Francisco to New York under the most favorable conditions was at least six months, now it is just seven days.

MRS. AOUDA: To think that this land, too, might still be under British influence if the Americans hadn't fought for their independence.

FOGG: British influence is not necessarily a bad thing, Mrs. Aouda.

MRS. AOUDA: For many people whose countries are no longer their own, it is indeed, a bad thing, Mr. Fogg.

Fogg takes that in.

MRS. AOUDA: (cont'd) But what I can not figure out, putting aside one's ability to understand why the world must be conquered at all, is why the English need to remake everything in their own image . . . the language, the names, the buildings, the shops, making every place, the whole world, the same.

Fogg looks at her, taking that in.

FOGG: Perhaps we just don't know how to see things any other way.

For me, although brief, this was an important scene that brought the play into the current moment and showed how Mrs. Aouda's thinking was beginning to affect Fogg.

The moment when love finally cracks Fogg open needed to be

unique and beautiful. In the novel, Indians attack the train in America (changed to "bandits" in the play for obvious reasons in 2008) and the group is forced to ride a sledge—a sled with sails—across the frozen plains to make their train connection. The scene is described in the novel, with no advancement in Fogg and Aouda's relationship, like this:

> But the breeze, far from lessening its force, blew as if to bend the mast, which, however, the metallic lashings held firmly. These lashings, like the chords of a stringed instrument, resounded as if vibrated by a violin bow. The sledge slid along in the midst of a plaintively intense melody. "Those chords give the fifth and the octave," said Mr. Fogg. These were the only words he uttered during the journey. Aouda, cozily packed in furs and cloaks, was sheltered as much as possible from the attacks of the freezing wind.

I wanted something magical to happen, something that would clearly indicate Fogg and Aouda's feelings for each other and bring the story to a more emotional place. I decided to make the sledge ride another physical sequence. The sledge was built by lifting a large piece of the stage deck on four wires, anchored at the corners but rigged so the platform could swing. It was big enough for the five actors playing Fogg, Aouda, Passepartout, Mr. Fix (an inspector from Scotland Yard who chases Fogg around the world mistakenly thinking he is a bank robber) and Mr. Mudge, the sledge driver, to sit on. As the sledge rocked back and forth, simulating gliding across the American plains, a giant white sail billowed behind it and snow gently fell from the sky above. As the group looked with wide eyes and open hearts at the amazing sights around them, they sang a lovely, wordless song written by our composer, Kevin O'Donnell. Fogg and Aouda huddled together, singing with their faces close, holding hands without really realizing it. It was a moment of pure openness for Fogg and although he backed off a bit for the rest of the journey, it let us into his heart in a way that lead the audience to both root for Fogg and Aouda to get together and to feel it was justified when they did, which isn't totally the case with the novel.

Often in adaptations you are faced with more characters than there are actors and you must double or triple (or more) cast from your ensemble. This show was no different. The four major characters in the play are Fogg, Aouda, Passepartout, and Fix. I wanted the audience to feel very connected and invested in the journey, both physically and emotionally, of these four main characters and for the development of their character arcs to be clear, unbroken, and constantly visible to the audience from beginning to end. That would have been challenging if the actors played multiple roles, as the development of their arcs would be interrupted by playing other characters with different motivations. So, I decided to have the actors playing the four main characters only play that role except in the "Day in the Life" sequence at the start of the play. In this sequence, the actors playing Passepartout, Mrs. Aouda, and Fix played unnamed ensemble roles before they appeared as their main characters.

In the adaptation, there were forty-nine other characters that appeared during the journey. Through careful planning, I was able to cast only four actors, three men and one woman, to cover these forty-nine parts. Each of these brave souls played at least eleven different characters, each with a head-to-toe costume change. I was told the action backstage rivaled the action onstage.

One of the smaller roles I reinterpreted that I was most pleased with was the role of Brigadier-General Sir Francis Cromarty. In the novel, Sir Francis, an English General, meets Mr. Fogg on a ship, the *Mongolia*, and then joins him on the journey across India. For the play, I wanted Fogg to encounter people who were not British who would push against Fogg's assumptions about people and the world. I reimagined Sir Francis as Mr. Naidu, an Indian businessman. In the novel, Sir Francis and Mr. Fogg have a conversation about Passepartout accidentally stepping into a temple in Bombay with his shoes on and almost getting arrested. In the Verne, the text reads:

The train entered the defiles of the mountains, with their basalt bases, and their summits crowned with thick and verdant forests. Phileas Fogg and Sir Francis Cromarty exchanged a few words from time to time, and now Sir Francis, reviving the conversation, observed,

"Some years ago, Mr. Fogg, you would have met with a delay at this point which would probably have lost you your wager."

"How so, Sir Francis?"

"Because the railway stopped at the base of these mountains, which the passengers were obliged to cross in palanquins or on ponies to Kandallah, on the other side."

"Such a delay would not have deranged my plans in the least," said Mr. Fogg. "I have constantly foreseen the likelihood of certain obstacles."

"But, Mr. Fogg," pursued Sir Francis, "you run the risk of having some difficulty about this worthy fellow's adventure at the pagoda." Passepartout, his feet comfortably wrapped in his traveling-blanket, was sound asleep and did not dream that anybody was talking about him. "The Government is very severe upon that kind of offence. It takes particular care that the religious customs of the Indians should be respected, and if your servant were caught—"

"Very well, Sir Francis," replied Mr. Fogg; "if he had been caught he would have been condemned and punished, and then would have quietly returned to Europe. I don't see how this affair could have delayed his master."

The conversation came to an end.

In the adaptation, the same scene goes like this:

SCENE 10: ON THE WAY TO CALCUTTA

Fogg is playing cards with Mr. Naidu on the train. Passepartout, still shoe-less, sleeps with a little blanket over him. Naidu glances at Passepartout.

MR. NAIDU: You are lucky, Mr. Fogg.

FOGG: How is that, Mr. Naidu?

MR. NAIDU: If Passepartout had been caught for not taking off his shoes in the temple, you would have met with a significant delay. Your government takes a very serious view, and rightly so, of disrespect towards the religious practices of the Indian people.

FOGG: Mr. Naidu, if he had been caught he would have been condemned, punished, and quietly returned to Europe. I don't see how it would have delayed me.

MR. NAIDU: I see. (*Glancing out the train window*) When I was a boy, the railway stopped at the base of these mountains. We were obliged to cross on ponies to the other side. Never did I imagine the train would one day climb the mountains, too. The world is surprising, isn't it Mr. Fogg?

FOGG: That all depends on what one is expecting, Mr. Naidu.

MR. NAIDU: And what do you expect of the world, Mr. Fogg?

FOGG: Only that it can be traveled in eighty days.

MR. NAIDU: Does nothing hold interest for you?

FOGG: Anything that can't be found in the *Bradshaw Guide* isn't of much interest or expectation to me. *(Laying down cards)* Hearts are trumps.

The train begins to slow. Passepartout wakes up.

The conversation is strongly influenced by the Verne text, but the lines are contextually very different when spoken by a native Indian man. We were also very lucky in that the actor of Indian descent who played Mr. Naidu, Anish Jethmalani, spoke Hindi. This enabled us to incorporate a few conversations in Hindi into the play, which added authenticity to the play's depiction of India and its people.

The final inspired invention of the adaptation I will mention came out of a suggestion from the actress who played Mrs. Aouda, Ravi Batista. She was interested in Mr. Fogg and Mrs. Aouda having a moment of cultural transcendence, where both she and Fogg knew something that didn't seem to be from either of their worlds. Ravi suggested a song somewhere, perhaps when they were on the sea. I worked with our composer and we found a sea chantey that we both loved. It was sung on board by the whole cast as the *Henrietta* sets sail.

Three Henrietta crewmen appear and the crew, Fogg and Aouda sing a sea chantey as the boat is built. Fogg and Aouda both recognize the other is singing along and are surprised. They look to each other.

MRS. AOUDA: I used to sail with my father.

FOGG: As did I.

The cast all continue to sing as the boat building is finished and the boat heads out to sea.

On paper it is hard to capture the delight this moment contained—the whole cast broke into song as the ship's rigging emerged from traps in the floor and was hoisted in the air. Fogg and Aouda sang the familiar song, enjoying each other and the moment. It was a delightful and highly theatrical sequence.

The sea-chantey moment was one of dozens of suggestions made by the cast that made the show richer and deeper. Which leads me to an important side note—collaboration. The rules of every collaboration between playwrights, directors, and actors need to be decided and agreed upon, but an important lesson of adaptation is that when you are collaborating with artists that you trust and respect, you won't be the

©Sean Williams (www.seanwill.com)

only one to have good text or content ideas. In my experience, actors, directors, dramaturges, designers, and stage managers have all had extremely valuable ideas that have helped shape shows. When developing adaptations, like any kind of my work, I find it invaluable to have collaborators who challenge me. These are typically fellow artists who don't let me off the hook easily, but do encourage me a hundred percent. That is what I have as a Lookingglass Ensemble member and with other trusted colleagues with whom I have had the pleasure to collaborate. My work is immeasurably better because of these relationships, some longstanding, some just beginning, and I am more grateful for them than I can ever adequately express.

My silent collaborator on *Around the World in 80 Days* was Jules Verne. Being long dead, he didn't have much to say about my adaptation. Because of this, I felt very comfortable straying from the source material and making the adaptation very much my own. Verne devotees and/or critics would complain about what was missing (including some things that don't actually exist in the source material, as often happens) or that I had misinterpreted something (their subjective interpretation of the text, of course, always being correct). But I also knew *Around the World in Eighty Days* is not a novel that is as known or loved in America as *Adventures of Huckleberry Finn* is. I assumed my inventions would generally be ascribed to Verne, as was most often true, and/or met with general approval, which was the case.

Adapting *The Coast of Chicago*

The Coast of Chicago was an adaptation of several short stories by Stuart Dybek, the Chicago native and MacArthur "genius" award-winning writer, from a collection of the same name. The stage production of *The Coast of Chicago* predated *Around the World* by two years. Many things I learned from *Coast* help to inform future adaptations and, although it was a more difficult script to write, I gained invaluable new insights through the process and developed new adaptation tools.

Walkabout Theater bought the project to me in the summer of 2004. Walkabout's artistic director Kristian Schmidt and the show's producer Betsy Ingram commissioned me to write a play adapted from the book that they were committed to producing in the summer of 2005. Walkabout is a company that often performs in non-traditional theater spaces. The plan was to perform the play version of *Coast* on the rooftop of a performance venue in downtown Chicago with the actual city as the backdrop/set.

Luckily, only one of the short stories from the collection had been optioned by a film company. Walkabout was able to secure the stage rights for the rest. So often with contemporary works of literature exclusive stage rights are bundled with the film rights. This prevents playwrights from adapting these texts for the stage, even if the film company has no interest in ever making the optioned text a play and the plans for the film version have stalled out, leaving the novel or collection of stories sitting on a shelf in Hollywood somewhere. In my own experience, there have been a dozen novels in the last fifteen years that Lookingglass wanted to adapt that were put aside due to film companies owning both the film and exclusive stage rights. With only one exception, the potential films that prevented Lookingglass from getting the stage rights were never made. At this point, I rarely consider modern literature for adaptation, knowing the difficulty acquiring rights. I wish authors would give film companies non-exclusive stage rights instead, keeping the door open for adaptation. But it is currently standard. So I was shocked and beyond delighted that all but one of the stories of *The Coast of Chicago* were available to us.

I had read the collection of fourteen tender and unforgiving stories of life in Chicago's gritty ethnic enclaves and found the weaving of crushing reality with phantasmagoric images of "dreams escaped from dreamers" stunning. Although I knew the adaptation would be challenging, I thought the venue was a great fit for the tone and themes of the stories. I was also thrilled that the commission came with a guaranteed production. I began working on the adaptation in the fall of 2004.

My approach with the commission of *The Coast of Chicago* was to be very flexible and make sure Walkabout was happy with the end result. As an artist, I want to believe in everything I create, but with a commission like this one, I am a hired gun brought on board to do a job. The danger in this kind of relationship is that one can be too deferential to whoever is in charge of the commission. One might not make strong enough choices or might not commit as deeply to the choices made because you want to be open to the wishes of the people who commissioned you and make sure they are pleased. Some of the challenges I encountered in the process of this adaptation were a result of that dynamic, although the formal challenge of adapting a collection of short stories is huge in and of itself.

Adapting short stories is different and more difficult than adapting a novel because you have to invent a whole structure that builds in the way a play would. In a collection of stories each one has its own narrative structure, but there is no overarching structure for the whole collection. I decided with my collaborators, Kristian, Betsy, and Gary Zabinski, who directed the piece, that the adaptation would mostly be centered on two larger stories "Chopin in Winter" and "Hot Ice." The big question was how to frame the story of the play and build a dramatic arc.

Unlike the narrative voice in *Around the World*, which was not overly compelling to me and was not included in the adaptation, the narrative voice in *Coast of Chicago* became essential in capturing the tone and spirit of the stories. I knew I wanted narration to somehow frame the piece. Generally, the use of the narrative voice must be rigorously examined because sustaining long narrative passages in the theater is difficult. It is the old "show don't tell" problem; long narrative monologues make for un-dynamic story-telling if the audience is not asked to do the work of figuring out a character's motivations and feelings, or if much of the play's action is described instead of seen and experienced. I found Dybek's voice to be about mood and atmosphere more than a traditional narrative taking the audience from event to event. Thus, his narrative voice would still leave plenty of "work" and involvement for the audience.

I imagined the narrative frame as abstract, coming from an unnamed narrator who was not in any realistic context but simply a man thinking of his past, giving the feel of a performance piece more than a traditional play. Here is how I described this in the initial proposal:

> The play will weave together a variety of stories to create an overall effect more like a collage than a traditional journey with a single protagonist. Like the book, as explained by Mr. Dybek in an interview with James Plath, the show will "proceed more by association—the way we do in dreams" rather than by cause and effect. Realism will be combined with the surreal and lyrical—music, abstract images and text will be interlaced to tell the story.

This approach would support a very poetic narrative framing the piece.

In the collection, there is a story called "Nighthawks" that is made up of nine shorter stories with different titles. I was drawn to one of these inner-stories, called "Silhouettes," that describes a boy looking out a window and seeing the shadow of people passing the "mouth of the alley" in the rain. The story continues to describe characters in neighboring apartments and ends, surprisingly, with the narrative voice moving from omniscient third person to first person as our narrator calls out to his love, saying it is a night "shaped like a shadow thrown by your absence."

I took this spare, poetic piece, shaped it and put it in the mouth of our narrator. The first draft opened like this.

NIGHTHAWKS—PART ONE

The NARRATOR walks forward, carrying a copy of The Coast of Chicago. *Perhaps he is mic'd so his voice is close in the audience's ear. Maybe he reads from the book.*

NARRATOR: The alley became a river in the rain—with clattering cans and a floe of cardboard. The boy would lie listening to the single note of drops pinging the metal hood of a blue bulb that glowed above the garage door. Finally, he'd go to the window and look.

Above the narrator, perhaps the face of a young boy appears in a window set into a wall.

NARRATOR: On a street whose name and number had been washed away, shadows moved aimlessly through the rain.

Cast members cross to various places in the playing space, creating different images in relation to one another.

NARRATOR: He could catch glimpses of them passing by the mouth of the alley. Even when he couldn't see them, he could sense their presence; shapes that he had named silhouettes—shadows that threw shadows, that inhabited the hourless times of night stolen from dreams. He couldn't remember when he'd first become aware of their presence, or when he first thought of them as silhouettes, but he had never thought of them as anything else—not ghosts or spirits. Silhouettes were enough to haunt him.

As the narrator speaks of the following characters, they emerge from the shadows and come to life.

UKRAINIAN KID: The Ukrainian kid downstairs who slept with his arms in the shape of the cross to ward off the dead.

THE PUERTO RICAN GIRL: Across the alley, in a basement flat, the Puerto Rican girl who prayed as if begging before the candle flickering the picture of the Virgin on her bureau.

As the neighborhood characters continued to emerge, the frame gave way to the first story, "Chopin in Winter." The narrator watched and narrated what became clearly his own experiences as a boy and then as a young man in "Hot Ice." The first draft ended like this:

NIGHTHAWKS—CONCLUSION

The sound of rain.

NARRATOR: In the rain, the alley becomes a river that winds through sleepers. A man unable to sleep imagines that he can hear the river, too, although he knows that listening for it may merely be a way of occupying his mind, which should be dreaming. Between wakefulness and dreaming, with his eyes closed he can see the light reflected by the falling river of rain; fogged streetlamps and taillights streaked along the Outer Drive, a downtown of dimmed office buildings and glowing hotel lobbies, acetylene sparking behind blue factory windows, racks of vigil candles in the cathedral, always kept open, across the street from the neon-lit bus terminal. He's drifting on a flood of night thoughts—thoughts he may try to dismiss in daylight, the way dreams are renounced and forgotten, but his restless nights have begun to inform his days. Almost dreaming, with the river flowing beside his ear . . .

Characters from the stories reemerge from the shadows.

NARRATOR: Images from the past appear to remind him that there is only so much time to change the direction of a life, to show him it may be time to release his memories so that they can begin to assume a life of their own.

The Boy appears.

NARRATOR: And what about the memory of the boy left at the window, staring out past his own spattered reflection? The boy could disappear behind a single breath fogged on the glass, then wiped away. The room has fallen away behind him; the bed, without his weight, is light enough to levitate. Downstairs, The Ukrainian kid . . .

UKRAINIAN KID: A maestro now . . .

NARRATOR: Has begun a fiddle nocturne to pacify the dead. Across the alley . . .

THE PUERTO RICAN GIRL: Prayers rise like an attar of roses from a basement flat.

NARRATOR: Love, rain drums on the helmet of blue light. Each drop contains its own blue bulb, and when they shatter they collect into a blue river that continues to gleam. The river, the same river sweeping them both away, is all that connects the boy and the man. It flows through the inland city, down streets it submerges, to the slick highways that bank a black sea prairie. It empties by the piers where the rusty barges are moored along the ghostly coastline.

Slowly one by one, the cast leaves the space. Perhaps the Boy appears in the window, repeating the first image of the play. The Narrator takes out The Coast of Chicago *book and reads, looking at the Boy,*

NARRATOR: From his window overlooking the alley that has become a river, the boy can see this. He could glimpse the future passing, reflected in the current, if he weren't watching the streetlight slowly sinking as it swirls into the vortex of a sewer, if he weren't still waiting for the silhouettes to come for him.

The boy disappears. The Narrator closes the book.

NARRATOR: He doesn't realize—he won't ever know—that, like them, he's become a shadow.

The sound of rain mixed with snatches of Chopin and conga drums and text from the show as the Narrator follows the rest of the cast away, disappearing into the night.

I read and reviewed the first draft with my collaborators, Kristian, Betsy, and Gary, and several things came to light. It was generally overwritten. We all felt that there was too much narration in general throughout the piece and that I needed to be more aggressive in looking at the scenes with a theatrical eye. The desire to have the piece be more performative gave way to the desire to have something less conceptual that felt more cohesive and relatable. Finally, the narrative frame was too abstract and poetic. The goals for the frame were discussed—that it needed to grab the audience and set up the tone and "rules" of the play—but there was a general lack of clarity on all of our parts of how best to achieve that. Finally, it was clear that the draft stayed too true to the source material. The tendency to make a first draft very close to the original text was amplified in this process by Stuart Dybek having power of approval over the adaptation. Knowing Stuart would review the final draft of the material and sign off on it—or not—made it scary to step away from the original text and invent as much as I needed to invent to make the stories work in a theatrical context.

The other major response to the adaptation from my collaborators is that they wanted the whole piece, which was quite dark, to reflect more "aspiration to the lyrical—reaching/yearning for a transcendent/ecstatic moment that moves the characters beyond the restrictions of their oppressive environments." This was something we all had discussed in our initial proposal for the adaptation, and I agreed.

As I've said, the second draft is always where I feel the real adaptation begins to emerge, and adapting *Coast* was no different. In the second draft, the play was still anchored by two main stories, "Chopin" and "Hot Ice," both about a Polish boy growing up in the increasingly Latino neighborhood of Pilsen. We made the boy in Chopin a younger version of the narrator and the young man in "Ice" his teenage counterpart. In both stories, the characters reached for a moment of transcendence, which is music overheard from an upstairs neighbor in the first story and the discovery of truth behind a long-told urban myth in the second. The adapted shape of these stories remained essentially the same from the second draft through the four pre-rehearsal drafts, needing many small changes but nothing radical.

The script developed through several drafts and was approved by Stuart Dybek just before rehearsals began. He was incredibly generous and supportive in his response to the script. Based on the rehearsal draft, he gave us permission to continue to develop the script through rehearsal and previews as we saw fit. He explained that making a play was not his expertise and that he trusted me and my collaborators to finish the play in the way we thought best, feeling that whatever changes we made through rehearsals and previews would be good ones. He was a supporter of the show, coming to many previews and performances, but he never asked to be notified of further script changes, gave very few notes but offered much praise for the show. I continue to be deeply grateful for his openness and support of the adaptation and the production.

The issue that ended up being challenging until the end was the frame. After the first draft or two, we learned that we would be unable to perform the show at the outside location for which the piece was originally conceived. The new performance venue would be an interior theater space, which ended up being, coincidentally, the Lookingglass Theatre. As with anything, there were pros and cons to this move, but in terms of the text, the expectations that inherently come along with being in a more traditional theater space led me in a more traditional/narrative direction for the frame.

All during the piece's development, my collaborators and I had many lingering questions about the frame: How narrative should it be? How clear should the identity of the narrator be? How realistic/naturalistic should the narrator's reality be? How should the stories connect to the frame and the narrator? Unfortunately, we were not able to answer these questions successfully for a long while, and I rewrote the ending at least five times. We found the final version of the frame somewhere in the blur of the last two previews. Very different from the more abstract first pass, the final draft of the opening included much of Dybek's text but pulled from different places and arranged by me with a little invention to have it all add up to something cohesive. Most significantly, the narration was changed from third person to first person and clearly established the narrator as an older version of the boys in the stories to come, struggling with where he is in this moment in his life, looking down from a fancy glass tower onto the streets he used to walk as a poor, young kid from a working class neighborhood. In the final draft, the narrator also presented a question that seemed to be at the heart of his struggle, "Will I ever leave this city?" The final opening went like this:

NIGHTHAWKS—PART ONE

The sound of rain. A man stands at a "window."

NARRATOR: Through the window, I can see the rain falling past the buildings. The buildings that tower up to form the glass cliffs of the gold coast I've drifted to, kept awake by an ache for something I can't name . . . but know is missing, knowing that I'll soon drift away again for no reason I can understand.

The Boy from "Chopin in Winter" and Eddie from "Hot Ice" enter unseen.

NARRATOR (CONT'D): How did I end up here —looking down from the thirty-seventh floor to a street where as a kid—

He sees the Boy and Eddie standing below him as if out of a dream. A gesture or costumes clearly indicate that they are younger versions of the narrator. He looks to the Boy.

NARRATOR (CONT'D): I might have stopped and looked up, seeing an older guy like me looking down in the middle of the night, unable to sleep, thinking . . .

BOY: I wonder if I will ever leave this city.

He sees Eddie.

NARRATOR: How did I end up here? Where, as a teenager, a buddy and I spent our nights exploring and I remember both the awe and contempt we felt towards this "gold coast."

EDDIE: I wonder if I will ever leave this city.

NARRATOR: Will I ever leave this city?

The sound of the El train in the distance.

NARRATOR (CONT'D): The El in the distance, clattering. Its lighted windows like a strip of blue movie. I imagine it streaming by the places I once lived, the people I once knew.

The cast begins to gather.

The neighborhood characters are introduced as in the first draft, but with the addition of meeting characters that the audience would see in later scenes of the play. The opening frame ended with the following line before launching into "Chopin in Winter":

NARRATOR (CONT'D): In my mind, I see them, wandering free, like dreams escaped from dreamers.

After "Chopin in Winter," we created a little "check in" with the narrator before launching into "Hot Ice." This helped us stay in touch with the narrator, root him back in his location and helped the feeling of time passing.

NIGHTHAWKS—PART TWO

Lights and sound take us to the Nighthawks timeline and location and our Narrator.

NARRATOR: I hear the sounds of the night—the rain and the clatter of the El train merging with the sound of sporadic traffic. I know now it's something other than insomnia that's keeping me here, wanting to dream, but succeeding only in remembering.

The final version of the ending, constructed primarily of Dybek text that was manipulated by me, went like this:

NIGHTHAWKS—PART THREE

Light and sound transition take us back to Nighthawks.

NARRATOR: It isn't dawn yet, still a gradation of night, but night with tomorrow close behind it. I hear the El, picking up the last of the night passengers, then speeding past brick walls and gray windows, roofs and treetops —the landscape I've memorized over a lifetime of rides.

Cast enters slowly, going to their first position from Nighthawks.

NARRATOR: One day, I will leave this city . . . but this city will never leave me. The places I once lived and the people I once knew are forever gathered . . .

(He gestures to his head)

Here.

The characters from the stories step towards the narrator and circle him as key lines of dialogue from previous scenes are heard in the sound design.

Marcy (V.O): I used to wish I could help you, as long as we were both up together in the middle of the night.

Dzia-Dzia (V.O): Deep down, you know more than you think.

Pancho (V.O): There's miracles happening everywhere.

Manny (V.O): I heard them calling me, so I turned around.

NARRATOR (CONT'D): The images from the past appear to remind me . . . that there is only so much time to change the direction of a life.

Final sound and lights. Blackout.

The invented line, "but this city will never leave me" was important to add as an answer to the question posed in the opening. This line provided a realization for the narrator that came out of him revisiting the memories of his past: that no matter where he is, his past made him who he is and it will always be a part of him. Interestingly enough, this final draft of the conclusion, in staging and with the line callbacks through voice over, had an abstract quality to it that was fairly close to my original impulse.

There was, however, a third option of the frame that was worked on early in rehearsal but discarded, although I was particularly fond of it. This version of the opening and closing, that I called the "Gold Coast frame," more fully incorporated a story from the Nighthawks section called "Gold Coast." We ended up using a couple of lines of the Gold Coast story in the final draft, but much of it was left out. The "Gold Coast frame" opened the show like this:

NIGHTHAWKS/GOLD COAST—PART ONE

The sound of rain. A man and woman are lying in "bed." She is clearly asleep. He is awake and restless. He gets up and crosses to a "window."

NARRATOR: Through the window, I can see the rain falling past buildings. The buildings that tower up to form the glass cliffs of the gold coast we've drifted to.

He turns and looks to the sleeping woman for a moment. He looks back to the "window" and out to the audience, too, as he speaks.

NARRATOR: I know that every city has these strips, and I don't trust them. No matter how elegant they might appear, I think of them as illusory, removed from the real life of cities, as places that are really no place, reflections floating like illuminated scum on the surface of a river. I remember how as a teenager, a buddy and I spent our nights exploring this gold coast, and I remember both the awe and contempt we felt towards it.

The BOY and EDDIE appear. Somehow it is clear that they are younger versions of the narrator. They look to the narrator as he looks to them.

NARRATOR: How did I end up here—looking down from the thirty-seventh floor . . .

And then it continued much like the final draft. The "Gold Coast frame" ending, though, was quite different than the ending we finally decided on. Several versions of the "Gold Coast frame" ending were developed, but this one was included in the rehearsal draft that Stuart reviewed and was my favorite:

NIGHTHAWKS/GOLD COAST—PART THREE

The Gold Coast room forms around the narrator, including a woman in bed. The Narrator still looks out the "window." The sound of rain.

NARRATOR: It isn't dawn yet, still a gradation of night, but night with tomorrow already luminous. I envy those still sleeping and pity them for missing this sky.

The sound of the El mixes with the sound of rain.

NARRATOR: I hear the El in the rain. I imagine it carrying a kiss across the city, traveling along streets named for coasts—North Shore, Lakeside, Waveland, Surf. The kiss finds me, floating face-down like a reflection over dreamers gazing up from a neighborhood of flooded basements and attics.

The cast begins to emerge from the shadows.

NARRATOR: And I see them all.

The characters from the stories emerged and spoke lines or mentioned images from the stories. It then continued . . .

The cast steps away.

NARRATOR: And suddenly I know WHY. The images from the past appear to remind me that there is only so much time to change the direction of a life.

Gold Coast Woman stirs awake and looks out the "window."

GOLD COAST WOMAN: Look at the sky! Look at the light!

NARRATOR: I know.

He sits next to the woman. They look out the window.

GOLD COAST WOMAN: (*After a moment*): I'm not sure if meeting you has been the most lucky or unlucky thing that's ever happened to me.

The narrator laughs.

GOLD COAST WOMAN: I wasn't kidding.

NARRATOR: I know. I'm only laughing because that's exactly what I was thinking about meeting you.

GOLD COAST WOMAN (*After a moment*): It smells like rain.

NARRATOR: Yeah.

GOLD COAST WOMAN: What's it supposed to be like today?

NARRATOR: (*Looking at her*) Beautiful.

GOLD COAST WOMAN: So . . . what do we do now?

NARRATOR: I don't know. . . . Let's go somewhere.

GOLD COAST WOMAN: Where?

NARRATOR: I don't know. (*After a moment*) How about I take you to where I used to live? Where I grew up. I haven't been there in a long time.

GOLD COAST WOMAN: Yeah? (*Smiling*) OK. (*Looking out the window*) Look at that sky.

NARRATOR: (*Looking out the window*) Look at the light.

They look out the "window" as the lights fade to black.

The scene is very close to the Dybek story, except the narrator's suggestion to return to the old neighborhood, which was my invention. Stuart thought this line and this ending in general was a little soft. I thought them visiting the old neighborhood was beautiful and an encapsulation of his moving on without abandoning his past.

With the frame we finally committed to for the production, I think we found a solution that tied the stories together, unified the narrator and our main stories' protagonists, and activated a journey for the narrator by giving him a question he was actively turning over in his mind. It took a lot of time and many conversations with my collaborators and the cast, but the text we finally settled on worked well.

If this had not been a for-hire commission with a company that was not my own, however, I might have pushed harder for the "Gold Coast" ending. Rooting the narrator so realistically in the stories of his past, but not giving him a real person to interact with at the end of the play that represented his future felt unsatisfying to me. Our final ending also seemed rushed and abrupt, not landing quite as fully as I would have wished. I liked the feeling of moving forward that the Gold Coast frame contained.

I think the difficulty of finding my way with the frame goes back to the original conception of the piece as an outdoor project and also the inherent challenges that come with trying to create a traditional dramatic structure (exposition, rising action, climax, falling action, dénouement) out of unconnected and unrelated short stories. When the project was imagined for a "rooftop," the concept of a more poetic and open frame seemed right. I didn't look for an explicit "big why" of the frame but thought more about image, mood, and tone as a set up for the other stories. With the show moving into a more traditional theater venue all kinds of questions about the frame and how it connected to the stories arose—motivation, character, conflict—the traditional dramatic questions that perhaps I should have been more rigorous about asking in the first place. Without total clarity on our frame's "big why," my collaborators and I struggled for a long time and I am not totally sure the ending was all it could have or should have been. But the production turned out great and was very well received by both critics and audiences. Who knows how it would have gone if the frame had been different?

Casting

There were a few other aspects of *Coast* that differed from *Around the World*. The most interesting to me was casting. As is often the case with adaptation, actors in both casts played multiple roles. It is very important to consider the ways in doubling (or tripling or quadrupling) parts can be "read" by the audience. In my adaptations, I always think very hard about this issue and give specific directions of what actor should play what parts, what I call a "character track."

In *Around the World*, the main criterion in conceiving the character tracks was variety. It was important that the audience felt as if they were constantly meeting new characters during the journey. So, the use of actors was staggered and no actor was seen as a new character two scenes in a row. This allowed time and space for the actor to recede in the audience's mind before reentering as someone new. It also allowed time for full costume changes. There wasn't a great deal thematically that played into the doubling, although I did have fun re-imagining several of Verne's characters as women so that there could be more female roles in the show.

In the *Coast* production there were a lot of thematic strands that ran through the double casting/character tracks as I imagined them. Although I had strong feelings about how the doubling/multiple casting could work, because I was not directing, casting was a joint decision between the director and me. In the first draft, I had the cast at eight, three women and five men. With the addition of one story and the desire for less double casting, the cast expanded in the final draft to twelve actors, four women, seven men, and one boy.

The most significant casting change was around the role of the Boy in "Chopin" and Eddie in "Hot Ice." Originally, the Boy and Eddie were to be played by the same actor who was in his early twenties. Gary, our director, suggested a young performer around age twelve play the boy in "Chopin." I readily agreed and it was a great change. Having an actual child in the cast added an increased vulnerability to the play and helped the feeling of time passing when we met his teenage self.

We were not of such like minds around the role of Dzia-Dzia, the Boy's Grandfather in "Chopin," and a character named Antek in "Hot Ice." Gary felt that the two characters were very different in tone and soul and wanted them to be played by different actors. I liked the idea of the same actor playing both as each are the gateway, as it were, to the more lyrical and magical aspects of their specific stories. In the end, we went with two actors, although it was a big compromise for me.

Development

One great thing about both of these adaptations is that I was able to develop them in relation to a company with an actual production in mind. In both situations, we were able to have development readings, but between the two shows I had another experience that helped shape *Around the World* in a profound way.

In the summer of 2007, I adapted Elizabeth Crane's book of short stories *When the Messenger is Hot*. Jessica Thebus, whom I frequently collaborate with, directed the play as part of Steppenwolf's First Look program. First Look provides development support for new plays and includes three weeks of rehearsal, a few days of tech and eight performances scattered over three weeks that run in repertory with two other shows. Basically, it provides a production—script development, rehearsal, tech, and previews—but the show never really "opens" and isn't reviewed by the press. I had only been working on the script for about six months when we went into rehearsal. We had done several readings and both Jessica and I felt that the script was in very good shape when we entered rehearsal. We were shocked by how much came to light and how much work needed to be done when we got the play on its feet.

The situation reminded me a lot of *The Coast of Chicago*. Although I wasn't able to be in the room during the whole *Coast* rehearsal process, I was surprised by how much needed to be changed during that rehearsal process, too, considering how well the script had read at first rehearsal. During *Messenger* I had what was a really obvious realization, I suppose, but one that took me many years to come to: as a development tool for adaptations readings are not very helpful. Because they used to be books, adaptations usually read well. It is only when you get an adaptation into the hands of actors who are "on their feet" that the true state of the script is revealed. Only when a script is explored in a three-dimensional dramatic context can the unique challenges that adaptations pose be explored. For example, the way an adaptation moves through time, place, and space is often very different from a traditional play script and requires a theatrical fluidity. Navigating and activating narration requires specific techniques and skills that many actors and directors have not had the opportunity to develop. Long scenes can read beautifully but they often can't sustain the stage-time. The creation of multiple characters by single actors requires chameleon-like abilities. These challenging aspects of adaptation are very demanding of everyone involved in the process of bringing a project to fruition. Actually being in the room with the text on its feet (beginning with the second or third draft) being brought to life with a director, whether it is the adaptor or someone else, and a group of actors is definitely the best way I have discovered to meet these challenges. When developing a new adaptation, I would recommend, at the very least, a one-week script workshop where the show is quickly put on its feet with the text as the focus. I did this for *Around the World in 80 Days* and learned a tremendous amount about what was going to play well and what still needed work. This allowed the script to be much further along when the actual rehearsal process began.

Credit

After much thought, I have come to a new place in relation to the credit I ask for when doing an adaptation. I no longer ask for an "adapted by" credit. Instead I ask for a "written by ____ adapted from ____" credit. This is important to me for three reasons. First of all, the playwright wrote the play. Period. Yes, it is adapted from another text but the work of playwriting is no less than if the play were original and that should be acknowledged. Secondly, a play title is not always going to be the same as the title of the book that was adapted. For example, I called my adaptation of *The Adventures of Huckleberry Finn* by Mark Twain *Huck Finn*, but I could have called it *Huck and Jim* or *River Adventures* and saying *River Adventures* adapted by Laura Eason isn't correct. Finally, and most importantly, the "written by ___ adapted from ___" credit acknowledges the separateness and the uniqueness of the two properties, like the mansion and the house of your own.

Stuart Dybek

The Terribly Lonely & Deadly Serious Business, or You Will Never Have to Teach Again

Years ago I was invited by a composer from New York to adapt a story of mine for a musical in four acts that would play on Broadway. Theater in Chicago had already entered the era of dynamic creative growth that continues to this day, and I went regularly to plays by companies like the Remains, Steppenwolf, Victory Gardens, and the Lookingglass, but only as a spectator. I had never tried writing a play, at least not since I was an undergraduate. The composer who had contacted me lived on Manhattan's Upper West Side, a quick cab ride from Symphony Space. He'd been attending the popular Symphony Space series featured on NPR, in which professional actors read short stories. He believed that musical theater needed to be revitalized through crossbreeding with the other arts, and that a synthesis with the short story could make for a fresh and successful musical. His concept for the project he'd contacted me for was that each act would be based on a story by a writer from a different geographical area of the country—East Coast, West Coast, the South, and the Midwest. I was the Midwest.

He flew to Chicago to talk the project over, and to see Little Village, the South Side barrio where many of my stories are set, including the one for the play. We drove down to Twenty-sixth Street to eat at a Mexican restaurant I liked, a storefront place that featured an automated corn tortilla machine they claimed was one of only three in existence, the other two being in Mexico City. I parked on a side street, locked my Mustang convertible, hoping it would be there when we got back, and we walked through *ranchera* music along a crowded sidewalk past spray-painted murals, graffiti, tattooed gangbangers, tamale carts, a man in a sombrero attacking green coconuts with a machete—it was a little chilly for coconuts. The composer paused to take the place in. "This is it?" he asked. "I thought it would be colorful, but it's just, well, depressing wouldn't be too strong a word."

The composer's had two requirements for the story we selected: it had to be set in Chicago, and it had to be unpublished so at least to seem as if it had been written to order for the musical. I'd shown him a few in-progress stories, and he chose "Orchids." From the start, I was concerned that I had never adapted a story before. "Orchids" was a story I liked, but it had a sprawl to it. At over fifty pages it verged on novella length, and I worried it was too long for a single act. What's more, it employed flashbacks; the interplay of past and present was integral to the story's structure. The flashback is a natural convention in fiction, and that it is defines fiction as a temporal genre—on the turn of a transitional phrase an author can travel in time and the reader will instantaneously follow. But in so far as scripts for film and theater I'd heard flashback described as the f-word.

"Orchids" was autobiographical, and when a writer turns autobiography into fiction some of the allegiance one has to memory and to his past remains. I'd worked especially hard on the dialogue, trying to make it pop, to catch that nonstop patter of wisecracks and repartee that transforms aimlessly riding around in beaters when you're seventeen into joyriding. Sentence by sentence, it wasn't polished enough for magazine publication yet, but the composer pointed out that aside from the dialogue, the quality of the descriptive sentences wasn't a problem for theater. If I wanted a street at dusk described there would be set designers and lighting experts to do that. I had sent the story prematurely to one magazine, a noted one that paid, and that had invited me to send them a story. But the editor there rejected "Orchids," not for its lack of polish, but because she said that she didn't believe that two guys from an inner city neighborhood would do something like cross town to hike along the North Branch of the Chicago River up near the Bahai Temple to find wild orchids.

The composer didn't have credibility problems with it. In fact he looked forward to writing a song called "Orchids" to be sung when the characters find them on the riverbank. He'd read the story with an eye for where the songs would naturally arise from the action, and heighten it to a lyrical level. There was a scene, for instance—it took place in flashback in the story—where a high school prom date goes bad when the narrator takes his date to a fire truck graveyard along the Chicago Sanitary Canal, i.e., Shit Creek. The composer turned that into a *tour de force* duet complete with the ringing of a rusty fire truck bell. That duet brought to mind the articles I'd read in which he been mentioned as a successor to Sondheim. He'd phone me at odd hours from his place in New York, set the receiver beside his piano, and play and sing over the telephone some song hot off the keyboard that he'd just written for our collaboration. If a friend was present when I got the call, I'd mouth, "he's singing," and hold the phone so we both could listen.

It was fun. It was seductive. Except for a few student films I'd worked on in grad school, and the marching band and the amateurish jazz combo in which I played sax back in high school, it was my first real experience with a collaborative art. While at the Iowa Writers' Workshop, I'd studied, so to speak, with a writer named Fred Exeley who had written a book called *A Fan's Notes* in what was at that time a new genre, the nonfiction novel. The book was about a drunken loser named Fred Exeley who spent his time at New York Giants games. Fred had a phrase for writing that some of us appropriated: "the terribly lonely and deadly serious business of getting on with it." He was a maintenance drinker and that phrase was usually slurred when delivered. That first couple of years of working on the play seemed like a release from the terribly lonely & deadly business, etc. The composer would call and sing and every few weeks I'd send him scenes I'd adapted from "Orchids," scenes we'd discuss at length. Every few months I'd fly to New York from Michigan, where I was teaching, to get together with the other writers at the composer's condo overlooking Broadway in order to assess how far along we were. With each such trip there'd be more people involved, more collaborators—the director, the musical director, the choreographer, the set designer, musicians, dancers, and the backers—investors, another word for the gamblers who were bankrolling our show.

The composer dismissed my worries about adapting "Orchids." Theater was his life. He'd dropped out of high school and went right into writing for musicals, and he had the resume and clippings to prove it. He assured me that between the two of us there'd be no problem. There wasn't any money in it as yet, but the composer, who, besides the condo, owned an eighteenth-century manor with stables on the Hudson (purchased, he said, with the proceeds from music he had written for a then famous movie star's workout video) told me that if—when—our play hit, "I'd never have to teach again." That became a kind of mantra over the three years we worked on the piece, especially when he or one of the backers would suggest essential changes to the story that seemed to me inauthentic—more *West Side Story* than Southwest Side of Chicago.

"Stuart, just try it another way, once we nail it you'll never have to teach again."

I'd write—adapt—a scene from my own story and then worry aloud that it didn't seem as alive anymore as it had on the page. What seemed to me to have vitality as a story seemed manufactured once I turned it into a scene.

"You're not writing for the page. You're writing for the stage where it's the job of the actors to bring it to life," the composer reassured me.

About two and half years into it the writers moved for a month into the Paramount Hotel right off Manhattan's Theater Row to begin rehearsals. By then there was a lot of talent assembled. The dancers and choreographer had come from *Jerome Kern on Broadway*, which had won a Tony that year. Over the next year, on its march to Broadway, the musical had test runs as a work in progress at the Pepsico Theater, Vassar, and then was mounted as a full production that ran a month at the Cleveland Playhouse as part of their Fiftieth Anniversary Celebration. *Good Morning America* did a short feature on it. The play seemed Broadway-bound. People—the actors, the director, some of the backers were complimentary about the play in general and my act in particular which opened the show. "You'll never have to teach again," they told me.

I admired the music the composer had written for the show and told myself the music and the quality of the performances would carry it, despite nagging concerns I'd had about my adaptation. Sometimes one of the songs would sneak into my mind, and I'd have the strange feeling that it came from a show I'd seen, one I'd had nothing to do with. There was a song about Perry and Stosh, the two kids in my story, who'd planned to go to Mexico on the profits from the orchids they'd found, that I especially liked. To heighten conflict in the play, we'd added to the original story a twist in which Perry gets so involved with a girl that he has second thoughts about leaving for Mexico. In the song Stosh wistfully sings: *but Mexico, what about Mexico, hey, bro, go slow . . .*

But in my heart I was dissatisfied and knew there was something wrong with my adaptation. The actors were working their butts off to bring it to life, but it lacked something I hadn't managed to get into the script—so that it might be translated to the stage. "Orchids" on stage seemed inauthentic to the point of being faked. The snappy dialogue I'd congratulated myself on didn't seem that funny upon delivery. Even though the story had been an account of something that had actually happened when I was seventeen, what I saw on stage didn't seem credible to me. I'd made a habit of telling students in the creative writing classes I taught that lack of credibility was a way a story had of telling the writer he had to lie better—to invent. For all the skilled efforts of my collaborators something on that basic level where one sits alone in the terribly lonely deadly serious business of getting on with it had not been invented.

I didn't know what that something was, but to try and right things, I'd advise myself to let the story be my guide and to simply tell the story on stage. What drew me to certain theaters in Chicago was their powerful way with story. Yet, gradually I began to wonder if telling the story was part of the problem. To stage "Orchids" we'd changed the structure—a common enough change in adaptation. We'd made the story linear, eliminated flashbacks, made judicious cuts to speed up action, condensed what had been over fifty pages into a scene that ran over a half an hour and was still too long given that it was only the first act. But for all the frenetic energy, the dancing, the music, sets, lighting, costumes, what was on stage by way of dialogue was narrative—telling a story—not dramatic. I'd never really thought about that difference between the narrative and the dramatic before.

I wish I could say that arriving at that recognition empowered me to do a rewrite I felt better about. Simply telling the story wasn't the solution. The story about two guys from a working-class, Southside neighborhood who go to the wealthy Northside on a quest for orchids seemed, when reduced to its chronological linearity, too anecdotal. On the page it was the very interplay between past and present that had given the story the richness it required. The magic, energy, and immediacy of music and theater didn't in this case replace what was given up. After three years of working together I bluntly told the composer over lunch that I didn't think "Orchids" was working on stage. This time, instead of reassuring me that it was just a few adjustments away, he said, "Then fix it."

When the composer had told me at the start of our collaboration about his idea that musical theater would be enriched by crossbreeding it with another art, that made perfect sense to me. I'd always worked in more than one genre. I read as much poetry as I did fiction. Several of my stories—"Orchids" wasn't one of them—began as poems. When, at Iowa, my friend, Ray Carver, who also wrote poetry and fiction, said that, if he didn't write poetry, he couldn't write fiction, I knew what he meant.

Genres aren't simply academic divisions between the various literary arts that permit for an organized historical study. Genres are about ways of thinking. Each genre has its own signature way of thinking, and of engaging the reader to think. Poetry's signature mode is lyrical. That doesn't mean it doesn't employ the narrative, the expository, the dramatic. Of course it does, and the counterpoint between those various modes makes for its beauty and complexity. Thought in poetry is metaphorical thinking. The song-like aspects of language, especially meter and rhyme, are mnemonic.

Fiction thinks through narration, organizing events along a narrative line, and that organization implies cause and effect. As individuals we remember through stories. Nations and cultures remember through stories. There can be great lyrical thinking in prose, as well, and, in fact, that combination of the narrative and the lyrical makes for some of my favorite fiction writers: Joyce, Borges, Kafka, Calvino, Welty.

In essays the signature mode is expository and in plays the signature mode is dramatic. They employ multiple modes as do the other genres. If "poetic" or lyrical thinking might be defined as thinking through the association of sound and image, and the patterns of language that accommodate such thought; and if narrative thinking might be defined as the arranging of events into the form of stories, then there must be dramatic thinking. What characterizes it?

I haven't asked the question in order to try to answer it here. I am not even sure the question itself stands up to scrutiny. Poetry, fiction, and the essay are literary genres, genres written in the terrible loneliness of isolation that separates writer and reader. The unseen audience is an audience of readers. Readers are active participants. The closest analogy to reading is dancing to music. One writes with that in mind. But a play is written to be performed. The audience is not an audience of readers, but of viewers. The action on the page must be translated to stage by actors, set designers, etc. In other words, a play might be rightly considered a literary genre when read by a single reader, but when performed it is a different medium, one that takes place in real time as words on a page never can, and because it exists in real time, devices such as flashback, while possible, are not natural to it.

All that said, I trusted as the composer did, that drama could gain from a crossbreeding with fiction. And I believed, and had hoped, that the converse would also be true: that a hands-on experience with theater would improve my fiction.

After the musical's run at the Cleveland Playhouse, there were negotiations for it to play the Garrick in San Francisco, but then the Garrick was damaged in an earthquake, and the run there put on hold, and another production of the musical, in which "Orchids" was Act One, was never mounted.

For years after, "Orchids" didn't seem to me like my story anymore. It sat in wooden wine crate in the corner of my writing studio, a third floor office I rented for the terribly lonely & deadly business of getting on with it. Drafts of the original story were buried under all the rewrites of scenes we'd done for the play. I'd piled all the scripts in the crate, complete with the lyrics of the songs the composer had written. When I paged through them I could still hear the tunes in my mind. Sometimes I thought of digging out the original story and giving it the polish it needed before sending it out to a magazine. I'd wonder if in rewriting the story for publication I would borrow anything from the adaptation we'd done. That thought alone was enough for me to leave it to further gestation in the crate.

Finally, I knew I needed it as a chapter for a book, a novel-in-stories that I was working on in which Perry and Stosh appear. One day in Chicago, I went for lunch in Little Village. The restaurant with the complicated corn taco machine had gone out of business, so I went to Playa Azul and had a huge ceviche called a Vuelva La Vida, then drove the route the characters in "Orchids" drive north to the Bahai Temple. Somewhere along the drive it came back to me that the story I had written if, no longer mine alone, had happened to me.

Rewriting "Orchids" back from adaptation to story, I remembered a rehearsal when Peter Gallagher, the wonderful actor who played Stosh in the musical, improvised a line of dialogue for a scene in which Perry and Stosh pull into a gas station to fill up on the way to look for orchids. The beater Stosh is driving is having fuel pump problems and each time the engine conks out Stosh has to suck gas up through the fuel line to get it to start.

"I was making out the other night and the girl kept complaining my breath smelled like Texaco," Stosh says.

The next line, as I had it written, was for Bigbo, the demented gas station attendant. He says, "She even knew the flavor . . . Chicks! Too fucken much, man."

But on stage Peter Gallagher as Stosh adlibbed, "No, it was Marvel. Sometimes she can be so wrong."

I left that in.

Jana Harris

Grace: Thoughts on Adapting Excerpts of an Early Social Science Textbook for the Stage

by their fruits ye shall know them—Matthew 7:16

By Grace, I don't mean the Three Graces or a prayer before eating, but Grace Abbott, certainly one of the modern goddesses of charity. A wisp of a girl from Grand Island, Nebraska, who together with her older sister Edith and other residents of Chicago's Hull House changed the study and dispensation of social welfare as we know it. Adapting a text or source book for the stage isn't an original thought; E. B. White's *Elements of Style* was adapted for Broadway. But converting a section of a more than eighty-year-old sociology text into theater? As the Abbott sisters' Nebraska neighbors might have said: "That's a hard row to hoe."

Immigration, Select Documents and Case Records, by Edith Abbott (University of Chicago Press, 1924).

I stumbled on this text, the original 1924 publication authored by Edith Abbott and published by the University of Chicago, when I was doing research for a short story I was asked to write for the Washington State Council on the Humanities.[1] My interest was in the lives of immigrant children at the turn of the twentieth century, particularly those who, for whatever reason, were denied entry into the United States. As I studied the social case records of immigrants trying to avoid deportation just before, during, and after the First World War that Abbott had included in her book, I was intrigued by the interviews, letters, notes, and memoriam. They were conducted predominantly between a woman named Lydia Gardner on behalf of the family or friends of many a beleaguered immigrant trying either to come to Chicago, remain there, locate a lost relative, or get one into the country. Most of the subjects originated in Eastern Europe; a handful were from the Middle East. None spoke much if any English. Lydia's focus seemed to be the welfare of "unaccompanied" women—women without a male relative—and children detained at Ellis Island in New York.

Lydia Gardner, whoever she was, said she was employed as superintendent of the Immigrants' Protective League[2] with offices strategically located across the street from the Chicago train station. The case studies began in 1912 and continued into the early 1920s. Some of the complaints are heart-wrenching if not horrendous miscarriages of justice: A young woman who could read and write in addition to understanding three languages ordered deported for feeblemindedness. A woman blinded by a rejected suitor who had thrown vitriol in her face was not allowed to board a ship for the United States with the rest of her family. Women lost in transit between Ellis Island and Illinois. Children separated from parents and detained because of disease, mainly trachoma or ringworm. Women ordered deported because their husbands died in detention; families trying to get an aged (52!) mother into the country. Other stories were not so heart-wrenching but were contrived to cover up the traffic of women for illegal purposes. These nefarious cases Miss Gardner sniffed out like a bloodhound. But in each hardship situation, Lydia Gardner helped the client or his or her relatives mount a case against exclusion. Not all were successful. If the cases were read in chronological order, 1912 to 1918, the drums of war beat louder, and I cringed each time a young girl was ordered deported to an uncertain fate. Finally, the deportees could no longer be returned to Europe because passenger ships were prohibited from crossing the Atlantic. And because they had been excluded from the United States, some, it appears, lived on ships in the New York harbor.

Miss Lydia Gardner proceeded on each case with aplomb. More than aplomb. She proceeded with a sense of entitlement mixed with skilled diplomacy. She wrote astonishingly persuasive letters to charitable agencies who might help her client: the Jewish Women's Aid Society, the

Catholic Home Bureau for Dependent Children, the Slavic Society, the Polish Home. Her appeals to government agencies—the State Board of Charities, the United States Immigration Service—were heartfelt, sincere, well-crafted, and to the point. This was not a woman who minced words. Nor did accusations of meddling deter her. When necessary, Miss Gardner acted decisively, knowing just how to lobby which congressman or judge for his intervention.

Who was this articulate, educated, modern, well-spoken woman? I couldn't find any mention of Lydia Gardner in any Chicago database or publication. Unlike Edith Abbott, Lydia had never lived at Hull House or any other settlement that I could discover. She seemed to have fallen from the sky in about 1912 and then disappeared into the 1920s.

After reading several hundred pages of these case records published in Edith Abbott's text, I began to envision a theater piece: a three-act play titled *Dear Miss Gardner*. What I was aiming for was a pastiche of intertwined case studies from the offices of the Immigrants' Protective League as presented in Edith Abbott's 1924 publication. Act 1: the years just before World War I, 1912–1914; Act 2: the years during World War I, 1914–1918; Act 3: the years immediately following. The rhetoric of anti-immigrant sentiment in the first quarter of the twentieth century had an astonishingly familiar ring to it. Many of the sponsors, loan companies, and employment agencies claiming to help non-English-speaking new arrivals bore a striking resemblance to those of the present. Where, I wondered, is the Miss Gardner of the twenty-first century?

In these case studies, the individual immigrants were identified by name, nationality, religion, and the ship which transported them from Europe, or in a few instances by their Ellis Island file number. According to a footnote, the given names and some of the particulars of each case study had been changed to protect the anonymity of the subjects. It never dawned on me that the names of case workers at the Immigrants' Protective League had been changed, that Lydia Gardener was a pseudonym.

Indeed, it was the name assumed, for this 1924 publication, by Edith Abbott's sister, Grace, the director of the Immigrants' Protective League (IPL). More accurately, it was the name that Edith chose to use instead of her sister's name. Why would Edith Abbott want to protect her sister's identity? I imagine that there were many reasons: anti-immigrant sentiment ran extremely high in 1924 for one. For another, perhaps Edith worried that if everything seemed to be originating from two sisters—who were well-known figures in their field—the text would have less credibility than if another person were involved. Why the name Lydia Gardner had been chosen was, to me, a more interesting question. It wasn't a name that either of the sisters, the author Edith or the younger by two years Grace, the supplier and selector of these case studies, just pulled out of a hat. I have found no evidence that either of the Abbott sisters believed in fairy godmothers, but if they did, Lydia Gardner was theirs.

Born in Grand Island, Nebraska in 1878, a town built between two channels of the Platt River, Grace was the third child and second daughter of Othman and Lizzie Abbott. Grace had one elder and one younger brother. Her lawyer father was a Civil War veteran, her mother from an Illinois Quaker family that had helped facilitate the Underground Railroad. Grace's mother attended the same female seminary (but at a different time) as Jane Addams, founder of Hull House, and trained as a teacher. Grace's parents had known each other since high school but didn't marry until Lizzie Griffith was twenty-eight and working as a grammar school principal. Lydia Gardner was Lizzie's aunt, her mother's sister, Grace's and Edith's great-aunt. Miss Gardner left her niece Lizzie a legacy which I suspect paid for the refinements her grand nieces enjoyed in their prairie home: piano lessons, instruction in the German language (in Grand Island, everyone looked to the German culture), a library of interesting books, and magazine subscriptions. Possibly it helped embellish the Abbotts' comfortable Victorian home built in 1884 across the street from Court House Square where Edith's and Grace's father practiced.

Othman Abbott encouraged his daughters to visit his courtroom. At home, he discussed his practice with his wife and children. Lizzie Abbott was a suffragist and instilled these beliefs in her daughters, as well as the Quaker dictum that women be of use. The family's first home was humble and without amenities, including a guest room. When she was four, Grace's six-year-old sister Edith shared a bed with Susan B. Anthony when the famous activist came to Grand Island to speak on women's rights.

Before the town of Grand Island began to prosper, when it was just a hamlet founded by German farmers, one can visualize the dailyness of the sisters' lives led on the threshold of the frontier. Imagine life on a Monday: up at four, water aboil on the wood stove, a scrub board and wooden bucket on a plank table in the kitchen next to stacks of laundry, much of it scrubbed and wrung dry before the girls went off to school. Tuesday: the same kitchen table piled with baskets of ironing—bed sheets, pillowcases, their father's white shirts, their aprons. Wednesday: an endless kneading of bread dough and rolling out of pie crust. Thursday: a hard-bristled brush submerged in a bucket of lye soap; the young sisters feeling soreness in their knees and suffering a redness of hands as they cleaned floorboards, cupboards, the kitchen table itself, windows and doors, not pausing too long to gaze outside for fear of never getting done. Friday: after school, their fingers blackened by soot, the girls helped their mother disassemble coal oil lamps and spread them across the kitchen table for cleaning.

But then the railroad brought commerce. The city of Grand Island was incorporated and residential land sales instigated. Othman Abbott was one of the first town commissioners. His legal practice began to thrive and he expanded into business enterprises, including a farm, a commercial building, and the Citizens National Bank of Grand Island. Even with the advantages afforded the sisters by their father's growing prosperity, Aunt Lydia Gardner's legacy, their close family circle, and their spacious new home, the sisters were witness to the fragility of life. There was chronic worry about the wrath of tornadoes and blizzards. Infestations of grasshoppers brought crop failures and food shortages.

Grace grew up not far from the great trails of western migration and certainly witnessed a trickle of people still heading west—those who couldn't afford train fare, or who had too many animals and possessions to move by rail. Native Americans were by now herded onto reservations, but many Sioux and Pawnee still lingered on the streets of town and on the shores of the Platt. Looking ragged and bedraggled, they incurred Mrs. Abbott's sympathy; Lizzie taught her daughters that the trail to the public lands set aside for the native population was the trail of injustice. During the last quarter of the nineteenth century, more German immigrant farmers congregated in central Nebraska. The population of Grand Island grew from 500 in 1866 to 7,500 in 1890. The Abbott girls were tutored in German, the language of commerce. Flour mills flourished, railroad expansion facilitated the opening of a cigar factory; sugar beets were introduced and the first processing plant in the country was built. Soap factories, breweries, a broom manufacturer, a steam laundry, and a patent medicine company prospered. When a tornado destroyed the first Catholic Church—Grand Island was predominantly a Catholic community—it was immediately rebuilt. A Methodist Episcopal Church Society thrived and a Baptist college opened—as did a post-secondary business school. At its peak, the community of Grand Island published three newspapers, including one in German.

Then, in 1893, the bank where Othman Abbott invested Aunt Lydia's legacy failed. Three years of drought brought crop failures, shortages, and bankruptcies. Everything the Abbotts had that could be sold was, except the house—a mortgaged white elephant. Lizzie's bright dreams for her daughters' further education dimmed. Before she attended the University of Nebraska and the University of Chicago, Grace had to earn her way through the Baptist college by teaching school, walking to class through sandstorms, grasshoppers, hot winds, prairie fires, forests of dead trees, and denuded pastures of starving animals tended by men who went to the snowy winter fields binding gunny sacks to their feet. The legacy of Lydia Gardner was lost. Grace's father worked for years afterwards to get out from under indebtedness due to loans taken on during the prosperous 1880s.

One bright reminiscence of these hard times must have burned through Grace's memory until she died just before World War Two. The Abbott sisters traveled by train to visit the 1893 Chicago World's Fair. Edith was eighteen and Grace sixteen. According to Edith, it was their last carefree outing for many years. In Chicago they saw the beginnings of the great university they would one day attend. They had already begun to imagine that a life other than that of becoming educated and returning to Grand Island to teach and to marry was possible; but now they saw where that life might begin to take root.

So: a theater piece concerning the altered and abridged records of the Immigrants' Protective League as represented in Edith Abbott's 1924 text. One of my purposes was to take a look at the treatment and circumstances of immigrants a hundred years ago. Another was to probe the character of this Florence Nightingale of immigration, the Grace Abbott of her Immigrants' Protective League (IPL) years: could I ever know what made a woman like her tick? She never married or had children; no tell-all biography or autobiography exists. Most of what has been published about her is written from an academic stance. One thing I have ascertained by reading Edith's reminiscences of her sister was that Grace was the more adventuresome and outgoing of the two. In 1911 she took a leave of absence from the IPL to visit the Eastern European cities and villages from which many of her clients immigrated. I longed to know more about her. Was she afraid of spiders? Did she call turnips "mangles" and slice them, eating them raw? Was her favorite color the deep amethyst of a Nebraska winter sky? It has been said in many different permutations that *by their deeds, ye shall know them*; so when I see Grace Abbott as the Lydia Gardner of my play-in-progress, I look for her in the case studies presented there. In Edith Abbott's text, was Grace pseudonymously named Lydia Gardner because Grace hoped to enrich the lives of immigrants the way the Abbott sisters' lives had been enriched by this great-aunt's legacy? I have no idea, but I like to think so. Visualizing Lydia Gardner at her Immigrants' Protective League desk, I see her past and present; I see her as the sum of her parts.

When I imagine the stage set, I see a stark office and waiting room in the building across a wide cobbled street from the Chicago train station, circa 1912. The room has a sixteen-foot-high ceiling and a pair of ten foot high windows. Wooden, straight-backed mismatched chairs line one wall, stage right. Women dressed in dark Eastern European pre-World War One garb sit in the chairs, their heads coved by scarves, tied bundles at their cloth-tied feet. They hold cloth dolls wrapped in blankets. Larger cloth dolls perch on their laps and sleep on the floor. Men wearing worn shoes and ill-fitting suits sit next to the women; some crouch on the floor, others sit at the edge of the stage with their legs dangling.

In the center of the stage is a long plank table, not unlike the kitchen table in the Abbott sisters' first prairie home. Two doors stage left are both closed. Stage right amid the seated immigrant masses, a double door hangs open. From outside this double door comes the noise of hundreds of pairs of feet shuffling along the sidewalk and the muffled voices of people bantering in many languages. Once in a while, a ragged person falls into the double doorway and then is pulled off stage. Occasionally someone knocks on the wall near the double doors. Sometimes it is more of a banging. In the distance behind the stage a train whistle bellows and iron wheels rumble and screech over railroad tracks. The Chicago Union Station is partially visible from one of the tall windows stage right. Outside the other tall window, stage left, the window closest to the two separate closed doors, is a view of sky, high clouds, the tips of tall prairie grass, the bend of a river. At the back of the theater behind the audience, a drum beats as if to accompany a slow march of soldiers. As World War One approaches, the tempo quickens and the drum beat gets louder. During the war, the drumming mirrors skirmishes on the Western Front. After the war, the drum beat is mildly chaotic and then morphs into the rhythms of jazz music.

On a scaffold above the stage is a barred room that goes across the IPL office below. Or maybe it is an iron-gated room symbolic of both

Ellis Island and Eastern Europe. Inside are more female immigrants and a matron. The immigrants silently wave and call. Some rattle the locks, others shove their arms through the bars. A few are called upon by people on stage below to answer inquiries, others silently weep, ring their hands, hold their heads; one holds the hand of a sick cloth doll who sleeps on the floor of the elevated room.

Occasionally, during the play, a well-dressed man stops at the window with the view of the train station to read current newspaper headlines; he also reads newspaper commentary about the number of immigrants overrunning the United States. A shop girl stops at the same window, talking with factory girl about immigrants taking their jobs. Two well-heeled women pause at the window to gossip about how uneducated and backward their immigrant charwomen are and how immigrants are all becoming wards of the state. Can't they learn English, one says to the other. Two men laugh about how odd Jews look; how strange their customs. Two society matrons engage in a friendly argument: who is more superstitious, Polish or Irish Catholics?

At one end of the long plank table, stage right, sits a thin thirty-four-year-old woman with a high forehead and dark hair. She is dressed in a tailored gray suit, white blouse, gloves, and hat in the fashion of 1912. This is Miss Gardner, a.k.a. Grace Abbott, well educated and articulate. She is well traveled and from a tolerant Quaker background. There is nothing dewy-eyed or naive about our Grace. She is a witness to change: the vanished frontier of her childhood. She has experienced climactic and environmental disasters and knows what it's like to lose almost everything.

Behind Miss Gardner is the window with the view of the Chicago train station. She hovers over binders and files, often writing on a blotter with an inkwell near her right hand; occasionally she pauses to blot what she's written. Sometimes she types forms on the typewriter positioned to her left. At the other end of the plank table, stage left near the two closed doors, sit a scrub bucket, a washboard, rolling pin, and a large china bowl. A portly gray-haired woman in a long gray dress and white bibbed apron stands at the table, silently instructing two girls in reading, sums, washing clothes, rolling dough, and kneading bread. Sometimes one or the other of the girls scrubs the floor or the table legs near her. Occasionally one of the girls or the mother glances out the window with the view of the prairie, looking for rain or a visitor.

During the play, various people will appear at this window: A bedraggled Indian woman asks for food. Another comes offering to sell a basket of berries. A neighbor, down on his luck, offers to sell Mrs. Abbott his copy of *Huckleberry Finn*, which delights Grace. An unemployed brewery worker begs help with a broken-down wagon. A mailman/clerk appears with a letter from Aunt Lydia Gardner, then again with a magazine, *Harper's Weekly*, and again with a book. The young Edith unwraps a copy of *The Old Curiosity Shop*. Othman Abbott, dressed in judge's robes, comes to the window and gives a thumbnail lecture on the elements of debate. Mr. Abbott was not, in real life, a judge, but I use the robe here as a symbol of his practice and as symbol of his just treatment of his children regardless of gender. These characters occasionally interact with the immigrants sitting in the chairs on the other side of the stage. One of the immigrants dressed in the fashion of a raggedy Mendelssohn steps forward, crosses in back of the table and the prim woman writing at it, and produces a one-by-six board with piano keys painted on it. He brings a chair with him. One of the young Nebraska girls steps away from the table. The two are seated and Mendelssohn begins to instruct young Edith in piano. Another immigrant carrying a chair approaches the table and knocks on it. Mrs. Abbott leads the young Grace towards him. The two sit and he instructs Grace in elementary German. Susan B. Anthony appears at the window and confers with Mrs. Abbott.

Now and then residents of Hull House—Sophonisba ("Nisba") Breckinridge, an adult Edith Abbott, Julia Lathrop—step out of one of the two closed doors. Crossing the stage, they speak with Lydia Gardner, Superintendent of the Immigrants' Protective League. The women consult about a particular case. The Hull House visitors are accompanied by their driver, Mr. Solomon, a Syrian immigrant who lives in their neighborhood. At various times in the play the women ask after Mr. Solomon's ailing wife and about the activities at his Greek Orthodox Church. The Hull House women inquire after his son, who is training to be a chauffeur. They encourage Mr. Solomon to send his daughter to classes at their settlement, an idea he finds distasteful, though he is too polite to say so. When Mrs. Solomon dies, the ladies send their condolences. At times Mr. Solomon serves as a translator for other Middle Eastern immigrants who come to the League for help. Other translators appear through these two doors. Meanwhile, Mr. Solomon, who is trying to get a relative into the country, listens to the goings-on of deportation cases with more than a passing interest.

Sometimes Mrs. Abbott crosses to the other end of the table and reads a letter from one of the immigrant aid societies to Lydia. Sometimes one of the young girls (the young Edith and Grace) crosses to the other end of the table and reads a letter from a beleaguered immigrant concerning his/her detained child. Othman Abbott reads letters of correspondence from foreign government agencies.

The basic structure of the play is delivered through the reading and scripting of the documents, correspondence, narratives, and explanations published in Edith Abbott's 1924 text. The story line entwines four narratives that stretch across all three acts. In each, Lydia and the League champion the subject's cause, facilitate his/her legal entrance into the United States. The first is the tale of the Aronoff girls. April 1912—Mr. Joseph Aronoff comes to the office of the Immigrants' Protective League to ask for help in getting his family into the country. His son Nathan, eighteen, and daughter Rose, sixteen, are detained at St. John, New Brunswick, Canada. His wife and four other children remain in Russia. The two older children came with prepaid steamship tickets, but the father has no home yet and boards with a cousin, so authorities will not allow his children to enter the country. When Lydia Gardner finds a boarding club for Jewish girls for Rose, Aronoff's two eldest children are admitted and come to Chicago.

In early 1914, Joseph Aronoff returns to the League. His wife with four children, Rachel age ten, Kazia age eight, Isaac age four, and Anton age three have arrived in Baltimore on S.S. *Koenigin Luise*. The Commissioner of Immigration at Baltimore has excluded all of them because Rachel and Kazia have been certified for contagious disease: ringworm of the scalp. These health problems will require an indefinite period of treatment, so the commissioner wants answers. Has Mr. Aronoff taken out a declaration of intention to become a citizen? What is his situation? Lydia pleads his case: Aronoff, age forty-two, works as a presser in Chicago's garment district at $12 per week; his son Nathan, a peddler at $10 per week. Daughter Rose, finisher on ladies' waists, receives wages of $7 per week. The Immigration Commissioner wants to know: is Mr. Aronoff in a position to pay for hospital treatment for the children, if indeed the children are accepted for treatment?

Lydia Gardner telegraphs the Hebrew Immigrant Aid Society of Baltimore. The Hebrew Hospital will accept the children if payments are sent regularly. Miss Gardner appeals to a "friend of the League," Mr. X, a wealthy Chicago merchant not unlike Julius Rosenwald, asking for his assistance for the ringworm treatment. She describes the Aronoffs as an unusually attractive family making good progress learning English at night school. Alas, the process of deporting Rachel and

Kazia continues. During the play, Mr. X makes intermittent appearances at the Immigrants' Protective League office on his way to and from philanthropic events. A robust man, he is dressed in a tuxedo and carries a walking stick.

The older brother Nathan volunteers to return to Russia with the Aronoff girls, so that the mother and the two healthy younger children can leave detention and continue to Chicago to be reunited with their father. At first the Immigration Commissioner at Baltimore refuses this plan, because a mother is the natural guardian. Mr. X agrees to sponsor the ringworm treatments, but this information is misdirected. The girls are ordered deported, but with their brother as guardian. Mr. X's sponsorship is discovered and Nathan and the girls are sent from Baltimore to Ellis Island for treatment in early July of 1914. The authorities in New York decide that treatment could take years, and the children are again ordered deported. The ship carrying Nathan, Rachel, and Kazia departs for Germany, but is turned back at sea due to the beginning of the war in Europe. The three are held on the boat adrift in New York Harbor. The only way they can communicate with the outside world is to tie a letter to a heavy object and throw it onto a passing ship. Finally the girls are allowed to land and be treated for ringworm at the Ellis Island hospital, the treatment sponsored by Mr. X. The treatments go on for a year without cure.

In 1915 the girls are transferred to a hospital in New York City where they begin a new serum treatment. This treatment has no effect, so one year later in 1916 Mr. X considers withdrawing his financial support. Miss Gardner asks the Hebrew Immigrant Aid Society to appeal to him. The treatments continue. The girls have their hair removed and begin X-ray treatment, sponsored by Mr. X.

Finally Kazia is cured, but Rachel is not. Rachel is returned to Ellis Island Hospital. In June of 1916, four years after they first applied for entry, the girls are certified cured and admitted to the United States. Rachel and Kazia are reunited with their parents in Chicago and enrolled in school. The girls graduate from the third grade. Each year the father sends the League a Christmas card summarizing the family's progress. In 1921 Lydia Gardner drops in on the Chicago apartment of the Aronoff family. The girls have an abundance of hair and will soon graduate from grammar school. Rachel plans to take a business course. Kazia wants to go through high school, but her father's ailing health dictates that she stay home and care for the younger children. Lydia applies to the Jewish Charities for help for Kazia to continue her education.

The second entwined narrative stretching over all three acts of the play concerns a Polish national. In 1913 he is admitted into the United States but his Lithuanian girlfriend and their baby are not. He applies to the League for help. The woman has been ordered deported because she has an illegitimate child. Miss Gardner petitions the Immigration Office not to deport the woman and baby. The woman and child are admitted on a Saturday and housed in a League boarding house over the weekend. On Monday morning, Lydia Gardner personally escorts the couple to City Hall where they are married by a judge who gives them the needed marriage certificate and waives the fee.

A year later, the Polish man returns to ask the League for help in finding work as a printer. The League helps the new wife take in boarders. The husband starts a newspaper printing lists of Eastern European casualties of war. When the war ends, the paper fails. The wife's boarders leave. The man finds a job in a print shop, but when the shop is raided by the Industrial Workers of the World (IWW), an international trade union founded in Chicago (1905), the man is arrested and ordered deported. Because his statement is given in Polish, Lydia Gardner finds a translator to read his statement in court. The man is released from jail and finds another job. The man attends English classes. In 1921 the man is naturalized as a citizen with Lydia as a character reference.

The third narrative: In 1913 Stephanie Woloski, an Austrian woman, is ordered deported for immoral behavior. The League cannot determine who the father of Stephanie's baby is nor can they discover the whereabouts of her present husband. When Stephanie's deportation is interrupted by the war situation, Stephanie and her baby are housed in the Home for the Friendless. Relatives are located, but cannot or will not help her, all except a very young unmarried sister in Chicago. Stephanie is sent to New York and put to work in domestic service. There she boards her baby, but never pays the board. The young sister marries. When Armistice is declared, Stephanie abandons her baby and disappears before she can be deported. The woman's young sister wants to find Stephanie so that she can report what has happened to their family in Europe during the war. She also would be willing to take in the baby. Stephanie cannot be found and the young sister believes this is a case of suicide. The young sister wants Lydia to find the baby. Lydia discovers that baby has been put up for adoption. The sister pleads for a picture of the baby, believing that Stephanie has committed suicide out of grief for her lost child. The baby is adopted and the records sealed. No one at the League believes that Stephanie is dead.

The fourth narrative: In 1912 a man applies to the League for help in bringing his two sisters over from Russia, Hedwig, age twenty, and Raisa, age sixteen. Hedwig was engaged to be married, but when she broke it off, her fiancé threw vitriol in her face, blinding and disfiguring her. Hedwig's mother, two brothers, and two other sisters are in the United States, but the steamship company refused to allow Hedwig to come onboard ship. Because of her blindness, she was likely to be deemed a public charge by immigration officials and denied entry into the United States. In cases such as these, the steamship company was responsible for the passenger's return trip to Europe. It was decided that Raisa remain in Russia with her sister. The brother wants to know how he can get Hedwig on a steamship and into this country.

Lydia seeks the advice of various shipping lines. New tickets are purchased just before the war starts. When the Germans destroy the train tracks to the town in Russia where the girls live, it is no longer possible to communicate with Hedwig. The brother decides not to cancel the girls' tickets, because when things improve the girls can use them. When the Germans occupy Hedwig and Raisa's village, the brother asks Lydia how he can send money to his sisters. Money is sent to the American Consul in Berlin, but never received. The war ends. Now it is even more difficult to get Hedwig into the country, because quotas have been instated. To add insult to injury, the criminal ex-boyfriend who ruined Hedwig's sight has been allowed into the United States. The girls receive money, but not visas. The family moves to California and Lydia waits to hear from them.

Interspersed with these four entwined narratives are several intrigues. A man comes to the League offices because his sister is about to be deported from Ellis Island. She was engaged in Prague, but her fiancé could find no work and came to America. The sister, who worked as a cashier, had agreed to follow as soon as she could save enough to purchase a steamship ticket. Instead, she embezzled money from her employer at a daily Prague newspaper and sailed for America. The brother asks Lydia to save his sister from shame and disgrace to the whole respectable family. Miss Gardner tells the man that if his sister took the money, the League can do nothing. The brother pleads: the situation will kill his mother.

A Persian asks the League for help. He is to be deported for illiteracy, because he has flunked his English literary test. He studied but flunked the second test. Lydia negotiates a third test. Mr. Solomon, the driver of the women at Hull House, is called in to help tutor. The Persian passes his English literacy test, his deportation canceled.

Mrs. O'Brien, a blatantly proud, well-to-do woman who immigrated to this country from Denmark and married an Irish-American, comes to ask advice about her sister, Mrs. Peterson. Mrs. Peterson, her husband, and two sons are detained on Ellis Island. The oldest child, Carl Peterson, hurt his leg onboard ship and now the leg has become infected. Surgery is suggested. Then the younger brother gets sick and Carl develops osteomyelitis. If Carl loses his leg, he is in danger of becoming a public charge and will not be admitted into the United States. Carl has surgery on the leg and improves, but slowly. When the youngest child gets well, the family, except for Carl, is admitted into the United States. Just as Carl can begin to stand on his troublesome leg, he develops diphtheria and is declared a diphtheria carrier. Then Carl comes down with measles. Carl recovers from both contagious diseases, but contracts scarlet fever. The mother, Mrs. Peterson, and her sister, Mrs. O'Brien, are worried sick that the child will get pneumonia. In the Ellis Island Hospital there is a shortage of blankets and the windows are left wide open due to fear of the spread of communicable diseases. With Lydia's help, the child is discharged from the detention hospital, even though he needs another surgery. Afterwards, according to the records presented in Edith Abbott's text, Mrs. O'Brien visits Lydia Gardner and apologizes for her haughty behavior.

A fifty-year-old unmarried Russian pharmacist wants the order of deportation for his twenty-one-year-old "relative" Rosa cancelled. He brings the girl's great-aunt with him to the League office as a witness, but the elderly woman can't seem to remember anything about her young niece.

Another Russian wants his twenty-four-year-old "niece," Axenia, who is detained at Ellis Island, to be allowed into the country so that she can keep house for him. He says that his wife has died and his three children live with the wife's parents. When questioned, the girl says that the man's wife is in the old country. Lydia visits the man's two-room apartment and finds other men living there; empty beer bottles litter the floors. The girl says that she had no idea that she was supposed to keep house for her "uncle."

The characters from these narratives interact when they visit the Immigrants' Protective League office. They return again and again looking for work or help in getting a relative into the country or English language classes. The characters are familiar with one another because they or their children meet at the Ellis Island facility or on the train from New York to Chicago; when they board with the Lithuanian woman married to the Polish man; when they find housing in the neighborhood of Hull House; when they frequent Hull House, take classes in bookbinding, receive nutritious food, and frequent the public baths; when they recognize the door-to-door peddler; when they help Stephanie's sister search for Stephanie's baby; when they buy and read the Pole's newspaper looking for names of war dead; when they visit the Russian's pharmacy; when they work as domestics in the home of Mrs. O'Brien; when they work in the same sweat shop, garment, or button factory.

At the end of Act Three, Lydia Gardner (a.k.a. Grace Abbott) prepares to leave the Immigrants' Protective League for a new job at the United States Children's Bureau in Washington, D.C. The fruits of her labor lie in case files on the table in front of her: the Aronoff girls are well situated and able to continue their education, the Polish man with the Lithuanian wife has become a citizen, Stephanie's sister continues to plead for a photograph of Stephanie's baby and says she will be satisfied with never actually seeing the child, and, though Hedwig's family has dropped out of sight, Lydia still hopes to hear from them and to get Hedwig into the country. As Miss Gardner muses, some sour fruit, some sweet, a very distressed Mr. Solomon bursts into her office.

Mr. Solomon has been trying without success to get his grand niece, Rachel, into the country. Mr. Solomon's wife is dead, his house in complete disarray. As an answer to his difficulties, Mr. Solomon has arranged a marriage between his son and this eighteen-year-old girl from the Solomons' village in Syria. The son has readily agreed to this arrangement. Mr. Solomon has a daughter, but she is Americanized and not interested in keeping house for her father and brother. The daughter is modern and makes her own living, and we cannot help but wonder if this is because of Hull House influences. Mr. Solomon has come to the Immigrants' Protective League office to apply for the League's help in getting Rachel into the country.

Miss Gardner points out the problem of arranged marriages. The Hull House women appear. They are too diplomatic and too skilled at the art of persuasion to burn Mr. Solomon at the stake; besides he is a friend, a neighbor, and the age of militant feminism has not yet reached its apex. The women of Hull House, the women of the Immigrants' Protective League, Lydia Gardner, her translators, the young Abbott girls, their mother, Susan B. Anthony, Mr. X, the immigrants who have appeared in the various cases, "Judge" Abbott, the Pawnee and Sioux Indian women, and everyone cast in the play converge on Mr. Solomon. All give their arguments pro and con regarding arranged marriages, everyone speaking at once, their voices rising and running over each other. Mr. Solomon ends up agreeing to giving Rachel the right of choice in marrying his son or not when she arrives, and Miss Gardner facilitates the young girl's entry into the country.

Grace Abbott went on to a job at the Child Labor Division of the United States. Children's Bureau. She spent the rest of her life lobbying for the rights of children and immigrants and worked in the Roosevelt Administration helping to draft the Social Security Act. In 1939, at the age of 60, she died of leukemia. Grace believed that the immigrant citizenry was just like the regular American citizenry: some good, some bad, but most hard working and intent on bettering their lives and the lives of their children. In 1942 a liberty ship, the SS Grace Abbott, was commissioned in her honor. Though she did more to help the plight of individual immigrant women and children than perhaps any other single person of her era, today her name and works have been largely forgotten.

Notes

Hull House: A Chicago center for women engaged in social reform and a safe haven for the poor. Founded by Jane Addams and Ellen Gates Star in 1889. The original records of the immigrants' Protective League are available on the Northwestern University Florence Kelley website: florencekelley.northwestern.edu.

1. The Writer's Workshop Review, Seattle, WA (The Writer's Workshop, Vol. 1, July 25, 2008) "Stone Lambs," short story. www.thewritersworkshopreview.net/issue.cgi.

2. IPL: Immigrants' Protective league, founded in 1909 by women living in Hull-House Settlement. The organization's mission was to help immigrants adjust to life in America.

Sources

Abbott, Edith, *Grace Abbott*, "A Sister's Memories," Social Service Review, (Sept. 1939).

Costin, Lela B. *Two Sisters for Social Justice* A Biography of Grace and Edith Abbott, (University of Illinois Press, Urbana and Chicago, 1983).

Kirkland, Winifred and Frances; *Girls who Became Leaders*, Grace Abbott, *Guardian of 43,000,000 Children*, (Ray Long & Richard R. Smith, Inc., The Branwell Press, New York, 1932).

Gonzalez, Suronda, *Immigrants in Our Midst: Grace Abbott, the Immigrants' Protective League of Chicago, and the New American Citizenship, 1908–1924* (PhD. dissertation, Binghamton University, NY, 2004).

Gonzalez, Suronda, (Director, Global Studies, International Studies Certificate Program, Languages Across the Curriculum, Binghamton University, NY) conversations and correspondence with the author, Jana Harris.

Meyerowitz, Joanne J., *Women Adrift*, Independent Wage Earners in Chicago, 1880–1930 (University of Chicago Press, Chicago, 1988).

Stebner, Eleanor J., *The Women of Hull House*: A Study of Spirituality, Vocation, and Friendship (SUNY Press, 1997).

Virgil Johnson

Memoirs of an
"Iconic Costume Maestro"

I was much amused to see myself referred to in the reviews of *Dangerous Beauty*, the summer 2008 premiere production of Northwestern's American Music Theatre Project, as an "iconic costume designer" and a "costume maestro. . . ."

I was born in Minneapolis, grew up at Lake Minnetonka, and graduated from Minnetonka High School. My father was a Chicago Blackhawk hockey player; my mother was an equestrienne. Actually my mother had worked for several years before getting married, first as a court reporter and later in law offices. They both were extroverts, independent, and very outgoing, social people. After the war my father left the Blackhawks and went into construction.

At graduation, I didn't have a particular idea of what I wanted to study when it came time to go to college. One thing was certain, my mother was very keen that I go out of state for school. She was an independent and adventurous person, very well read, self-motivated, although not with a college education herself. She always said: "Any woman who spends time pushing a vacuum cleaner or working in the kitchen washing dishes deserves it!" My Midwestern mother was very keen on traditional values, fair play, and the principles of liberal democracy. She did not welcome expressions of prejudice, snobbery, indolence, or self-congratulation in my brother or myself.

So, in 1957 at age seventeen, I took the train east to Boston

University (BU) to enroll in their new School of Fine and Applied Arts. This School offered a Bachelor of Fine Arts degree, something unusual in that day, and incorporated the Departments of Music, Theatre, and Art. I thought at the time I would probably major in art and end up in advertising.

I had four roommates in the freshman dorm Miles Standish Hall. Two of my roommates, Stanley Blackman and Franklin Keyser, had been in theater throughout their youth. Stanley had appeared as a child in the original Broadway version of *The King and I*. With Gertrude Lawrence! I was spellbound. My theatrical past was negligible. I had appeared in my high school senior class play, Kaufman and Hart's *You Can't Take It With You*, playing Mr. DePinna, the weird man found in the basement making firecrackers. Would my lack of experience prevent me from imagining a career in theater?

We went off to freshman orientation, where the dean of the school spoke. Then Francis Sidlauskus (Mr. Sid), the head of the Theatre Department, spoke and he was mesmerizing. He warned us, "You're going into theater, and you are going to be working there day and night." And I thought: "Fine!" After the orientation speeches, we got into lines for registration, and I squeezed into the line queuing for the Theatre Department. I've never left that line nor looked back since. The world of advertising would have to do without me.

Life is serendipitous. I always tell my students, I don't know how to advise them about securing work as a designer because I have never really looked for a job. Interesting projects lead to other interesting projects. People you meet and work with recommend you for new jobs. The doors that opened for me were the right ones. I seemed to be in the right place at the right time.

Mr. Sid was a theater impresario. The school hired him because they wanted to create a pre-professional program that would train people to be actors, designers, and directors. He hired Sarah Caldwell, the opera conductor, to head the opera program and advise him on other faculty hires. He persuaded Horace Armistead, who was at that time the house designer for the Metropolitan Opera in New York, to move to Boston. Then they hired David Pressman to teach acting. Pressman was a significant director for the stage and television. He had been blacklisted in New York after the House Un-American Activities Committee Hearings. BU did not avoid controversy. The theater program had the makings of what we would today call "cutting edge."

The head of costume design for the program was Raymond Sovey, a charter member of the United Scenic Artists Union (USA). He was someone who, in his heyday, had six to eight shows a year on Broadway, at a time when someone could do that. He was a designer for the Lunts, for example, some of the leading actors of their day. What a character! He was an unforgettable presence, and we adored him. Mr. Sovey designed both sets and costumes, as did Mr. Armistead, because that was the way designers worked in those days.

So I started taking design classes. I quickly realized that our job was to support the actor. I was very much in awe of actors. I still am in awe of actors. I saw how they could transform the play script and captivate an audience. What could be more thrilling? Night after night. How do they do it? I still cry at a good performance. And I am a sucker for a good story. To be a part of this world would be wonderful. I did not have a clue about how to go about it.

In the early part of the twentieth century the practice of designing stage scenery, costumes, and lighting design was not separated. A production designer like Armistead or Sovey would design the whole show. And all of them were men. Today, in America, a different designer is hired for each area of design. Designers have become specialists. And women are well represented in the costume and lighting fields since the 1950s. Women have made significant contributions in scenic design today in regional theater but much less so on Broadway.

Just before World War Two a number of superbly talented women who specialized in costume design broke the all-boy mold: Lucinda Ballard, Irene Sharaff, and Aline Bernstein, who became iconic in the field. Aline Bernstein was the first and only woman to design sets on Broadway in the 1920s and 1930s. Mr. Sovey adored her. In the late 1930s these women were the nucleus of the movement to recognize, within the USA, the category of Costume Design. Today, a young designer can take entrance examinations for as many of the design categories that he or she is qualified for.

But I digress. When I was an undergraduate in the Theatre Department at BU we produced a season of four theater pieces and two operas. My training from the very outset prepared me for a professional career in theater or opera. I was assigned by Horace Armistead to design five various operas at BU. I designed Puccini's *Madame Butterfly* and *Gianni Schicci*. The director was the legendary Sarah Caldwell, a dark-shrouded woman who was simultaneously nurturing and terrifying. I learned very quickly about the special needs of singers and staging on a big stage. And about working with eccentric directors. Mr. Armistead always said,

"If you can design opera well, you can design anything," What an indelible experience for me.

When I was in my senior year at BU the British theater director, Tyrone Guthrie, came to be a guest speaker. He was an overwhelming presence, six feet, three inches tall, and towering in every way. He talked about his plans to open his own theater in an American city where he would present Shakespeare, Shaw, and Chekhov (and later Pinter). And he did do just that. In Minneapolis! When I heard him, I knew I had met someone with extraordinary vision. He talked about founding a theater and presenting drama about the human condition and spirit. It was to be for the immediate community, *not* for Broadway. It was not commercial theater. He talked about working with skilled stage actors, people like Alec Guinness and designers like Tanya Moiseiwitsch. And when I heard him, I said to myself, this is what I want to do. So I wrote him a letter, saying I wanted to come and work at the Guthrie Theater. They put me on file, but years later I did come back to Minneapolis to design at the Guthrie Theater.

What is the importance of bringing distinguished guests before students? It's essential. Currently, at NU, we are privileged to have a program endowed by Hope Abelson (the Hope Abelson Guest Artist Program). This program guarantees that the students have annual visits by theater artists of caliber such as Meryl Streep, David Hockney, and Peter Sellars.

When I graduated from the School of Fine and Applied Arts, Mr. Armistead and Adelaide Bishop (the new head of the opera program) had arranged interviews for me at the New York City Opera, where Julius Rudell was the Artistic Director. I was hired to be a slave in the Costume Department. I was paid $50 a week and expected to do everything from sewing to gluing. I remained with the company for the next several years.

My pay increased. In those days (1961) my college roommate, Frank, and I could afford an apartment in New York City! On the Upper East Side no less. Frank became a stage manager at American Ballet Theatre and toured the world. So there we were: two twenty-somethings in New York City, coming out of Boston, and working with professionals in the New York theater right out of college. We were blessed to be doing what we were doing—to be paid to work and learn with some of the best professional artists in the country.

In 1964 I took a full time job at the APA (Association of Producing

Artists) at the Phoenix Theatre. The director of the company was the flamboyant actor Ellis Rabb, who was married to the actress Rosemary Harris. I ran wardrobe for three productions running in repertory, including *War and Peace*, complete with cannons. I needed this job to save money because I had decided to return to college and work toward a graduate degree. At that time there were only three high-profile programs offering graduate degrees in stage design: the Yale School of Drama, Carnegie Mellon in Pittsburgh, and Northwestern University somewhere in the Midwest. I didn't want to go to Pittsburgh, the Yale School of Drama wasn't giving me any encouragement, but I knew about Chicago, as I had spent the first five years of my life there with my sports-minded family.

The Chairman of the Theatre Program at Northwestern University (NU), Dr. Lee Mitchell, wrote me a letter back right away in response to my initial enquiry. NU only offered an MA program at that time. He wrote saying he was recommending me for acceptance and also asking if I would like to teach the second-year undergraduate course in Costume Design and Stagecraft. It appeared that there was no current faculty in costume design. It looked like I would be teaching both myself (and others) for the immediate future. I accepted Dr. Mitchell's offer.

When I arrived at NU in my father's station wagon with everything I owned, including my books and antique Worcester china, I was able to tailor my own graduate curriculum. Design Professor Sam Ball had just finished his MFA at Yale, but he was on sabbatical designing scenery at the Seattle Repertory. Because there was a kind of vacuum, or they were "between hires," as we would say now, I stepped right in and started doing things. I designed three wonderful productions during my tenure there, including a Midwest premiere of James Joyce's *Finnegans Wake*. Then Sam Ball came back, and the department hired a man who was working on a PhD in psychiatry to head the costume program. Actually, he did have something of a career in costumes, but he was getting his PhD at the time and was preoccupied with studying the behavior of both the characters in various plays and that of his students.

I received my degree after two years. A particular highlight for me were my peers in the program, including the now legendary actor/director Frank Galati, designers Mary Griswold and Geoffrey Bushor, Barbara Gaines, artistic director of the Chicago Shakespeare Theater, and Dennis Zacek, who went on to become the Artistic Director of the Victory Gardens Theater in Chicago. All lifelong friends. NU has always attracted the very top talent.

What NU excelled at in those days, and still does, was the teaching of theater as part of a liberal arts curriculum. We learned to read, understand and interpret the written word. I took all of Dr. Walter Scott's courses in theater history and dramatic literature. They were very difficult, but I loved them. Curiously, no play written after World War I was taught. Of course, I had intense academic coursework at BU with Elliot Norton, a Shakespearean scholar and Boston drama critic, who taught all of the dramatic literature and theater history courses. But I was now older and looking at the great dramatic texts with new eyes. What a world to explore! It was one that has served me very well with subsequent design projects as complex and diverse as *The Winter's Tale* and *The Visit*.

And one could go across the street and find even more excitement. In those days the theater's sister program was the Department of Interpretation (now renamed Performance Studies). The distinction lay in the "Interp" department's discoveries made from non-scripted works, unlike the Theatre Department's reliance on scripted text. The star teachers were Wallace Bacon, Charlotte Lee, and Robert Breen. Their classes were extraordinary. Particularly impressive was Dr. Bacon's Shakespeare class that every cunning theater student took. Barbara Gaines still refers to those classes in referencing her work today. It seems that my ongoing struggle to find meanings in plays or novels is cumulative from discoveries made years ago with Dr. Bacon.

The Interp faculty always performed annually reading their own dramatic readings or "interpretations." They read from podiums. Students cherished those memories. It was the intention of the Interp faculty to study, interpret, and perform non-scripted texts, a tradition that is carried on in public performance today, and seen in the work of my theater colleagues Frank Galati, Martha Lavey, and Mary Zimmerman.

But I digress again. Theatergoing in Chicago in those years was limited. One could see student productions at the Goodman Theatre and School of Drama. There were new young groups like the Body Politic, the Ivanhoe, and Second City. Some dinner theaters like Candlelight presented musicals. And the Lyric Opera had been organized in 1954. Off-Loop, for which Chicago is equally famous today, didn't exist, in fact or even as a firm concept. But I was kept so busy at NU, what did I know? I never went south of Howard Street and was unaware of all of them. So was I in the right city to start a career?

While I was still a graduate student at NU, Marna King, a costume designer (and NU alum) at the Goodman, was doing Brecht's *Man is*

Man as the fifth show of their season. Unexpectedly she became ill and invited me to finish the design of the play, which I did. Her health didn't permit her to return, and they asked me to apply for her position, which I did. I was offered the junior costume design and teaching position. So there I found myself again, with the right door opening at the right time.

What everyone in the business knew then was that Chicago expected to enter into a new phase in its theater history. The Goodman was identified as the leading classical theater in the city, under the artistic leadership of Dr. John Reich, a director who was the artistic disciple of the famous European theater director Max Reinhardt. Reich was a very imposing (some felt intimidating) and Teutonic figure, complete with accent and manner. He envisioned a theater with a resident company in the style of Tyrone Guthrie's theater in Minneapolis. Dr. Reich appointed the English director, Douglas Seale, as his co-artistic director, and they planned a season of Shakespeare, Shaw, and American classics. The senior members of the acting company were the English actors Douglas Campbell and his wife Ann Casson, the daughter of Louis Casson and Dame Sybil Thorndyke. This was all pretty heady stuff for me. After all, I had made a pact with myself to be designing in a major city by the time I was thirty. I was twenty-nine years old.

My co-designer was a fabulously talented woman named Alicia Finkel. She subsequently went east to be Head of Design at the University of Connecticut at Storrs. We shared the design and teaching responsibilities at the Goodman and worked together for years very compatibly. I designed two plays in that first 1969–1970 season: Kaufman and Hart's *You Can't Take it With You*, the same play in which I had played the part of Mr. DePinna in high school, and G. B. Shaw's *Heartbreak House*. And I turned thirty during the course of the year. It was the best of all possible worlds, and what I continued doing—teaching and designing—for the next thirty-nine years. Did I really design seventy-seven professional productions while being a full-time faculty member? Then last year I retired from teaching, and now I concentrate on costume design.

Alicia Finkel and I wanted to establish a costume shop of distinction in the British tradition, so we went to England with hiring plans. I was very influenced by Tyrone Guthrie, even though I didn't directly work with him or in his theater until years later. Tanya Moiseiwitsch designed the new thrust stage for Guthrie and numerous sets and costumes at Stratford, Canada, and Minneapolis. She became a patron saint for classically inspired designers.

At the Guthrie, and at the Goodman, if a director requested a period in which to set a play, the designer recreated the fashion and the interiors (scenic design) for that period. It was very precise. It was like Masterpiece Theater on stage. Both Alicia and I admired the skills we saw in the British theater, at Stratford, Canada, and at the Guthrie. Will anyone who saw it ever forget the Guthrie/Moiseiwitsch production of *The House of Atreus*? The Guthrie hired the English *costumier*, the head of costume construction, Annette Garceau. She was very famous, and her work set the standard for costume construction for my generation of designers. Costume cutters who worked at the Guthrie and Stratford then went to New York and opened shops there, people such as Barbara Matera and Ray Diffen, and they altered the nature of costume and design in this country. They upped the ante. Now costume designers were expected to know how period garments were actually made. You could not face Annette Garceau with vague ideas about your designs. A designer had to have a working knowledge of historical garments and that transformed the practice and also the training in America.

In England, we found the *costumier* Ann Hardie. She was a graduate of the Edinburgh School of Art. She was a veteran of the Welsh National Opera and Thames Television. One of her specialties was corset construction. And she became my friend and colleague until her death a few years ago. I wanted to incorporate precise British techniques in construction and design for our productions and coursework at the Goodman. These impulses were simultaneously felt in other training programs and theaters across the country. An entire generation of costume designers would be prepared with concentration in art history, costume history, and period accuracy. Although theories and taste have changed over subsequent years, rigorous design, craft, and skill issues continue to be felt even today. Go to the movies and enjoy *The Duchess*.

My teaching career has been dedicated to the idea of developing historically accurate costumes and teaching costume design based upon period style and construction. We have great costume study collections in the Chicago area, and I make students use them. Costumes for the stage have to be very durable, solid, and well built, even if they are historically correct. If I've been successful, training is rigorously historically investigative, but I urge students to make creative departures. I certainly did that on *Dangerous Beauty* last summer. If design training is solid, then theatrical departures are innovative and true to the artist creating them for a particular production, and not a violation of form or discipline.

We developed the academic program at NU over a period of years. In 1985 I was professionally designing and teaching at the Goodman Theatre and Goodman School of Drama. The latter had been relocated to DePaul University in 1978. Then I received a call from my old colleagues, Dominic Missimi and Frank Galati, who were both faculty at NU, about applying for the position in costume design that had been open for a year. It is hard not to be enthusiastic when either Dominic or Frank is in a persuasive mood. I thought this was an interesting career choice. The challenges were immense. The Goodman School was primarily an undergraduate training program. NU was the reverse. The MFA Program at NU was in transition and seemed open to collaborative development. Returning to NU offered me the opportunity to develop a graduate program of distinction.

My first year at NU, I had one graduate student in costume design, Kim Schnormeier, who applied and was accepted. There were also some really intense design undergraduates in the program. For example, both Tracy Christensen and Dan Lawson are now designers for Broadway and television in New York. With this little band of thespians we costumed the entire Theater Center's season. At the end of my first year Leslie Hinderckyx, then Chair of the Department of Theatre, appointed me Head of the MFA Program in Stage Design.

My classes were small initially, and the curriculum was interesting but not very inclusive. However, there were many possibilities, and there seemed to be little faculty resistance to some experimentation. In the early 1990s the faculty reenvisioned and reconstructed the graduate design curriculum. This was punctuated by a series of faculty hires culminating in the early 2000s with the hiring of Professors Anna D. Shapiro, Daniel Ostling, and Todd Rosenthal, which along with the directing presence of Frank Galati and Mary Zimmerman brought the faculty to an exceptionally high level. Due to astute decanal leadership of the School of Communication we were able to make these significant hires that established a tone for present and future MFA faculty. They all have extensive professional credits and national reputations.

The basic philosophy of the program has been the same since the new curriculum was endorsed in the early 1990s. The program mandates co-study between directing and design students. It is a program in collaboration. Many classes have directing and design faculty as well as students. Enrollment is up with top caliber students enrolling. Today, the enrollment in the three-year MFA program includes eighteen graduate designers, six in each of the three years of training, and twelve graduate directors. Admission is highly competitive. Our recruitment efforts are simplified by the fact that frequently our students often have to wait a year to be admitted.

Collaboration has become an overused word today and there are critics who claim it cannot be taught. But the faculty at NU is committed to this experimental teaching plan in the belief that it will prepare directing and design teams to reinvigorate the American theater. We expect directors and designers to interpret a text and develop viable plans for stage production. If the creative team imagines a unique and highly ambitious game plan, intellectually and visually, then the audience should be in for a treat. They may or may not consciously recognize the overall game plan, but telling the story should be exciting. A good critic should identify and critique the overall plan and analyze the experience. These things are very complicated and hard to understand. Some critics go to plays more than once, and most theater producers now produce texts and outlines to lead critics to an understanding of the goals of a production.

MFA faculty teaching in this program are really put to the test. All faculty teach undergraduate and graduate design coursework. NU hires very few adjunct faculty. The coursework demands a teaching range including lecture, skills (drawing and painting) training, and design and collaboration. Whee! I loved this program and shuddered like my colleagues at the prospect of rapidly developing new coursework I had not taught before as the collaboration coursework evolved.

When I retired from active teaching in the spring of 2006, I was very positive about my twenty-plus years at NU and felt that we had collectively established a program of national distinction at NU.

While I was chair of the Department of Theatre in the early 2000s, I was instrumental in proposing a new initiative that became known as the American Music Theater Program (AMTP). It is dedicated to the development of new music theater works using a combination of professional and student talent. The pilot program funded five productions. The last one suggested was *Dangerous Beauty*. I kept my eye on this project because it was a fabulous design opportunity.

In designing *Dangerous Beauty* I began working with the director, Sheryl Kaller, last spring, several months before the play would go into rehearsal. We met in New York to discuss her ideas of the play and its characters. This piece is very complex. It tells multiple stories of women and is set in Venice in 1570. The central character, Veronica Franco, is an historical figure, a poet, and a "courtesan," a *cortigiana onesta*. These women were exceptions to the strict social codes that divided the sexes. They were able to transgress seemingly fixed boundaries that separated private domestic residences, the quasi-public aristocratic salons, and the public streets of the city-state.

Our musical, *Dangerous Beauty*, is about the women of this time, who they were, what they did, and what happened to some of them who sought independence. Costumes also need to reflect the story, in addition to the personal trajectory of each woman. There was an admiration for female beauty and sexuality, and a repression of that admiration, and the costumes reflect that too. Then there was the gross prosecution for human transgressions by the church. The black costumes worn by Venetian men and women in the finale are worn by those who enforce the rules of the Inquisition.

Interest in Veronica Franco's life has been revived as the result of a PhD thesis written about her that was subsequently published as a book. Veronica's story had survived centuries. Tintoretto painted her and was also purported to be one of her lovers. His paintings show her, sitting up or reclining, as a bare-breasted voluptuary. The paintings are spectacular. She was a published poet in her lifetime, and it is a matter of the historical record that she was tried twelve times by the Inquisition; she spoke in her own defense and each time she was acquitted. The book writer for this production, Jeannine Dominy, used the research material to write the script for the 1998 Warner Brothers film of the same title. Dominy dramatized this historical material for both the 1998 film and for our stage version. The central character has become the subject of gender studies in recent years. And Veronica Franco's poetry survives.

Dangerous Beauty was produced at NU in July 2008. I envisioned the costumes for the show as a crazy quilt. And why? The director, Sheryl Kaller, was interested in exploring "rock and roll" production elements similar to the recent movie *Marie Antoinette*, directed by Sofia Coppola. This was to be an historical but also a contemporary production. Sheryl is one of a new generation of directors who have come to the fore today who have little passion for period reproduction. Times have changed since Tyrone Guthrie. Current directors may be reacting to the fastidious *Masterpiece Theater* production styles of their youth. Which is OK. Or, many of them may not have the kind of liberal arts training that I was fortunate enough to have had in the 1950s. The evolution of directors in my design career has been interesting. At the beginning of my career the directors I worked with were of my parents' generation. Later

I worked with my peers. Now I primarily work with younger people such as Sheryl Kaller, Gary Griffin, and Anna D. Shapiro.

Dangerous Beauty is emblematic of this kind of contemporary approach. Kaller wanted to combine past and present, but find a visual idea particular for this production. We developed a concept which we called layering. The natural woman is one who is unrestrained by clothing. As one adds outer layers, one gets farther away from one's real self. The outer layers of garments, often restrictive, tell society who you are: a wife, a courtesan, a schoolgirl, a whore. A woman can only experience freedom, in our play, by removing layers of clothing.

I put Jenny Powers, who played Veronica Franco, in an unconstructed linen shift (a basic white slip). Over the shift goes a laced corset. Over the corset goes a series of gowns that read: schoolgirl or courtesan. If she would put on a gauze-hooded cape she could enter a Church. This layering is true for all of the female characters. Then a black gauze layer is worn over everything for the finale, the trial at the Inquisition. A woman can be this, but also that, then in one moment something else. Always in motion. Always a new identity.

The costume that the principal actress wears at one point is laden with opulent jewelry and fabrics of contrasting colors, weights and patterns. And it has a zipper—not invented until the 1890s—up the back of the bodice! Rock and Roll! Yet the drama is set in Imperial Venice in 1560. This is an era when Venice was already declining in political power, a time of change, threatened invasion, a time of great social and military conflict. Venice in the late sixteenth century was not part of Italy, but a city-state with its own dialect, social customs, and autonomous government, balancing the interests of the state, the church, and the ecclesiastical legal system.

From the outset I was sensitive to the fact that Veronica Franco had become a feminist heroine. Her life story is powerfully theatrical. There were the poems, then other contemporaneous historical figures wrote about her and remembered her. She was a self-empowered woman at a time when women were relatively powerless. There was no equivalent to Elizabeth I in the Doge-controlled Venice of 1590. Women had few choices outside marriage or the Church, and most importantly they couldn't own property in their own name. Veronica's power stemmed from the liberal life style associated with being a courtesan at a time when a rich, aristocratic social class had leisure and cultivated and supported the arts.

The piece is also about several other women in Veronica's genera-

Photo: Bill Arsenault.

tion. Before the play was to go into dress rehearsal the Director and I discussed various trajectories. During the rehearsal of the play the stories of the other women began to shrink. To exclusively tell Veronica's story, it still took two hours and fifteen minutes, including intermission!

At the beginning of the piece you see two girlhood friends, Beatrice and Veronica; one is upper class, and one is from a family that has fallen from wealth and is now impoverished. To distinguish the two ladies, I put Beatrice in beautiful expensive transparent silk fabrics. Veronica's fabrics were, by comparison, woven, and her bodice was plain. The latter was dressed in warm, hot colors; the former in a cool blue, like the sea.

Beatrice, also the sister of Veronica's lover Marco, goes from maiden to wife in the course of the play. As a wife her hair is dressed up, and her body is totally covered except for the hands and face. Her wife costume is worn over her maiden's dress. Layers! It is a lustrous blue silk satin, richly trimmed with embroidery and pearls. The evolution of before and after is reinforced by the costuming.

By contrast, the other young wife, Guilia, is in an arranged marriage to the man Veronica remains in love with, has only one costume because her stage time was significantly reduced. We see her only in three scenes. She enters as a fiancée; next we see her publicly accusing Veronica of being a whore, and finally in support of Veronica during her trial by the Inquisition. She is the only character in black, owing to her nun-like demeanor. By contrast, the movie version of the story has the men who loved Veronica save her by standing up against the Inquisition and defending her. In our rendition it was the women who supported one of her kind against the prosecutions of the Church. Both choices were dramatically effective.

Thus, the basic concept for the clothing for all of the women in the play was: the natural woman is clothed in a free-flowing silk shift. When a woman enters "society" she puts a steel boned corset over the shift, then adds a heavily decorated dress, followed by a gauze cape over the dress when she gets married, goes to the trial, goes to church, or appears in public. This layering is meant to demonstrate the encasement of women in Venetian culture. The natural woman is now lost as society dictates what is proper.

Veronica becomes a courtesan in a dressing scene dictated by her mother, herself a former courtesan. She is presented to the Venetian senators as marketable property at a festive masked ball wearing an opulent red dress. Actually, all of Veronica's costumes were in red tones that progressively get bolder and brighter. Over the red dress, she wore a transparent gold coat emblazoned with gold leaves and embroidery. She is masked. She is voluptuous!

One of the most popular of Veronica's garments, cited by the audience to me, was her seductive peignoir. This garment was the simplest design and cut in the show. It was made from a cream silk jersey and cut in a T-shape. The fabric has tiny rows of ruffles of the silk jersey stitched horizontally that shimmered under the stage lights. Veronica gave the impression and appearance of a gorgeously draped Greek goddess.

Another of Veronica's startling costumes was her fencing outfit. The trousers, complete with a male codpiece, were skintight. Made from white suede (I preferred doeskin but could not locate it in white), they were intended to be a second skin. Worn with a blood red silk bodice, Veronica duels with Maffio, Marco's evil cousin, and wins!

For her final "presentation" costume to meet the masochistic King Henry IV of France, Veronica wore a shimmering red and gold cape. The cape covered a vivid fuchsia and red brocade court gown beneath. Worthy of a king and exotically dressed, Veronica was presented by the citizens of Venice as chattel. This gown is seen on the cover of this issue. The gown was heavily encrusted with metallic gold and jewels. When Veronica appears on stage she twinkles and glitters more than any other character. Everything about her appearance attracts the attention of the audience and the king.

Veronica was surrounded by a chorus of courtesans with exotic names like Imperia and Olympia. And they wore exotic gowns that also reflected the patchwork concept. The patchwork idea came to me from images of the uniforms worn by the Swiss Guards at the Vatican. It was also a budget necessity. They were in hot colors like yellow, orange, and pink. I raided the theater's storage bins for leftover fabrics. This combination of old and new materials was sewn together for a highly theatrical effect.

This show had seventeen characters, nine men and eight women, nine of whom were principal roles, meaning there were nine distinct stories to tell through the costuming. The men's clothing, except for the leading men, Marco and Maffio, did not change. Their conceived and written characters and clothing were, well, one-dimensional. Layered garments were not part of our concept for the boys, excluding Marco, as we did not want to diminish the women's stories. So how do we secure these male garments?

By having to rent the majority of men's costumes, my patchwork idea was not universal to the design. But I located a set of Metropolitan Opera costumes designed by Tanya Moiseiwitsch for Verdi's *Rigoletto* in New York. And they were perfect. The fabrics were cool colors, purple, green, and blue. And the feeling of the garments was similar to the women's gowns we were building. Additional garments were rented from the Shakespeare Theater Costume Storage, Stratford, Canada. That town is always good for a trip, and one can go to the theater every night. I took my student assistant.

Wig design and makeup is also the responsibility of the costume designer. My longtime colleague Maloo (Melissa Veal), who was trained at Stratford and is currently the wig designer for the Chicago Shakespeare Theater, was engaged for this project. Her work is artistically of a very high quality. For many of the student actors it was the first time they had to apply complex makeup and wear period wigs. An excellent training experience for the NU undergraduate! Veronica wore two wigs plus a tiaraed wig piece that had to be removed on stage, in the dark. It took several tries and re-dressings to make her hair suit the design.

The fabrics were not period but that was not a constraint for me. I mixed and matched rich Thai silks with shiny polyester fabrics. It all contributed somehow to a final patchwork product that did not highlight the component parts. One nineteenth-century velvet brocade textile, a former upholstered chair seat donated by the Parenteau Studio, was reworked into the doublet for Marco, my leading man. Whether the production of *Dangerous Beauty* came off and the audience could discern these subtleties, I don't know. I have grown to trust my instinct for what is right and wrong in building costumes. And I like to take risks and experiment.

My staff at NU, headed by Ryan Magnusson, rose to every occasion presented by *Dangerous Beauty*. So did the actors who wore the costumes. My job is actually to enable the actors to do their work. Some of my success is due to the critics who have acknowledged their success in production. And they have won awards for the theaters that produced them. Several of the designs have been American entries at the prestigious Prague Quadrennial. But costumes should not be intrusive. As Mr. Sovey told me back in Boston, "You have failed if you have the audience leave the theater whistling the costumes."

Bibliographic Note

Anderson, Barbara and Cletus, *Costume Design*, Holt, Rinehart and Winston 1984.

Edelstein, Terri J., *The Stage Is All The World, The Theater Designs of Tany Moiseiwitsch*, The University of Chicago Press, 1994.

Henderson, Mary C., Theater in America, Harry N. Abrams, Inc., New York, 1988.

Lehnert, Gertrud, *History of Fashion in the Twentieth Century*, Koneman, 1996.

Motley, *Designing and Making Stage Costumes*, Watson-Guptill, New York 1964.

Pectal, Lynn, *Costume Design*, Back Stage Books, 1993.

Two standard texts that integrate theater design with the world of art, a rarity in our field, are very old. Both authors are now dead.

Fleming, William, *Arts and Ideas*, several editions.

Russell, Douglas A., *Period Style for the Theater*, several editions.

David Kersnar

Sita Ram: Adapting the *Ramayana* in Chicago

In 2000, I was commissioned by Josephine Lee, the artistic director for the Chicago Children's Choir, to conceive an original opera that would reflect her organization's mission to bring the diverse cultures of Chicago together through the harmony of music. I suggested an adaptation of the *Ramayana*, a 24,000–line Hindu epic I had discovered while trawling the Internet for world stories. I came upon a passage describing Prince Rama's distress at losing Princess Sita. Having lost his love, Rama also lost his divine power. Hanuman the monkey warrior, an avatar of Shiva, rallied all the world's creatures to his aid. Monkeys, bears, and squirrels put aside their differences to help return Sita to Rama and rid the earth of Ravana and his demons, restoring balance and harmony to the universe.

The wild animals that normally fear and feed upon each other come together in the *Ramayana* to fulfill a spiritual purpose. This story seemed a fitting metaphor to celebrate the fiftieth anniversary of the choir's formation out of the civil rights movement in Chicago. The Chicago Children's Choir's mission is to mount performances of musical excellence to bring together young representatives of Chicago neighborhoods to pursue the same goals and share common experiences. Though the text seemed like a perfect match for a musical adaptation, little did I know that I would face six challenging years to bring this work from the page to the stage. Completing *Sita Ram* became a personal odyssey in which

I journeyed through one of the world's greatest pieces of literature, and absorbed more South Asian culture than I had imagined possible. Writing the book and lyrics for the opera required that I myself undertake an inner exploration. That introspection helped me clarify the mission of the piece to convey the message that we have to first look within ourselves to solve the world's problems.

What I want to track here is how I came to develop my own interpretation of the story, and how I harnessed a universal message of balance and harmony for a Western audience while still honoring a culture which holds sacred the words of the *Ramayana*. I will discuss how I researched cultural traditions associated with the text, developed my point of view for the adaptation, streamlined the scale of theatrical elements, made script revisions to avoid redundant imagery, and designed rehearsal systems, to successfully stage the ambitious production of *Sita Ram* at Lookingglass Theatre in the spring of 2006.

Meeting My Composer and Choreographer: Meeting the *Ramayana*

In India, the stories in the *Ramayana* are as popular today as they were when they were first told. A television series that dramatized the epic actually brought India to a standstill. Its weekly broadcast closed shops and silenced whole streets. There are several different versions of the story written in various regional languages and diverse sub-cultural tastes. The *Ramayana* follows the life of Prince Rama, his connection to his love Princess Sita, and his spiritual quest to save the world from the ego-driven tyranny of the demonic King Ravana. The primary texts that inspired the adaption were the translations of the two-thousand-year-old Sanskrit *Ramayana* of Sage Valmiki, and the sixteenth-century *Ramcaritmanas* of Tulsidas. Legend says that Valmiki was compelled to write the *Ramayana* after seeing a hunter pierce the heart of a male bird singing to his mate. As the female bird lamented over her soulmate, Valmiki cried out causing the hunter to feel the same pain in his heart he had inflicted on these birds. That cry became the first words of the *Ramayana*. I strove to make sure that cry informed my adaptation and drove the actions and motives of all my central characters.

The one who first pointed me toward those two particular versions of the *Ramayana* was Jai Uttal, who collaborated with me as composer of the opera. Uttal, a renowned world music recording artist, spent many years studying in India, mastering Eastern instruments and music forms. He built his career fusing South Asian music with Appalachian, folk, rock, and South American rhythms to create his signature fusion sound. Even before I met him, I used his recordings to energize physical theater exercises I led. When I began to write outlines for *Sita Ram*, I discovered that many of Uttal's songs used text from, or referred to, the *Ramayana*. I learned that Jai Uttal also led *kirtan* (devotional) call and response, Hindu chanting workshops that actually told the story of the characters and deities in the *Ramayana*. I suggested to Josephine Lee that we try to persuade Jai Uttal to collaborate on the project. Having never met Uttal, we took a chance and contacted his agent. Lee and I then flew out to Uttal's studio in Northern California for an initial introductory meeting. Won over by our enthusiasm, Uttal joined the production team. His deep relationship with the text became critical to our production.

Writer and directors bent on creating musical productions are not always given the luxury of working with a Jai Uttal, but at the very least a director must choose a composer willing to immerse himself in the world of the play. The composer must understand and share the writer's point of view. The music will be telling the story in alignment with the lyrics, book, and visual images. All of these elements must be synchronized.

In India, *Ramayana* reenactments can last for up to a month, telling the entire story. I needed to create a version of the story that could be contained in a single evening. The *Ramayana* is divided into seven *kandas*, meaning chapters or books, literally translated as "lakes" or "bodies of water." By "diving" into each one of these "lakes," the reader focuses on a different aspect of the teachings in the story. For instance, the first book, *Bala Kanda*, focuses on Rama's birth as an avatar of the God Vishnu, and how he exhibited the model behavior of a young boy and citizen. The second book, *Ayodhya Kanda*, depicts a family drama that results in Prince Rama's unjust banishment from his kingdom to preserve his father's honor and word. The third book, *Aranya Kanda*, illustrates how Rama survives trials in the forest, including the kidnapping of Sita by the Evil demon Ravana. In the fourth book, *Kishkinda Kanda*, Rama's hope is renewed as the Warrior Hanuman and his fellow monkey army join him in his search for Sita. The fifth and six books, *Sundara* and *Yuddha Kanda*, describe the epic battle between earth creatures and demons, the compassionate defeat of Ravana, and Rama and Sita's triumphant return to Ayodhya.

In the very last book, *Uttara Kanda*, Rama and Sita are united and return home to Ayodhya. Rama is pressured by his people to exile Sita because they fear that her purity has been ruined in Ravana's presence. Many scholars, including Jai Uttal, suspect that this section of the *Ramayana* was an addition to Valmiki with the purpose of reinforcing cultural misogyny. Uttal was very reluctant to include this section in our performance. Taking his advice, I constructed a resolution using Rama and Sita's "test of fire" depicted in book six, ending our production's adaption with their reunion. I have to stress at this point that writers only earn the right to interpretive freedoms by first immersing themselves thoroughly in the extant text. Though I did receive some criticism for the revision, I stand by our decision. Having developed an informed point of view on the text allowed me to make confident adaptation decisions.

As I became more exposed to those familiar with the *Ramayana*, I discovered that there were many vastly divergent opinions on the many variations of the text. To hold my own among these divergent opinions, I had to develop more than a cursory understanding of the story. At the outset, after listening to Uttal's recitation of the epic, I read eleven different translations of the story to gain inspiration for a version that I thought would be best for our production.

In 2001, shortly after our initial meeting, Uttal and I started to plan which sections of the *Ramayana* would be adapted through song and to start writing lyrics. Two songs Uttal had already written, *Be With You* and *Hot Button*, were perfect to give voice to Rama and Sita's longing for each other and for the final battle. The Artistic Director of the Chicago Children's Choir, Josephine Lee, interwove music from their choral repertoire and brought in string and vocal arrangements from Chicago Children's Choir associate Ted Hearne to emphasize the cultural connections between Eastern and Western music. For instance, in the section where Hanuman has to save Rama and his monkey army from their mortal wounds at the hands of demons, we fused the *Libera Me* section of Faure's *Requiem* together with Uttal's *kirtan* chant-infused *Hot Button* to express parallel pleas for deliverance.

As with Uttal, I received an unexpected boon when I was introduced to my choreographer, Krithika Rajagopalan. Lookingglass already had been invited to work with her and her company, the Natya Dance Theatre, to develop and implement in-school residencies using theater and South Indian *bharata natyam* dance choreography. *Bharata natyam* dance is one of six different forms of classical dance in India, not including the numerous regional folk dances. The highly stylized emotional facial expressions called *Abhinaya* and technical hand gestures or *Mudras* are connected to the very origins of dramatic performance in India. This style of dance has a long history in both South Indian court and temple performance and is considered much more distinguished than the modern *bhangra* dance forms often depicted in Bollywood films. I was fascinated by Krithika Rajagopalan's comparison between the work of Natya Dance Theatre, who borrow theatrical elements to create dance, to the work of Lookingglass, which often creates theater by borrowing from dance traditions.

Rajagopalan was at first skeptical when I announced to that I was working on a musical adaptation of the *Ramayana*. As with many South Asian dance forms, performing sections of the *Ramayana* was a strong tradition within *bharata natyam* repertoire. Fortunately Krithika, the daughter of company founder Hema Rajagopalan, was at the time beginning to experiment fusing other cultural forms with her own *bharata natyam* classical dance choreography. Krithika accepted the invitation to join the project once she learned that I had a respectful knowledge and understanding of the text. I was able to then use this unexpected opportunity in our Chicago Public Schools residency with Lookingglass and the Natya Dance Theatre to workshop different scenes from the *Ramayana*, experimenting with Uttal's existing recordings. Early drafts of the book and visual language for *Sita Ram* had its beginnings in these Lookingglass residencies with Natya Dance Theatre, as well as development in prior summer workshops with the Chicago Children's Choir and Lookingglass students.

Working with Jai Uttal and Krithika Rajagopalan made me realize that practicing Hindus relate to the *Ramayana* not as construct, but rather as a history. Later when discussing this with fellow Lookingglass Ensemble member Mary Zimmerman, she cautioned me in regard to adapting religious text. She remarked that she has adapted Greek myth, but the *Bible* or the *Ramayana* are living texts that are used in worship today. Adaptation by artists that are not practicing those religions comes with very specific challenges. By consulting with my collaborators, Krithika Ragagopalan and Jai Uttal, who both had a deep spiritual relationship with the text, I was satisfied that I was approaching the *Ramayana* with reverence.

Early Drafts of *Sita Ram*

After these initial workshops and music sessions the script was further refined through the Lookingglass Artistic Development Program. Lookingglass schedules these development sessions to work on promising scripts prior to committing to put the plays into production. I set out to forge common ground for both the spiritual significance and the dramatic thrust of the text.

Sita Ram was first performed by the Chicago Children's Choir in a concert version at Ravinia's Bennett-Gordon Hall in May of 2003, bringing together over sixty members of the Choir, sixteen members of Natya Dance Theatre, Jai Uttal and his ten-piece Pagan Love Orchestra, and a string quartet, all under the musical direction of Josephine Lee. It was a Herculean undertaking. Uttal's band alone took up over half the stage with a keyboard and organ, harmonium, several Indian string instruments, electric bass, several guitars, full rock drum set, percussionist, and two-headed Indian drum. Each organization had its own separate rehearsal schedule. We only had a few hours of tech together, and most of that time was devoted to sound checks. Nonetheless, we learned a great deal from the concert. Audience reactions to the songs, lyrics, and arrangements were overwhelmingly positive. I realized that although I had cut down much of the story, there was still too much material for one evening, and I would have to make significant cuts to give the remaining text room to breathe. I also realized that as exciting as it was to see that many people on stage at once, the logistics and financial limitations of staging that many bodies in a professional venue would be unmanageable. And, other than the costumes provided by Natya Dance Theatre and the stock lighting from the performance hall, we had no visual spectacle design for the show. Much more work needed to be done, but based on the concert's success, Lookingglass put the production back into development. After two more years of script development and music revisions, *Sita Ram* was voted by the Lookingglass Ensemble to be presented in the 2006 season in our new theater in Chicago's Water Tower Water Works.

Diving into the Lakes of Rama

To prepare myself to lead a full production of *Sita Ram*, I needed to immerse myself deeper in its cultural origins and the history of the text. I also needed to know how the text was traditionally performed in South Asian countries. Although I had done some background research on the text, I had a limited knowledge of India and the present cultural traditions surrounding the *Ramayana*. My exposure had been through Internet and travelogue research, a few scholarly analytical texts, conversations with Krithika and Hema Rajagopalan of Natya Dance Theatre, workshop sessions with Jai Uttal, and newly admired Bollywood movies. In order to make informed artistic decisions, I needed first-hand experiences with the present South Asian culture.

Krithika Rajagopalan had scheduled performances of Natya Dance Theatre to tour in India from December through January of 2005. She invited me to join her, to stay with her grandmother in Chennai and to meet her in-laws in New Delhi. I received a travel grant from a Lookingglass board member. In spite of the tsunami that had hit six days earlier, flooding the South Indian coastal region of Tamil Nadu, I took the twenty-two-hour flight to southern India. I was spurred on by Krithika Ragagopalan's insistence that all of her contacts were encouraging me to still come, even though the devastation from the tsunami had occurred only a few miles away. My short visit to India showed me one of the most sensual environments I have ever experienced. The whirlwind trip had us getting up early to tour temples or archeological sites, and then meet with numerous *Ramayana* scholars and local artists. I would then stay up late into the night talking to Krithika and her grandparents about what we had seen and how it related to the *Ramayana* and South Asian culture. Krithika's grandmother Pati cooked South Indian meals three times a day, preparing a wide variety of special dishes for my visit.

On our first morning we visited the Viswaroopa Hanuman temple in Chennai with the seven-story Hanuman statue made out of a single piece of stone. Hanuman, a pivotal figure from the *Ramayana*, was much more revered in India than I had expected, based on my earlier research. The impressive statue was specially adorned for the *Pongal* harvest festival, as were many of the cows that roamed freely in the streets. I was struck by how venerated the Hanuman temple was (we were not allowed to take pictures), yet across the narrow alley that lead to the temple was a billboard advertising the "Hanuman driving school." The Hindu pantheon was treated with reverence yet accepted as part of everyday life. That juxtaposition of the mundane billboard and the sacred temple became a central image for our production's set.

On the second morning Krithika's grandfather woke us up before sunrise for an audience with Dr. M. A. Vinkata Krishnan, a highly respected Brahmin priest associated with one of the oldest Rama temples in Chennai. Dr. Krishnan, dressed in a traditional white wrap with the V markings for Vishnu on his forehead, spoke to us in Tamil, which Krithika translated into English. We sat in a simply decorated receiving room on the ground floor, with windows open to the sights and the sounds of the street woven into our conversation. I had arrived in Chennai during the South Indian *Pongal* harvest festival. Doorway thresholds were decorated with colored rice-flour *rungoli* patterns. Cow horns were brightly decorated and *Surya* sun god deities were paraded through the streets.

Dr. Krishnan seemed amused that I was here to ask for "permission" to create a Western version of the *Ramayana* but pleased when I asked specific complicated questions about the conundrums the text presents to a Western reader. I asked how one was to interpret Rama's flaws, as exhibited in certain sections. He was quick to point out that Rama's failures are attached to his human existence. His human emotions only become out of control in Sita's absence, proving the force that love can play in our lives. He was sympathetic and encouraging when I put forward some of the alterations to the text we had planned for our version of the story. He reminded me that the *Ramayana* has been told in many different forms both inside and outside of India. What is important, he said, is to discover and maintain the messages that the *Ramayana* teaches. When I told him of my personal interpretation that the *Ramayana* teaches us to look within ourselves to locate greater truth, as exhibited by Hanuman looking inside himself to find Rama and Sita, he seemed pleased. Our meeting was interrupted several times by noises of *Pongal* festival celebrations, parades of the large deities pulled on special carts, and decorated cows peering into the street-level sitting room window.

The next day I visited the Mamallapuram archeological site where giant temples are carved out of the mountainside, each from a single giant stone. Two teenage sisters who lived in an orphanage for abused young women with polio accompanied me. The director of the program was a Chicago transplant and Krithika's childhood friend who asked if the girls could accompany us and test their English by being interpreters. The Shore Temple that juts out on a peninsula right on the beach miraculously had only received minor damage from the force of the tsunami. The severe damage to the surrounding grounds had already been repaired. New sod had been laid out and the corrugated metal and fiberglass tourist shops that lined the walkways had been hastily rebuilt

Photo: David Kersnar.

because tourism was so important to the local economy. The structures were being restored with whatever materials could be found. The scaffolding protecting these structures was mismatched. Steel poles and clamps were tied together with teetering bamboo and hemp lashing. Workers scampered up the temporary structures, apparently trusting the precarious towers that seemed about to crash to the ground at any moment. These scaffoldings and flimsy structures became another motif in the set of the Lookingglass production.

Another goal I had for my travels was to learn more about South Asian puppet traditions. A journalist I met, V.R. Devika, told me to visit A. Selvaraja, the puppeteer-in-residence at the Dakshina Chitra Cultural Center. Selvaraja was a third-generation puppeteer who had lost his beach home and studio to the tsunami. I caught him at the end of the day as he was packing up the few puppets that remained in his temporary studio at the Cultural Center. I offered him a donation to help him get started rebuilding his inventory and he graciously consented to give us an impromptu show, in which he manipulated the puppets to depict the Gods as well as comedic interchanges between monkey puppets.

His puppets were made of pigskin. They were translucent, so they projected vegetable-dyed, multicolored pigments onto the shadow screen in a manner similar to the Wayang Kulit puppets of Java or Bali. Wayang actually means "skin," and these puppets had their origins in India. As Hinduism spread, they found their way to Indonesia. That's why puppet performances in Java and Bali depict scenes from the *Ramayana* or *Mahabharata*. During the beginning of Muslim rule in sixteenth-century Indonesia, when it was forbidden to show images of the gods, the translucent skin puppets were rendered opaque, so that only the shadow could be seen and the Muslim clerics would not be angered. Thus the famous Indonesian shadow puppets were born out of a necessity to conform.

Inspired by my experience with Selvaraja, I attended an arts fair in Chennai and acquired several puppets that depicted the characters from the *Ramayana*. I was able to utilize some of these puppets for the Lookingglass 2006 production. The cloth and textile shops in both Chennai and New Delhi offered different styles of material for the costumes for the production. Different patterns and weaves were associated with a region or, in some instances, the caste of the person wearing the garment.

In North India I saw more of the urban sprawl. Many building sites were covered with the same rickety scaffolding structures I noticed in the south. In my mind I was continually taking pictures of the contrast between modern India and its ancient past. Everywhere decrepit slums stood next to gleaming modern info-tech complexes, which looked like spaceships that had landed in the teaming squalor. The check list for my designers would say we have to present three worlds at once: The ancient world still connected to the birth of South Asian spirituality; the stark contemporary reality of an impoverished, yet resourceful, population willing to make do with whatever materials could be found; and a very modern world proudly showing the latest technologies, Western influences, and vast wealth.

Over the next several months, I worked over these images with our design team as we developed our ideas for the visual language of the show. I showed set designer Scott Neale pictures of the archeological sites and he came back with his twisting creation of uneven scaffolding, wooden plank ramps, and the faux stone, lotus-patterned, raked stage. He made billboards surrounding the stage that were inspired by the actual homemade advertisements I saw repeatedly in India.

Let me say it again: you can't do a show like this without immersing yourself in the culture that inspired it.

While in North India, I visited Brindavan, the birthplace of Krishna.

Like Rama, he is an avatar of Vishnu. Brindavan is also home to the Ashram of composer Jai Uttal's Guru, Baba Shri Neeb Karori, who trained him in the art of *kirtan* chanting in the early seventies. Pictures of Baba Shri Neeb Karori were hung all over the ashram, and kirtan players performed over loudspeakers the entire time we visited. *Kirtan* "call and response" devotional chanting is at the heart of many of the songs in the show and is the basis for much of the choral singing from the choir. Standing in that ashram reminded me of when I first witnessed Uttal lead an interactive *kirtan* chanting workshop in 2001. Jai first explained to the audience the contemporary relevance of the ancient Hindu figures in the songs before leading each chant. Everyone was swept up in the enthusiastic singing. It is this very feeling of interaction between audience and performer that I have always tried to cultivate in the theater I create, and it was from that point that I knew that *kirtan* call and response chanting needed to be a vital part of the *Sita Ram* production.

In Brindavan, I reunited with Bhima, who played Bengali Mridangam, two-headed drum, in the 2003 Ravinia concert version of *Sita Ram*. At the ashram, I watched as he sat in with the *kirtan* musicians, who performed with slightly different instrumentation and melodic structure than Jai Uttal. However, Bhima and the ashram players had the same euphoric drive and *bhakti* (expression of devotion), confirming to me that at the heart of this style of chant is vocal and instrumental energy, as opposed to exact musical notation.

Whenever we visited a temple or sacred site we took off our shoes in reverence to the deities present. There was little delineation between the representations of the gods, or the gurus, and their actual presence. Both were revered equally. I witnessed this phenomenon countless times, whether in a home, miniature temple, or large Hindu complex thousands of years old.

In both North and South India, I attended concerts, folk art demonstrations, and dance recitals, professional and amateur. I only saw a fraction of the possible cultural presentations India had to offer. Yet I came away with a deep sense that these classical dance forms had to be preserved in our show.

I had intended to visit Bali to witness authentic performances of *kecak* monkey chanting we planned to use in the production, but the tsunami's timing and the far worse devastation in that area thwarted my plans. Upon returning from my trip, I was even more determined to connect with an authentic source to understand the interlocking rhythms that make up *kecak* chanting. *Kecak* chanting in its current form is actually a relatively new tradition in Bali. In the early twentieth century, the German painter Walter Spies was studying with the gamelan Master Wayan Limbak, who wanted to show elements of *Sanghyang* trance-induced exorcism rituals to westerners so they could better appreciate the culture of Bali. Wayan enlisted Spies to help him borrow from traditions that were not allowed to be viewed by Western eyes, to tell the *Kishkinda Kanda* monkey section of the Ramayana. No westerner at that point had seen the original dance and chanting forms. The current version of *kecak* chanting, however, is now very popular among world music enthusiasts.

In August of 2003 Jai Uttal and I attended a *kecak* session in San Francisco with some former students of Master Nyomen Wenten, who taught from his gamelan studio at the California School of the Arts. At that event, Jai Uttal experimented with mixing the *Hanuman Chalisa* (a translation of this Tulsidas epic appears in the final "Om Shanti" of *Sita Ram*) with a chorus of chanted, interlocking *kecak* syllables. That session inspired us to include *kecak* chanting in our rewrites for the show's music.

In Los Angeles in February of 2005, after returning from India, I met with Wenten and scheduled him for a workshop in Chicago with the choir in November of 2005. The result surpassed my expectations. In a short two-hour workshop he was able to draw out an artistically cohesive playfulness within the choir that would have taken me weeks to accomplish. The workshop gave us many different combinations of authentic interlocking rhythms to enhance the storytelling. Using only broken English and his own body, Wenten was able to communicate very clearly the way that *kecak* requires the chorus members to throw themselves physically into making the sounds and images come together. He taught members of the choir to listen with their entire bodies, to use soft focus with their peripheral vision, and to respond kinesthetically to aural and visual changes in the room. The skills needed to perform *kecak* paralleled those formal skills valued in the collaborative work at Lookingglass, as well as in Ann Bogart's *Viewpoints* techniques that are widely practiced today in the theater community. Wenten was teaching a heightened dramatic awareness with great clarity and, at the same time, teaching advanced musicianship. It quickly became clear that the use of *kecak* chanting would create a perfect illustration of both the original themes of the text (*kecak* was specifically created to tell the *Ramayana*) and to illustrate the Chicago Children's Choir's mission to celebrate many cultures working together through the harmony of music.

Script Revisions

My production choice to include foreign music and a novel form of storytelling in *Sita Ram* might have merely served to entertain if I had not been motivated by a strong desire to tell a clear story. The task of reducing the 24,000–line poem down to a two-hour musical was a challenge from the beginning. After we presented the songs and the early version of the book for the 2003 Ravinia concert, there was much work to do. In my next revisions of the script, I identified characters essential to tell the story. I compressed the roles of the narrator Sage Valmiki and Rama's brother Lakshmana into the single character Hanuman, who stood at Rama's side and told the story of his epic journey.

The music was strong, but many of the songs were too long for the musical theater format. The songs were great at illustrating heightened emotion, but didn't always move the story forward. In the 2003 version of the book, for instance, I used four different scenes to tell the story of Rama and Sita being distracted by a golden deer sent by the demon king Ravana to lure Rama away from Sita so Ravana could abduct her. As a result, there was too much dialogue between songs. To simplify the scale of this section and tell a clear story, Jai Uttal and I set out to create one song for this scene, *All That Glitters Is Not Gold*. This song now told the entire story of Sita's abduction by Ravana through musical changes, lyrics, and the visual language of the dancers. The goal of story clarity as a production guide had a positive effect on reducing the scale of all the elements in the production, including song interpretations, score revisions, and staging and spectacle choices.

While I worked with the show's collaborators to further refine the book and lyrics for the fully realized production at Lookingglass, I needed to come to terms with another huge challenge: How would such a massive production fit into the Lookingglass Theatre's intimate two-hundred-seat theater and retain the show's integrity?

The Challenge of Theatrical Scale

I was imprinted with a love of large-scale performance as a boy soprano in the San Francisco Opera. I shared the stage with Placido Domingo in *Carmen* and Luciano Pavarotti in *La Gioconda* and soloed in Mozart's *The Magic Flute* and Puccini's *Gianni Schicchi*. No wonder my senior thesis at Northwestern turned out to be a fifty-person, never-before-staged version of the Who's rock opera *Tommy*. I held onto those grandiose sensibilities for the next two decades. Unless I restrained myself, my motto would continue to be: think big, reach far, and stage my shows to soar on a grand operatic scale.

At Lookingglass my productions were known for being big. Every Lookingglass production must be voted on by the entire ensemble. I sold Lookingglass on my pie-in-the-sky proposals for shows such as *Brundibar* and *La Luna Muda* because I convinced them I could transform my bold and expansive visions into box office hits. Though Lookingglass at the time had limited resources, the ensemble eagerly voted *Sita Ram* into the 2006 season. This was an epic filled with many characters, high stakes, and big emotions. In order to tell the story of the *Ramayana* in *Sita Ram*, I felt it essential to create a spectacle using the Chicago Children's Choir singing Jai Uttal's East-meets-West lush score, Krithika Rajagopalan's complicated South Indian *bharata natyam* dance choreography, and Master Nyomen Wenten's Balinese *kecak* interlocking-rhythm chanting. I staged *Sita Ram* by retaining story elements and extant South Asian performance modes recognizable to those familiar with the text. At the same time, I used narration, dialogue, and contemporary American iconography to make sure the performance also spoke to Western audiences.

My first uncomfortable realization was that I had signed on to the Lookingglass production despite the unrealistic budget constraints of the season slot. Instead of waiting for a future producer with more resources, I hedged my bets and spent the year in production, finding ways to limit the scale of the show to fit the slot. I rationalized that producing the show was a gift to Lookingglass and that the limited budget would force me to inventively use and reuse existing elements on stage, matching the transformative aesthetic of our company's core values. However, there was a tension between the need to have the show fit into the relatively small new Lookingglass Theatre and my desire to delight the audience with pageantry and spectacle. Although both criteria always come into play in determining the scale of a production, a key question was not yet answered: what was the proper scale for telling *this* particular story?

To choose the proper scale for a show, a director must construct a researched point of view and a guiding thrust statement. Research on the world of the play and text analysis are necessary steps for a director to develop a point of view and to articulate an approach to a project. I have in the past devised original work in an ensemble atmosphere, where I let the group arrive at a mission statement by consensus. Getting that buy-in builds loyalty to the project. However, this technique is only effective when you have ample lead time to develop the piece. In this case, the point of view and thrust, or mission for the piece, had to be developed far in advance of the performers beginning their work. The thrust statement must use the least amount of words to state both the central idea of the play and to pinpoint the main conflict. Though this statement can be refined throughout the process, I have found the most success when I draft this statement before the adaptation process begins. The statement then guides all aspects of the production, whether it be development of the script, the design, or the rehearsals process.

I came to realize that much of my previous decision making regarding production scale had more to do with the needs of the company and my desire to harness elaborate pageantry than with my studied take on the story and text. Through text analysis and research, the following thrust statement emerged: "The answers we seek to change the world only come when we find the answers inside to change ourselves." Key moments of spectacle in the production had to be connected to the different characters finding answers within themselves. As an illustration, one of the main events involved the monkey warrior Hanuman soothing his despair by realizing that Rama and Sita's love is still in his heart. Somehow we had to show Hanuman ripping open his chest to find Rama and Sita inside. To depict this, we projected a heart logo onto a scrim, behind which the lights came up to reveal the actors playing Rama and Sita. My thrust statement gave me the confidence to justify the expense, time, and energy needed to create the image. I also began to use the thrust statement to identify other images which needed to be cut because they were off topic or redundant.

Theatrical Redundancy

My enhanced ability to clarify images by focusing on point of view was a direct outgrowth of developing a thrust statement. However, I still had a propensity for pageantry and visual storytelling that tended to expand the size of my productions. With *Sita Ram*, for example, in order to show how the consummation of Rama and Sita's love made a suffering, dark world bloom with color and bliss, I envisioned dozens of dancers with multiple costume changes. I encouraged my collaborators to write rich scores and choral arrangements, asked for expensive moving-light effects, video projections of supernatural images, and even compressed air cannons to catapult marigolds into the air. I didn't think I was just indulging a desire to delight the audience; I considered mine a valid attempt to communicate the story. I wanted to create a cascade of images to illustrate the depth of Rama and Sita's love. What I failed to realize was that this redundancy of images tended toward gilding the lily.

By questioning the duplicated images, I came to grips with the issues of redundancy. I knew that redundancy was a theatrical issue, but I didn't see how it undermined clarity and loosened the dramatic tension. I came to realize that if the sets, lights, costumes, sound, and actors were all conveying the same message, nothing will stand out; and therefore the thrust of the production would be lost.

Though final designs had already been submitted, I applied my new-found understanding of redundancy to the *Sita Ram* design revisions. Much to the relief of our production manager, I canceled all plans for video projections and condensed the lighting inventory. We also reduced the number of chorus members, dancers, and costume changes without in any way impoverishing the show.

Sita Ram Photo: Michael Brosilow.

I am amused that the show was called "Ramspell" and the "Hindu Hair" by several critics. If it made a vast and complex text more approachable, I am all for it. Some may argue that my efforts were borderline appropriation of the culture or a dumbing down of the text to pander to an American audience, but I whole-heartedly disagree. The fusion of performance forms was intended to communicate the story to an audience on multiple levels. That fusion was intended to tell the story more clearly. Using these different forms allowed me to convey the story and illustrate the core values of the text simultaneously. It was my intention to create recognizable markers for those familiar with the text and cultural elements, but at the same time to reinvent environments to be recognizable to a Western audience. If the Western audience only viewed the performance as a cultural exchange, and was not able to move beyond a simple exposure to the story, I would not be successful in fulfilling my storytelling goals.

Many new cultural challenges arose as we began to rehearse and word of the production spread. The fact that I strove to cast from a wide range of ethnic backgrounds actually alienated certain members of the South Asian community. Despite my intensive research into the text and the stamp of approval from Natya Dance Theatre, some still expressed that the text was in danger of being appropriated. Certain artistic choices, such as cutting out the character of Lakshmana, Rama's brother, a prominent character in the original text, or having Rama join Sita to walk through fire in the show's revisionist finale, were frowned upon by various members of the South Asian community. This example presented a cultural Catch-22 because politically correct westerners are offended that Sita alone has to walk through fire to prove her purity to Rama.

I then met with several members of the South Asian community, who had very specific and helpful suggestions. In response to these meetings, I added back into the final production earlier references to Rama's exile and to his father, Dasaratha, dying of grief. I remembered the words of the Brahmin priest in Chennai who reminded me that even within India there are numerous interpretations of the *Ramayana*, and not every member of the South Asian culture thinks the same way about it. In the end, my allegiance had to be to the message of the original text, as I interpreted it. The decisions I made in production had to be connected to maintaining the integrity of my interpretation of the text, as opposed to trying to please every person who took issue with single moments of my adaptation. Doing this while remaining respectful towards the thoughts and ideas of members of the South Asian community was, I felt, the soundest course of action. This required, however, a certain amount of proactive cultural diplomacy.

Krithika Rajagopalan was in an even more precarious position in having to defend the inventiveness of the show and its mission. She had to balance the show's objectives with her mission of promoting her own Hindu faith and the cultural awareness of her art form for both the South Asian community and the greater Western community.

Unexpectedly, another obstacle arose in casting Pranidhi Varshney as Sita. Pranidhi had spent most of her life growing up in a Michigan suburb of Detroit, but was born In New Delhi, India. She is a living example of the conflict between Eastern and Western culture. She is dealing with the dilemmas of wanting to excel in a career as a performer, while at the same time struggling with the cultural stigma a profession in the performing arts has among the South Asian community in the United States and abroad. When design choices involving Sita's costume did not have the traditional *dupatta* scarf covering her cleavage and naval, certain "aunties" who viewed the dress rehearsal made Hema Rajagopalan's phone ring of the hook with their concerns. Pranidhi did not personally know these women, but she took their complaints as a personal attack on her character as a performer, even though callers were merely reacting to what they saw as an offensive representation of Sita, the most revered symbol of female restraint and chastity in Hindu culture. In discussing this with Pranidhi, I was able to understand the extremely difficult position she found herself in as the actor depicting this deity. She knew full well that Hindus would see no difference between her as an actor and Sita the god, the character.

Anish Jethlamani, who played Ravana, while already an established actor in the Chicago community, experienced a different kind of pressure from other South Asian performers for participating in our intercultural production. He confided in me that his participation was frowned upon by some because we had chosen not to use an exclusively South Asian cast. But Jethlamani's passion and ability to bring truth to a very complex role as a professional actor won over many of those who originally doubted his intentions.

In the end, the production's success would have been impossible without the strong participation and support of the South Asian community. Lookingglass also formed a *Sita Ram* Community Committee made up of participants both in and out of the South Asian community. The Committee scheduled events and discussions that ran in tandem with the production and put certain difficult issues on the table in an effort to communicate the goals of the production. This was a positive step towards promoting long-term cultural ties for *Sita Ram* and Lookingglass both now and in the future.

Managing a Large Production

To direct my large-scale productions, I have always leaned on delegation to enable multiple tasks to take place during production rehearsals. I have used this technique in student theater, residencies, camps, and workshops. I assigned assistant directors or choreographers to work on different sections, while I oversaw and gave quick notes on each scene, and then worked with a smaller group of principals. I used this same technique with *Sita Ram*. The value of this approach is that I can get a great deal done within a short amount of time. The pitfall is that I generate a lot of material and thereby create redundancy. It takes time to remove this redundancy. Working in separate groups also can contribute to a disconnected feel to the production, if the different elements are not properly woven together. Without careful continual oversight, this separated production process favors undesired expansion of scale in accommodating everyone's work.

Working with two casts, one made up of twenty-four chorus members and the other with eight dancers from two separate companies, all with different rehearsal schedules, did in fact contribute to a disconnected quality in the final production. The different artistic contributors were all telling the same story, but sometimes telling it more than once. Others commented on this, and I agreed.

Conclusion

As much as I would love another life for *Sita Ram*, I am aware now that the logistics of mounting such a large production again mean that I may need to be satisfied with the Lookingglass production being the end of the theatrical journey for the show. If that is the case, there is much to celebrate. I am indebted to all of the collaborators who contributed so much time, energy, and funds to make this production happen. So many audience members have approached me to list their favorite moments, including members of the South Asian community expressing their appreciation that this cherished story is being told. I am proud that the many families who saw the production report that their children act out the stories and play the cast recording obsessively. To hear my own children telling their friends the stories from the epic confirms to me the lasting cyclical power of storytelling.

Witnessing the diverse audiences of Lookingglass, Chicago Children's Choir, Natya Dance Theatre, and Jai Uttal singing together in the show's *Kirtan*-inspired finale, *Om Shanti*, is for me a living example of a real way to build community. Cultural harmony through music: was this not the fulfillment of the mission of the Choir I was asked to reflect when first commissioned six years earlier? Perhaps our planet's conflicts are too complicated to be solved from our theater seats. But at least within the walls of our theater we can dream of the harmony and balance the world so desperately needs, and then carry that message outward. For whatever future productions I may be given an opportunity to lead, I hope to bring success by continuing to focus on my growth as a writer and director, striving always to pass on to my audiences the passion, drive, and sense of mission that I have felt for *Sita Ram*.

The *Ramayana* has much to teach a world that continues to fight wars over religion and cultural difference. We can choose to demonize and fear the other, see those different from ourselves as "the evil Ravana" and try to defeat them with might, aggression, shock, and awe. Or rather, like Rama, who compassionately helps Ravana rid himself of the corrupting power of greed, gluttonous desire, and ego, we can strive to look deeper and understand the "other" in an effort to recognize that there is more underneath us all that unites us, rather than divides us. *Sita Ram* is a story of "self." A story, as Hanuman states, of "our own inner battles coming to life, our own hidden demons, waiting to be tamed." What if we, like Hanuman, truly opened up our hearts? What would we find? Sita's love? Rama's wisdom and compassion? Our true selves? Each other? One's own personal spirituality? The very origins of the universe? My hope is, all of the above.

Bibliographic Afterword

The stories of the *Ramayana* have survived largely through oral, classical and folk traditions, all passed down through generations of South

Asian storytelling, dance, chanting, and puppetry. There are versions of the text translated from every region of India, each with slightly different twists to the story. Though I was saw many examples of these traditions, much of *Sita Ram* was primarily adapted from versions of the Ramayana stories translated and told to me by Jai Uttal and Krithika Rajagopalan. That said, I was inspired by several authors and translators in the creation of our production's book and lyrics.

For those new to the *Ramayana*, there are several versions of the original Sage Valmiki *Ramayana* that have been translated from Sanskrit into English. I highly recommend *Ramayana: A Journey* by Ranchor Prime (New York, Welcome Rain Publishers, 1999). Prime offers an abridged translation accompanied by illustrations of ancient paintings and a very clear glossary of terms and characters. Ramesh Menon's longer translation, *The Ramayana* (New York: North Point Press, 1999), includes larger sections of Sage Valmiki's text and captures much more of the poetry. William Buck's *Ramayana* (Berkeley: University of California Press, 1976) retells the story in the prose style of an adventure novel, a form much more recognizable to Western audiences. I also pulled stories from the sixteenth-century Old Hindi Version of the *Ramayana* told by Tulsidas. This text, also referred to as the *Ramcaritmanas*, captures much more of the devotional aspects of the story. The nineteenth-century English translation of this text by F. S. Growse, *Ramayana of Tulasidasa* (New Delhi: Motilal Banarsidass Publishers, 1978), is still very approachable despite its age.

A vast amount of critical theory has been written about the *Ramayana*. To begin to study the history and intercultural, socio-political significance of this text in India and the United States, I recommend starting with the works of two American *Ramayana* scholars I met during the production of *Sita Ram*, Philip Lutgendorf and Paula Richman. Philip Lutgendorf has written extensively on performances of the Tulsidas *Ramcaritmanas* in his book, *The Life of a Text* (Berkeley, University of California Press, 1991), as well as in his new book, *Hanuma's Tail: The Messages of a Divine Monkey* (Oxford University Press, 2006). Paula Richman has written two valuable texts, *Many Ramayanas* (Berkeley, University of California Press, 1991), which tracks traditional and alternative performances of the *Ramayana*; and *Questioning Ramayanas* (Berkeley, University of California Press, 2001), a book that revisits the teachings of the *Ramayana* in a challenging contemporary context.

To understand further the specific South Asian art forms that were utilized in the Lookingglass production of *Sita Ram*, I would suggest starting with Kalanidhi Narayanan's *Abhinaya* (Chennai, The Alliance Company, 1994), a well-organized manual of the codified facial expressions and gestures used in *Bharata Natyam* dance. *Inside the Drama-House: Rama Stories and Shadow Puppets in South India* by Stuart Blackburn (Berkeley: University of California Press, 1996) expands upon the *Ramayana* puppet performance we used in our production. To listen to authentic *kecak* chanting I would recommend the recording *Kecak from Bali* (produced by David Lewiston, 1990). I Wayan Dibia's book, *Kecak: the vocal chant of Bali* (Denpasar: Hartanto Art Books, 1996), offers much more extensive history of Ramayana monkey chanting than I was able to provide in this essay.

An audio recording produced in 2006 by the Chicago Children's Choir of the original music from the Lookingglass production of *Sita Ram* is still widely available. Finally, video and still images from the 2006 production of *Sita Ram* are featured in my directing portfolio online at www.youtube.com/watch?v=CvfCK_PrqAg.

Jillian Campana

Contemporary Acting in India: Authentic Exaggeration and Realism Unite

There is a performance space in the Bandra neighborhood of Mumbai called Pioneer Hall. I went there last week to discuss the possibility of leasing it for a production. I was met at the rickety gate by two dogs—one quite capable of scavenging for himself, even with only three legs, and the other, a mange-infested beast with a missing eye and a large, puss-oozing sore on its rear. The guard was asleep on the ground, but after waking him up I was able to convince him, in limited Marathi, that I was there to spend money. After speaking to four different men about the possibility of renting the space and being referred by each to the next with a head wriggle and a dismissive wave of the hand, I found Mr. Suarez, the manager of the building, who told me that a four-hour rental would cost 38,000 rupees (about 775 U. S. dollars). Mr. Suarez chose two of his many assistants to procure the listing of the lighting equipment not included in the rental fee, and when the mimeographed price list arrived twenty minutes later, we bargained on the price and shook hands on a flat 35,000 rupees. He offered me tea, and when we sat down he asked me when I needed to schedule the performance. When I told him I was looking for any two nights in January he wagged his fingers and abruptly took the tea cup out of my hands, "Oh no madam, this building has been sold. We are only here for the next three weeks. Then, it will become a restaurant."

The theater currently produced on the stages of urban India is a fusion of Indian classical and folk theater and Western realism. Most of the performances are heavily codified and hyperbolic. The acting styles in many of the plays are enlarged beyond truth and do not hold a mirror up to real life or seek to present people as they actually are. There are flashes of subtlety and moments of character dimensionality, but more often than not the acting on the stages of cities like Mumbai tends to be purposeful exaggeration, communicated through a well-orchestrated system of non-verbal languages, involving gesture, movement, dance, music, and makeup. In addition, many forms of Indian theater make use of tonality, resonance, distended vowels, and heavily punctuated bursts of sound to communicate emotion and emphasis in the dialogue. Stock plots and characters, gestures, and vocal inflations go back as far as the ancient Sanskrit dramas of the first century, and story plays such as the ones that recount the *Ramayana* are so familiar to Indian audiences in rural villages that children can often recite large portions of the plays out loud.

Against this backdrop of exaggerated performance aesthetics, there is a strong movement afoot to cultivate actors who allow their characters' behavior to develop out of their personal identification with the circumstances both given and imagined. But many artists who are becoming increasingly interested in performing in realistic productions are finding it difficult to disentangle their voices from oral embellishment and shed the many gesticulations so present in the ancient theater. With realistic actions butting up against the gestures, voices, and characters of classical and folk Indian drama, there is a sudden confluence of styles on the stage. This mixture is of course more noticeable in the major metropolitan areas of India, most notably the populous Mumbai, the world's third largest city and the most densely populated. The elements of traditional Indian performance have followed the mass influx of population that has moved from the country to the city and taken root on the professional stage, producing an interesting and sometimes successful mix of amplified exaggeration and contemporary realism.

There are many reasons why Indian artists and spectators have tended to gravitate toward non-realistic and melodramatic performances. To begin with, this tendency toward amplification can be accounted for in the very foundations of the art form in the subcontinent.

As in many ancient cultures, the connections performance has to ritual, religion, and moral guidance are strong. In essence, actors are honoring ancient stories and gods that are otherworldly. Size in these performances often equals reverence and thus, subtle characterization just does not fit the purpose. In addition, the use of gesture as a means to communicate emotions and language on the stage is rooted in the very beginnings of Indian theater and is still a principal component in the folk performances of today. In the Southern Indian theater form of *Kathakali*, which translates to "story-play," the plot is mimed by the actors who appear on stage. This example of modern folk art (*Kathakali* is approximately three hundred years old) relies on *hasta mudras* (hand gestures) and on eye, eyebrow, and other facial movements made by actors to convey characters ideas and feelings to the audience. For example, an actor portraying Kamsa the antihero in many *Kathakali* performances would have his eyeballs, eyelids, and eyebrows follow the movements of his hands (Venu, *The Language of Kathakali*, 2002), which would make use of single and mixed hand gestures as both suggestion and specific symbol.

A third reason non-realistic acting can be said to prevail in Indian theater can be located in the importance of *Rasa* and the corollary *Bhava* which can best be defined as "the external manifestation of a feeling by the appropriate symptoms" (Venu, 2002. p. 175). *Rasas* are said to be the aesthetic experience gained by the audience after witnessing a specific *Bhava* and they are a central element in India's oldest book detailing performance and dramaturgy, the *Natyasastra*, written between 400 BCE and 200 BC by the legendary Bharata and his students. And finally, another reason Realism is slow to take root in India has to do with the sheer number of people in the country; India is expected to overtake China as the most populated country in the world. Home to some of the largest slums in the world, seven major regional languages, and hundreds of dialects, India is itself a theatrical place. Today 1.6 billion human bodies are competing for attention, space, money, and food, and these individuals have helped to create a culture of drama present in everyday life where everything is bold, loud, and amplified. This culture of amplification has had a profound impact on everything in India, from the driving to the clothing, from birth to death and everything in between, including contemporary acting styles.

Indian performance has historically been a community-based form of religious worship, identity expression, and celebration. Its connections to ritual have been strong and ever-present from the start with the Sanskrit Dramas of the 400s BCE and continuing in the folk performances taking place today. In his essay, *Notes on the Invention of Tradition*, Rustom Bharucha explains the urban construct of Indian folk theater: "The clientele of 'folk drama' is not the 'folk,' but city people who need to be reminded of their 'roots and native places' from which they are irrevocably displaced" (p. 82). These performances honoring deities and their traditions have moved from torch-lit temples in villages to the auditoriums and stages of Mumbai and Delhi, but they are still a way by which the performer and spectator can make closer contact with gods. Undoubtedly, these reenactments, performed and witnessed on a regular basis, have factored significantly in the style of acting that is both appreciated and reassuring to actors and spectators alike, lending to very representational acting that focuses on providing morality and spirituality to guide spectators toward the divine rather than on being true to mortal or common life.

This connection of performance to worship is seen on a daily basis in the numerous Indian festivals and celebrations, each marked with its own performance of music, dance, and drama. Each Hindu temple has its own festival to celebrate the local deities or gods, and festivals large or small are connected to a specific story, which is more often than not retold through theatrical performances. The purpose of the *Dussera* Festival, for example, which takes place annually at all Hindu temples, is to teach and reflect upon the story of Ram and Sita. Principal to this festival is the play performance of the *Ramayana*, the ancient Sanskrit epic compiled between 400 BCE and 200 BCE. The *Ramayana* is one of India's most well-known pieces of literature, with the character of Rama now considered to be a symbol of Hindu piety. The story transcends faith and is told in Buddhist and Jain temples throughout Asia and into Muslim Indonesia. The Ram plays, or Ramlila (lila translating to "play"), pit good against evil by showcasing Rama as a hero in love with the chaste and uncorrupted Sita. Rama is heir to the throne, but his father's third wife convinced her husband that the throne belonged to her son. Rama and his wife Sita and brother Lakshman are forced into exile in the forest. When the evil king Ravana, who by the way has ten heads, kidnaps Sita and takes her to Lanka (modern day Sri Lanka), Rama enlists the help of Hanuman the monkey god and other noble monkey gods to return his beautiful and virtuous wife home. Of course Rama kills Ravana to win back his wife, and we see good triumph over evil when the demigod Rama becomes the rightful king and his dutiful wife the queen.

Rama plays are performed all over India during the *Dussera* Festival and again at the festival of *Ramanavami*, which marks the birthday of its hero in the summer. In addition to the importance of spreading the morality story, the play is marked with many layers. There is a formal narration that depicts each scene as it occurs, and audience members, who can number well over one thousand, generally carry their own copies of the narration with them and join the performers in the readings at times. Central to this classical play, and the many others like it is the idea that common people can be transformed into mythical figures. Like Rama, the common man of India can become a hero by doing good and refusing evil. In the Ramalila the actors, all men, who portray Hanuman the Monkey god and Ravana the evil king are handed their roles by their father, and before that the role is played by their grandfather. Roles for these actors are responsibilities that bring with them the opportunity to lead an entire community in the religious act of worship. The divine roles in the Ramayana must be played by innocent actors who have not yet been tarnished or jaded and who show no signs of hair on their faces (Rajendran, 2002), and typical performances end with audiences so overcome by their feelings that they often faint with devotion. Not only is the plot of the Ramalila overly dramatic and non-realistic, but the characters are hyperbolic in both their representative emotions and in their personality and actions. Hindus grow up seeing this performance alone several times each year. The story and characters are a part of their identity, as are the gestures and expressions.

Much of Indian theater is also rooted in an intricate system of codified gesture. The most extreme example comes from the South Indian tradition of *Kutiyattam*. The only surviving traditional Sanskrit theater in India, it is perhaps lesser known outside of India than its modern relative *Kathakali*, and like *Kathakali* it uses multiple levels and patterns of voice to communicate emotion and plot. In addition *Kutiyattam* employs the acting techniques outlined in the *Natyasastra*, which are based on the elaborate set of *mudras* developed as early as the fourth century BCE. Actors communicate verbally but also by making use of the thousands of hand gestures in forms which each convey a specific meaning. There is a classification so complex in this form and so scientific and physical in approach that novices have a difficult time forming even one *mudra* correctly. For instance, the mudra *pataka* (meaning flag) can convey about fifty different meanings from sun to peace when it is accompanied by appropriate body movements, face expression and movements with the eyeballs, eyelids, and eyebrows. In one scene from a *Kutiyattam* play depicting the Ram and Sita story, an actor must disconnect his right and left body sides in order to perform two different roles simultaneously (Venu, 2000, pg. 40). Because of the complexity of the gestures and movements, actors can begin their *Kutiyattam* training as young as six and work for many years to perfect their craft. Gesture may be the privileged medium of communication in *Kutiyattam*; gestures are also prevalent in many other Indian folk theater, including, but not limited to, the popular forms of *Nangiar Kotthu* and *Krishnanattam*, and, as mentioned earlier, connotative gestures still reside on the contemporary stage, most notably in plays depicting religious or folk stories, but also in some of the more realistic family dramas.

As mentioned previously, the *Natyasastra* identifies Rasa as the central element of drama. "Nothing proceeds on the stage without Rasa" (pg. 71). *Rasa* can be felt when appreciating any of the arts, but it is especially poignant in theater arts, where it can best be defined as the experience the spectator derives from witnessing the gestures, movements, makeup, and costuming for the characters. In other words, an appropriate *Rasa* can be aroused in the audience through the actor's presentation of an external manifestation meant to express an emotion. Called *Bhavas*, these external manifestations signaling specific feelings are used in many forms of Indian theater. Bharata identified eight *Rasas*: *shringara* (the erotic); *hasya* (the comic); *karuna* (the pathetic); *raudra* (the furious); *rira* (the heroic); *bhayanaka* (the terrible); *bibhatsa* (the odious); and *adbhuta* (the marvelous). A ninth *Rasa* was added later by one of his pupils—*shanta* (the quiescent). Thus when a performer presents a *Bhava*, the audience feels the corresponding *Rasa* (Rajendran, 2002. pg. 17). Not only do we again see the importance of gesture with the performance of the *Bhavas* and the feeling of the *Rasa*, but mostly profoundly perhaps this concept signals a different type of relationship between audience and performer. In realistic theater, the audience is meant to feel that they are witnessing something private—whereas in Indian theater, though there may be a fourth wall, the actors and audience work and commune together. Though plays often intend to manipulate the spectator's emotions in realism, the intended result is not nearly as specific as it is in traditional Indian theater where all audience members are literally told how to respond emotionally through showcasing of the specific *Bhavas*.

A brief look at the *Times of India* newspaper reveals the drama in everyday life: Catholic Nun Raped, Dragged Naked through Streets; Tiger Kills Family of Three outside Bangalore; Man with Rabies Escapes Hospital. It is virtually impossible to escape drama in India. From the city to the country, life is dramatic, and this holds true for everyone here regardless of station in life—from the blinded ox pulling a car through the overcrowded and narrow street who contends with motorcycles holding families of five, busses, cars, rickshaws, and other livestock to the shoe-walla who resides on a small block of broken down bricks outside the posh flat for someone to come outside and bargain to have his shoes resoled for ten rupees instead of fifteen. Lack of basic necessities certainly adds to the drama of the street, and the growing population of the cities compounds the spectacle. The Population Foundation of India estimates that roughly one sixth of the world's population is currently living in India, and this number of people translates to a lack of space. With little or no privacy, emotions, problems, and personal dramas often become public. The cities are so crowded that the sounds swell to deafening proportions and in many neighborhoods one must yell and gesticulate aggressively in order to be understood. Even securing a theater space to perform a play in takes a great amount of time, emotional energy, and aggression. And so what might be categorized in the West as exaggerated non-realism can be for this country and her performers and spectators, Truth, both on and off the stage.

The verbal communication off the stage is often accompanied by hand, body, and head signals in order to punctuate or even just to communicate. Like the *mudras* of *Kathakali* and *Kutiyattam*, there are specific gestures to communicate numerous words and there is the infamous head wiggle that no one who has been to India can forget. Perched on top of the shoulders, buoyant and graceful, as if it were suspended by an invisible thread, the head simply wiggles left to right very rapidly almost like it is being manipulated by a puppeteer. This commonly used head movement has numerous meanings and connotations depending on the perceived need or relationship between the parties involved and the accompanying facial expression and the eye movements. It can mean anything from "yes" to "no" to "go away." These gestures, which play a considerable role in everyday life, also show up on the stages of realistic plays. If as Uta Hagen said in *A Challenge for the Actor*, "any tendency to mark, indicate, show, illustrate, or externally react to what we are hearing is the mark of someone not really listening" (pg. 115), then the complicated codified gestures of classical Indian theater must disappear from the realistic stage production. Certainly however there are times when gesture can work in Realism. Often depending on the play, the setting, and the size, gesture can lend a dramatic reality to the work, but it does seem more often than not in India that the exaggerated gestures present in traditional performances make their way even into realistic plays.

Though there are, and have been for years, Indian theater practitioners who have understood and cultivated realistic acting, there has not been a demand for or a subsequent focus on realistic acting in the country. In general because performance is so embedded in Indian culture there has been a dearth of acting classes and programs in higher education. Children grow up learning and practicing music and dance and participating in local play productions honoring temple gods and famous stories, but this training is done either informally or ends before the age of seventeen, when such classes give way to more practical considerations. Recently, though, there have emerged a few actor-training programs that view realistic acting as the lynchpin of the actor's training and that seek to utilize the actor's personal experiences and self as the gateway to character development. The focus of this movement is the employment of the tenets of the Stanislavski system that has been the center of much of Western acting for years.

This philosophy and subsequent approach has only recently become mainstream in India, and there has emerged a strong group of personalities here who are striving to offer artists and audiences a new acting style that seeks to capture the psychological realism of the West. With the current urban trend of bringing realistic acting to the fore, the professional theater scene is changing with the emergence of schools like Whistling Woods and the Academy of Theatre Arts at the University of Mumbai and with theater groups like Motley and Cinematograph. These groups are producing not only a new crop of young and talented actors well versed in the techniques of realistic acting, but they are also cultivating an appreciation of both realism and realism fused with traditional Indian theater in the theater patron. With some actors and directors rebelling against the established norms of gesture-based Indian acting styles, actors' movements are becoming more natural, and stock characterizations are fading. Many successful plays are fusing elements of traditional Indian theater with Western realism, and this is offering spontaneous, dimensional characters capable of feeling and expressing a multitude of emotions simultaneously to audiences.

Whistling Woods International Film and Media Institute is the first program in India designed to train actors solely in the traditions of realism. Though the National School of Drama (NSD) remains India's first and more known conservatory program, it is Whistling Woods that is at the forefront of promoting realism in acting. Started in 2005 by Mukesh Arts Limited CEO Subhash Ghai, the acting program is run by NSD graduate Naseerdduin Shah, who is one of the more famous actors in India and is certainly one of the most well known theater personalities in the country. Western audiences might remember him for his portrayal of the bride's father in Mira Nair's 2001 film *Monsoon Wedding*, but he is also known for his theater acting and directing. He is the artistic director of the theater company Motley which he started in 1977 with Benjamin Gilani and Tom Alter with the staging of Beckett's *Waiting for Godot* in Mumbai. Shah has studied with Peter Brook, made more than fifty films, and won numerous awards for his work including the National Film Award for Best Actor and Filmfare's best actor award. In 2005, frustrated with seeing only inflated, stock characters in both theater and film, he took on the direction of the acting department at Whistling Woods with the goal of training actors in the theatrical techniques of the Stanislavski system.

Grounded in the belief that acting in India is in dire need of a makeover, this conservatory is located in Film City, a gated parcel of land home to most of the Mumbai film studios. Situated alongside the numerous stock settings for the Hindi film industry known as Bollywood, Whistling Woods trains actors in Realistic acting in an effort to cultivate actors and audiences who appreciate the more internally nuanced aspects of psychological realism. Though it is only a two-year program, the acting classes here run for five to seven hours a day, six days a week. Additionally there are early morning classes in dance, yoga, and voice training, and rehearsals for various plays and short student films, after dark. A typical acting class at Whistling Woods focuses on the theories of the Western acting guru Constantin Stanislavski and the exercises and ideas created by his American students, Lee Strasberg, Harold Clurman, and Stella Adler. The goal above all is to produce truthfulness in performance akin to the realities of life. Imagination is taught to be the most important tool for the actor and the idea of the "magic if" is the key to entering into the actions of the characters. Objectives and obstacles are employed and tactics are explored. Students work with objects first before moving onto working with other actors, and emphasis is placed on the specificity of relationships and intentions. This may seem simple, but for most of the students these are new concepts and vocabulary terms that disregard much of the traditional techniques of Indian theater.

For example, at Whistling Woods the concept, "as if" is explored in depth in exercises that take actors from themselves slowly in an effort to first nurture the ability to engage in private moments specifically. Once students have grown comfortable in this arena, they then begin to work outside of their own selves to develop characters distinct and different from their real selves. They engage in action exercises and in scenes that make use of Uta Hagen's six essential questions: Who am I? What are the circumstances? What are my relationships? What do I want? What is my obstacle? What do I do to get what I want? (Hagen, p. 134). The idea of answering questions like these is new to many of pupils who find them to be contradictory to the nature of portraying a character. For the representational style of acting in traditional Indian theater such questions could be considered irreverent. Imagine an actor groomed for years to play Hanuman the monkey god in the *Ramayana* approaching his role by asking, "Now how would I behave if I were a monkey god?" Not only would this approach be considered disrespectful and possibly blasphemous, but unlike a realistic approach where actors seek to live through the characters, the traditional Indian actor captures the character physically and vocally and any transference to character comes about through the external.

The Academy of Theatre Arts at the University of Mumbai, which opened in 2003, is a graduate program offering an MA degree. Though it is much broader in scope than Whistling Woods, it is important to note that it teaches realistic acting alongside classical Indian drama, privileging both and by doing so making a statement of things to come. All graduate students are trained in the Stanislavski System and once a year a contemporary and realistic play is mounted. Started in 2003 under the direction of Marathi theater artist Waman Kendre, another NSD graduate, the program believes the actors must be flexible and conversant in all areas of theater and styles of acting. By offering the students an opportunity to study the work of Stanislavski, the faculty has found that the acting work in classical Indian theater also improves. Milind Inamdar teaches the modern and contemporary Western acting class and focuses his students on lending a lifelike air to their stage acting by having actors analyze the text and characters in depth to understand the super-objective of the characters. "The super-objective," he says, "will provide the context and the motivation for all actions." The terms super-objective and motivation, so widely used in basic acting and theater classes in the West, are new concepts for the Indian actor, and students at first have a hard time grasping these concepts which segregate wants and suppose that individual needs drive behavior. In order to combat this much time is spent discussing Western philosophy and the techniques of realistic acting prior to any practical work. Students spend much time improvising and performing their selves in different situations before even dealing with character or text.

The Prithvi Theatre in Mumbai is leading the country in bringing realism to the stage. The theater was conceived by the late actor Prithviraj Kapoor, who did not have a permanent space for his acting troupe, but rather traveled across India to bring quality theater to the people. Prithviraj's son, Shashi Kapoor, dreamt of a permanent space for this group of actors that could be a home to all types of theater. Shashi bought a plot of land in Juhu, and in 1978 the Prithvi Theatre opened its doors to the general public with theater management being conducted by his wife, Jennifer Kendal. In 1990 their daughter, Sanjna Kapoor, took over as executive director of the theater and sought to continue her parents' and grandfather's vision of providing excellent, experimental theater at a low cost to both theater companies and the public spectator. One of the most well-known theaters in India, the Prithvi has always focused on and supported what they call Experimental Theatre, which includes plays written, directed, and acted in styles outside of the traditionally performed classical and folk plays which had owned the stages of India for so many years. Many of the plays that are staged at the Prithvi fall under the category of realistic drama, also considered experimental in India today. The Prithvi hosts several annual festivals that showcase the best new plays from all over India, and acting classes are taught at the theater on a regular basis. This theater has provided Mumbaikers and professional artists from all over India a platform to try out unique and sometimes innovative ways of staging and performing. There is no permanent company of actors; rather theater companies of repute can apply to the Prithvi for show dates. Tickets are sold by the Prithvi, so that for 100 rupees (about $2.25 US) theater patrons can see their favorite personalities experiment with new techniques, roles, and staging devices.

Of course the work of these institutions is only making a small dent in contemporary theater. Many performances seeking to capture verisimilitude are still mired in the hallmarks of non-realism: magnified and exaggerated physicality, melodramatic vocal choices, and over-the-top, demonstrated emotions. Add to this the fact that the reality of India is a far cry from the reality of the West. Born out of the backlash of Bollywood *masala* movies and with a foundation of stylized and gesture-based performance, Indian realism is hyper-responsive. In the West we might call it exaggeration, but for this country and her performers and spectators, the realism offered on stage, and that holds on to elements of folk and classical theater, is true to life. And so with the solid traditions of the past merging with the more Western notions of realistic acting some interesting work is emerging, successful to various degrees, but interesting nonetheless and in the forefront of a new type of Indian theater.

In a recent acting workshop in Mumbai a prominent theater director explained to students that George Bernard Shaw's plays offered them the best example of realism and that contemporary plays touting "realism" are actually often disguised farce. Farce is highly popular in India, and I have heard many theatergoers hold up farcical plays as excellent examples of reality. The improbable situations and automatic behavior in farce is not problematic for audiences seeking a glimpse into the world as it actually is. There are also productions written as realistic dramas that suffer precisely because hyperbolic elements are mixed with actors seeking to present realistic characters and feelings. One such production was the *Marathi* adaptation of *Twelve Angry Men* performed at the University of Mumbai last year. This production failed to reconcile these vastly different styles in many ways. First, the production made use of tableaus in order to convey relationships. Now, tableaus can work. But here it was also the code behind the gesture that was non-specific but rather melodramatically one-dimensional. After each conflict was presented in the play, a new tableau was formed, I assume to showcase the relationships. What this production failed to remember however is that with solid realistic acting, relationships need no clarification. Audiences do not need to be told what is going on through narration or gesture or pose. They know what is going on and appreciate the work that it might take to unravel a character's dimensionality and relationships.

On the other hand, theatricality and the aliveness that comes with largesse and exaggeration is never dull, and though not all practitioners are getting it right this time around, they are exploring in ways that have not yet been examined in India. A recent production of Anouilh's *Antigone*, performed by the theater company Motley, and adapted and directed by the renowned director Satyadev Dubey, is clearly set in India and asks the audience to see Antigone as a Muslim woman being punished for her beliefs. Creon is played by Naseeruddin Shah and Antigone by Shah's real life wife, Ratna Pathak Shah; though she is nowhere near young, she does a tremendous job of portraying the single-minded determination of the youthful Antigone. Though the scope of the play is large and the issues tragic in nature, the production offers the audience a fine example of realistic acting. Firstly, rather than focusing on the things the characters represent, the play focuses on the characters themselves. The Sophoclean conflict is exposed and the typical roles of protagonist and villain disappear and are replaced by dimensional beings. Creon is torn apart by his ideals, and we see this struggle early on so that in the end we are unsure who was right and who was wrong. There are in this play also elements consistent with traditional Indian theater, including musical accompaniment, tableaus, and costumes designed to connote status, relationships and religion. This play has performed over sixty times in the past two years, always to a packed house and has given rise to many subsequent productions that have also sought to ride the rails between Western and Eastern aesthetics.

Another very successful production that beautifully merged these two vastly different approaches was Rajat Kapoor's *Hamlet, the clown prince*, in which the play Hamlet is performed by seven clowns. This play might be described as constructivist to the hilt, but the acting in the production owes much of its success to the ability of the actors to portray believable, truthful emotions. Spoken half in gibberish and half in English, the actors weave in and out of portraying natural emotions and regularly break the ubiquitous fourth wall. And though there is much spectacle in the play in the sense that lighting, sound, and costumes are intended to be quite noticeable and over-the-top, the acting remains honest and offers a true sense of situation, character, and need. Atul Kumar, who plays Hamlet, ridicules the audience over and over and when gearing up for his famous speech asks the front row to ponder the options of choice when he says, "to smoke or not smoke . . . to eat or not eat . . . to stay for the second act, or to go . . . ?" But when he finally settles the spectators down and offers them Shakespeare's words, "To be or not to be . . . ," the audience is exhausted enough from the laughter and nonsense language thrown at them to really watch and listen to a young man in the throes of despair. The clown costume disappears and the heavy makeup slides away to reveal such vulnerability in the character that we understand life better.

Though clowning is highly physical and is often built upon non-realistic situations and problems, the actors in this production worked as an ensemble with Rajat Kapoor to create their clown, out of their own personalities. They focused on their personal anxieties and fears and from there explored objects and situations to allow the clown to emerge naturally from the exploratory circumstances and their own demons. And the success of this fusion of realism and hyperbole does not exclude performances outside of the subcontinent. The Oregon Shakespeare Festival's

2008 production of *The Clay Cart*, directed by Bill Rauch in his inaugural season as the company's artistic director, was a good example of an American theater production that successfully embraced elements of both traditional Indian theater arts including gesture and vocal exaggeration, *mudras*, and stock characters and Western realism. This production, one of Ashland's best last year, was able to hold onto the subtlety of realism. Sure, there was a big song and dance number, but the live musical accompaniment and the dramatic and often sculpted movements by the actors only served to add clarity and depth to the relationships presented on stage. The actors seemed to claim ownership over their physical and vocal choices, quite the opposite from the regional acting styles in India that impart the feeling of actors being guided through the plays by some mystical force, larger and greater than any one man.

Being an American living in Mumbai, I am grateful for the theatricality of Indian theater. The purposeful exaggeration of characters' personalities, emotions, and abilities makes for a highly interesting performance. And so though many productions seeking to offer reality are short-sighted, they are certainly not dull. The fact that most productions seeking to achieve a realistic feel or to adequately blend styles to strike the proper balance may not be successful in their endeavors, the success is incidental. What is far more interesting is the idea that Indian theater is interested in considering new approaches to acting and also in merging vastly different approaches and styles. The United States has of course experimented with fusion for years in all areas of art, but India has been slower on the uptake. Who can blame them? With claim to some of the oldest surviving theater art forms, scripts, and dramaturgy, there is a strong belief that traditional and classical theater should be preserved. The purposeful exaggeration of characters' personalities, emotions, and abilities certainly makes for a highly theatrical performance, but, at the same time, it is electrifying to see actors deepening their work by also examining their characters' wants and behaviors. It is an exciting time for Indian theater practitioners and patrons. I am glad to be here and look forward to seeing what happens next on the Indian stage.

References

Rustom Bharucha. Notes on the Invention of Tradition, in The Twentieth Century Performance Reader (ed) Michael Huxley and Noel Witts. Routledge, 1996.

Rosalyn D'Mello. Budget Theatre in TimeOut Mumbai. Volume 5, Issue 5, 2008.

Manomohan Ghosh and Manisha Granthalaya (trans). *The Natyasastra of Bharata Muni*. Calcutta, 1951.

Uta Hagen, *A Challenge for the Actor*. Scribner, 1991.

Farley P. Richmond, Darius L. Swann, and Phillip B.Zarelli. *Indian Theatre: traditions of Performance* Motilal Banarsidas Publishers, 1993.

Farley Richmond, "India," in *The Cambridge Guide to Asian Theatre*, ed. James R. Brandon. Cambridge University Press, 1993.

Jerry Pinto. "The Powerhouse," in *Verve*, July 2007.

H.S. Shiva Prakash. *Traditional Theatres*. Wisdom Tree Academic, 2007.

Ravi Prakash (ed.). *Ramayana of Valmiki: Sanskrit Text and English Translation*. (English translation according to M. N. Dutt, introduction by Dr. Ramashraya Sharma, 4–volume set) Parimal Publications: Delhi, 1998.

C. Rajendran. Performance According to Natyasatra" in Living Traditions of Natyasastra. New Bharatiya Book Corporation, 2002.

Nandini Ramnath. An Interview with Naseeruddin Shah" in TimeOut Mumbai. Volume 5 issue 2, 2008.

Richard Schechner. Performance Studies, an introduction. Routledge, 2002.

G. Venu. *Into the World of Kutiyattam*. Natana Kairali Research and Performing Center for Traditional Arts. 2002.

G. Venu. The Language of Kathakali. Natana Kairali Research and Performing Center for Traditional Arts. 2000.

Richard Waterstone. *India: the cultural companion*. Duncan Baird Publishers, 1995.

Emily Mann

A Seagull in the Hamptons

By the time I wrote *A Seagull in the Hamptons* I already had a forty-year relationship with Anton Chekhov, having read and memorized the astonishing part of Nina in *The Seagull* when I was a student in high school. I continued to study his plays throughout my life, but it wasn't until I was almost forty that I felt ready to direct one of Chekhov's great plays. Adapted by Lanford Wilson, my production of *The Three Sisters* played to standing-room-only audiences at McCarter Theatre in 1991, and it was that production that cemented my love for Chekhov as a director and my admiration for him as a writer. In 2000, I directed and wrote my own adaptation of *The Cherry Orchard*. I wanted to understand writer to writer just how he melded comedy and drama, just how he captured the way people truly speak and behave, just how he constructed character and events. I felt in constant conversation with him as I worked on the play. In 2003, I adapted and directed *Uncle Vanya*. And last year, I returned to the play that had started my love affair with Chekhov. After faithfully adapting two of his plays and directing three, I wrote a free adaptation of *The Seagull*, called *A Seagull in the Hamptons*, set in the present day in Quogue, New York. I sensed him on my shoulder as I wrote, and the writing felt effortless.

Though I have now directed all four of the plays considered to be Chekhov's master works and adapted three of them, I know I cannot (nor, perhaps more accurately, will not want to) ever stay away from him for long. I always seem to return to Chekhov's plays because I find with him, as with a few other great writers, there is always something I missed, some richness of observation that I didn't see because I was either too young to understand it the first time around or had not yet experienced it. I try to reread Chekhov, certain plays of Shakespeare, *Anna Karenina*, and other great literary works every few years because each time they are completely new experiences, perhaps because each time, inevitably, I bring more of my life to them. For example, just a few years ago, I reread *Anna Karenina* to prepare for directing Nilo Cruz's brilliant play, *Anna in the Tropics*. I remembered reading the book in college and being swept away by the passionate love affair between Anna and Vronsky. This time through, however, I found myself practically skimming through the love affair chapters to read about the marriage of Levin and Kitty. I hardly remembered those two characters from my college reading! Their relationship was riveting to me in middle age, just as Tolstoy's descriptions of the serfs and the fields spoke volumes to me now and were meaningless to me when I was a sophomore in college. Speaking with a Russian friend of mine who is in her eighties about my experience she told me the same thing had happened to her. "Wait until you're eighty!" she exclaimed. "I finally understand the book." It is something I look forward to experiencing.

For many years, both as a writer and a director, I have been working on how to make historical material or works of art from the past speak evocatively to a present-day audience who may or may not have any familiarity with the world where the events took place or the world in which the work of art is ostensibly set. It is a crucial hurdle to overcome and is much more complex than simply costuming Shakespeare in contemporary dress or setting *The Cherry Orchard* on a ranch in Texas. (Yes, this has been done . . .) As my colleague, the playwright Steven Dietz, said on reading my play, *Mrs. Packard*, which is set in nineteenth-century Illinois, "Of course we writers write 'historical plays' because it is the best way to write about the present day." Ditto for directing a play set in the past.

I had been thinking for some time about directing and adapting *The Seagull* partly because the people in *The Seagull* and the concerns of *The Seagull* had haunted me for decades, but also because it now seemed thoroughly contemporary and essentially relevant to me and my personal life. I felt I actually knew all these people. They were no longer "them"; they were "me"; they were "us." These were the friends, employees and family of a theater person not unlike me or people I know. I felt I knew her and her lover, the writer, all too well. I understood and personally connected to the leading lady struggling with balancing her career, her love affair, and bringing up her son, and I could finally forgive her failings. I felt great sympathy and love for her brother, a lonely, funny, retired lawyer who dreamed of having lived a different life. In short, I felt I now knew and understood the adults as well as I had always known and understood the children betrayed by them.

I wasn't quite sure how to begin working on a new production until a few summers ago when I spent time in a beautiful house on the beach in the Hamptons. I began hearing and picturing scenes from *The Seagull*, both in the house and on the beach. This Long Island estate struck me as having many resonances with the country estate Chekhov used to set *The Seagull*. The Hamptons is a place where artists—successful artists—used to go to work and vacation. And though now it is overrun by moguls and hedge fund operators, it is still a place where young and aspiring artists visit, hoping to meet up with more successful artists still living there. The constellation of characters in *The Seagull* set in Russia a century ago could easily be found on the estate I was visiting in Quogue, New York today—the actress and her younger lover, a writer; her son, an aspiring playwright; her brother, a retired lawyer; her servants and employees; their daughter; the daughter's local boyfriend; and a local doctor, who is a family friend and most likely, was once the actress's lover.

I knew the characters transcended time and place, but as I delved deeper, I found so, too, did the themes. Chekhov is the ultimate humanist. Perhaps the cultural and historical details change, but I see versions of these characters and their dilemmas around me every day at my own theater. I have witnessed the exploitation of the young, fragile artists by the successful older artists; the use of younger artists by older artists to refresh themselves artistically; the essentially depressive character of creativity, sometimes leading to suicide and self-destruction; the centrality of love and sexuality to all art; and the strength of character of the artist who will not give up working in the face of difficult circumstances and wracking self-doubt.

Like Chekhov, I revel in the comedy inherent in observing these miserable and all too human dilemmas. Arkadina, the central character, whom I call Maria in this new adaptation, continues to work, as she struggles with an actress's worst nightmare—aging past her prime. She is vain, foolish, self-indulgent, and self-absorbed, but no fool, and she is still working hard while everyone else stumbles around her. Though the people who surround her live off of her, they criticize her harshly (often rightly so)—but what do they do for themselves? Some of them can't get themselves up in the morning. They complain and wish they had more money. They whine about not being creative, and fantasize that when they retire they will have time to be artists, too. Maria's young lover who is experiencing a crippling writer's block, asks her to let him have an affair with Nina, her son's girlfriend, because "it's just what I need right now." Each person falls in love with the person who does not love him or her back, and the most decent people on the stage are often the ones least gifted with beauty, talent, or even brains. In our society today, just like in Chekhov's, people worship celebrity. People want to be close to it, or live it, and are too often destroyed by it.

It became my mission to bring Chekhov's people and their story to this country and make them as real to an American audience in the twenty-first century as Chekhov had made them for Russians in the nineteenth.

One day in Quogue, after visualizing the first act of the play from the deck overlooking the beach, I called my colleague and friend, the great set designer Eugene Lee, and asked him if he could put a beach onstage for me in the Berlind Theater at the McCarter, as I wanted to set *The Seagull* in the Hamptons and needed it to take place on sand—truly on a beach. He said of course he could do that, but I might be risking the ire of the theater staff since there would be sand all over the theater and it would take at least eighteen tons of sand to accomplish what I wanted! But I knew it was right. I called the production manager and he agreed to do it, so I began in earnest. I allowed myself to hear fully the characters speaking in present day American idiom, just as Chekhov had heard his characters in their present-day idiom. I could see them on the beach, staring out at the ocean, sticking their toes in the sand, drinking white wine as the sun set. One night, as the moon rose, I imagined Treplev's (Alex's) play performed, and I could hear the party music wafting down the beach. I saw it and heard it and realized I was already writing it. And since I had written two very faithful Chekhov adaptations before, going over the language word for word with Ellen Chances, a Chekhov scholar at Princeton University, bilingual in Russian and English, I felt Chekhov would trust me to make this leap.

The following summer, I took myself away for four weeks with an old literal translation in the public domain and wrote a draft of it. When I came home, I held my breath and gave the play to Professor Chances to read. She called me back a day later and said it was not only contemporary and moving and very funny, but the most accurate

Brian Murray and Maria Tucci in McCarter Theatre's production of *A Seagull in the Hamptons*, written and directed by Emily Mann. Photo: T. Charles Erickson.

and faithful adaptation of *The Seagull* that she had read in English. What an exhale! She recognized my intention. It was alive. It was funny. It was moving. It was real for us here and now. And it was absolutely Chekhov.

Let me show you the first few pages of my adaptation followed by a few pages of a literal translation from the Russian to show you the choices I made as a writer and director, though to get the full impact of it, I hope you will read the play in its entirety. This is the beginning:

ACT ONE

MARIA'S HOUSE IN QUOGUE. A MAKE-SHIFT THEATER ON THE BEACH. CHAIRS.

MILLY AND HAROLD ENTERING:

HAROLD

Maybe black just isn't your color.

MILLY

What? What are you talking about?

HAROLD

Well . . . why do you always wear black? It's summer for Chrissake!

MILLY

I'm in mourning . . . for my life. I'm unhappy, Harold.

HAROLD

Oh, come *on*! *You're* unhappy? Why? You live on a gorgeous estate! On the beach! Your parents make a great living working here! You—

MILLY

Will you stop? It's not *about* money! With you, everything's always about money. What's wrong with you?

HAROLD

Well, as they say, rich or poor it's good to have money!

MILLY

I never thought that joke was funny.

HAROLD

Look—do you hear me complaining? I live with my . . . crazy mother, two bratty sisters and my pathetic little brother in a three-bedroom walk-up in town . . .

MILLY

I know that, Harold.

HAROLD

I made $21,550 last year *before taxes*. My mother won't work; we can't afford health insurance; my sister needs—

MILLY

When is the play going to start?

HAROLD

I don't know. Oh, God . . . can you imagine what it must feel like to be them? He writes a play —she stars in it—they both get swept away by each other's genius. I mean, really . . . Some people are just born with it all—looks, talent, money . . . PLUS they're madly in love with each other.

MILLY

Don't make me sick.

HAROLD

I know. Who wants to marry a man who can't afford his own funeral?

MILLY

Look!—Harold! I'm well . . . touched by your affection; I just can't return it, okay? (pause) Cigarette?

HAROLD

No, thanks.

MILLY

You know . . . I would gladly be homeless? Begging on the street . . . if I was—if only I was . . . well . . . if only the right person would just—oh, God, never mind. You could never understand.

ENTER ALEX AND HIS UNCLE, NICHOLAS, CONVERSING.

ALEX

You should live in the City, Uncle Nick, and stop complaining about the country all the time.

NICHOLAS

I know!

ALEX

(SEEING MILLY AND HAROLD) What are you two doing here? I told you I'd call you when the play was going to start.

MILLY

Okay.

NICHOLAS

TO MILLY: Milly, I really wish you'd tell your father to do something about that dog. His barking keeps me up at night.

MILLY

I don't speak to my father. I can't stand him. So don't ask me. (TO HAROLD) Come on, Harold.

HAROLD

Don't forget to let us know when the play starts!

THEY EXIT.

NICHOLAS

Good God! Look at me! All dressed up with no place to go!

ALEX

Get a grip, Uncle Nick.

HE SHOVES ON HIS SUNGLASSES

NICHOLAS

I finally got to sleep last night and woke up at 10:30 this morning feeling like my brains were stuck to my skull. I thought sea air was supposed to be good for you, but my bowels are made of cement, I have this raging headache, and my mouth feels like a bog. Goddammit! That dog is going to howl all night again tonight, and tomorrow night, and the night after that—and I won't get a wink of sleep—ever! . . . Why do I come out here? Why do I even bother trying to have a nice time? Every year it's the same thing. I arrive and before the end of the first day—the very first day—I wish I'd never come! And for some incomprehensible reason, I have decided to retire! Out here! Can you believe it? What could have possessed me to do that? Retirement's a mug's game, Alex. Old people should never be born.

ALEX

Uh . . . Okay . . . What do you think of my stage? It's Peter Brook's empty space.

NICHOLAS

Who?

Now compare this to a standard, literal translation of the play:

Act I

The scene is laid in the park on SORIN'S estate. A broad avenue of trees leads away from the audience toward a lake, which lies lost in the depths of the park. The avenue is obstructed by a rough stage, temporarily erected for the performance of amateur theatricals, and which screens the lake from view. There is a dense growth of bushes to the left and right of the stage. A few chairs and a little table are placed in front of the stage. The sun has just set. JACOB and some other workmen are heard hammering and coughing on the stage behind the lowered curtain. MASHA and MEDVIEDENKO come in from the left, returning from a walk.

MEDVIEDENKO. Why do you always wear mourning?

MASHA. I dress in black to match my life. I am unhappy.

MEDVIEDENKO. Why should you be unhappy? [Thinking it over] I don't understand it. You are healthy, and though your father is not rich, he has a good competency. My life is far harder than yours. I only have twenty-three rubles a month to live on, but I don't wear mourning. [They sit down].

MASHA. Happiness does not depend on riches; poor men are often happy.

MEDVIEDENKO. In theory, yes, but not in reality. Take my case, for instance; my mother, my two sisters, my little brother and I must all live somehow on my salary of twenty-three rubles a month. We have to eat and drink, I take it. You wouldn't have us go without tea and sugar, would you? Or tobacco? Answer me that, if you can.

MASHA. [Looking in the direction of the stage] The play will soon begin.

MEDVIEDENKO. Yes, Nina Zarietchnaya is going to act in Treplieff's play. They love one another, and their two souls will unite tonight in the effort to interpret the same idea by different means. There is no ground on which your soul and mine can meet. I love you. Too restless and sad to stay at home, I tramp here every day,

269

six miles and back, to be met only by your indifference. I am poor, my family is large, you can have no inducement to marry a man who cannot even find sufficient food for his own mouth.

MASHA. It is not that. [She takes snuff] I am touched by your affection, but I cannot return it, that is all. [She offers him the snuffbox] Will you take some?

MEDVIEDENKO. No, thank you. [A pause.]

MASHA. The air is sultry; a storm is brewing for tonight. You do nothing but moralize or else talk about money. To you, poverty is the greatest misfortune that can befall a man, but I think it is a thousand times easier to go begging in rags than to—You wouldn't understand that, though.

SORIN, leaning on a cane, and TREPLIEFF come in.

SORIN. For some reason, my boy, country life doesn't suit me, and I am sure I shall never get used to it. Last night I went to bed at ten and woke at nine this morning, feeling as if, from oversleep, my brain had stuck to my skull. [Laughing] And yet I accidentally dropped off to sleep again after dinner, and feel utterly done up at this moment. It is like a nightmare.

TREPLIEFF. There is no doubt that you should live in town. [He catches sight of MASHA and MEDVIEDENKO.] You shall be called when the play begins, my friends, but you must not stay here now. Go away, please.

SORIN. Miss Masha, will you kindly ask your father to leave the dog unchained? It howled so last night that my sister was unable to sleep.

MASHA. You must speak to my father yourself. Please excuse me; I can't do so. [To MEDVIEDENKO] Come, let us go.

MEDVIEDENKO. You will let us know when the play begins?

MASHA and MEDVIEDENKO go out.

SORIN. I foresee that that dog is going to howl all night again. It is always this way in the country; I have never been able to live as I like here. I come down for a month's holiday, to rest and all, and am plagued so by their nonsense that I long to escape after the first day. [Laughing] I have always been glad to get away from this place, but I have been retired now, and this was the only place I had to come to. Willy-nilly, one must live somewhere.

JACOB. [To TREPLIEFF] We are going to take a swim, Mr. Constantine.

TREPLIEFF. Very well, but you must be back in ten minutes.

JACOB. We will, sir.

TREPLIEFF. [Looking at the stage] Just like a real theatre! See, there we have the curtain, the foreground, the background, and all. No artificial scenery is needed.

I found *The Seagull* to be absolutely contemporary once I'd cracked open the place to set it. It is the unchanging human comedy, repeating in every generation. Transcending time and culture, only the details change. On Chekhov's estate, the people play Lotto; in Quogue, they play Scrabble. In Chekhov's day, young people of a certain class spoke in complete sentences, grammatically and precisely. Our young people speak in a different rhythm, encoded for each other. In Chekhov's play, Masha takes snuff; in my adaptation, Milly smokes, but in both versions people still fall hopelessly in love with those who cannot love them back. People still hurt those whom they most want to cherish. Parents still unwittingly crush their children. What I hoped to accomplish with this adaptation is to introduce a new play into the repertory, written by Anton Chekhov, in 2008.

Note

For a copy of the full script of *A Seagull in the Hamptons*, contact Emily Mann, Artistic Director, McCarter Theatre, 91 University Place, Princeton, NY 08540.

CONTRIBUTORS

Leigh Buchanan Bienen is a senior lecturer at Northwestern University School of Law and a criminal defense attorney whose areas of expertise include capital punishment, sex crimes, and rape reform legislation. She is the Director of the Chicago Historical Homicide Project, work involving the analysis and exegesis of a handwritten data set kept by the Chicago Police of more than 11,000 homicides in Chicago from 1870–1930. Her essays and fiction have appeared in *Tri-Quarterly*, the *Ontario Review*, *Transition*, and *The O'Henry Prize Stories*. In 2001 her first book length collection of fiction, *The Left Handed Marriage*, was published by Ontario Review Press. **Jillian Campana** has worked in the theater in the Middle East and Latin America, as well as in New York and Los Angeles. Her last play, *The Puzzle Club*, about a group of brain injury survivors, was recently made into a film by Broken Pieces Productions and is being distributed to hospitals and rehabilitation centers throughout North America. A documentary about her playwriting process recently aired on PBS. Dr. Campana is a 2005 recipient of an award for directing from the John F. Kennedy Center for the Performing Arts and was named the 2003 Distinguished Faculty Member of the School of Fine Arts at the University of Montana, where she is an associate profes-

sor of drama. **David Catlin** has served as director of artistic development, studio teacher, managing director, and currently serves as artistic director of Lookingglass Theater. Directing credits include *Lookingglass Alice*, *Metamorphosis*, *Her Name was Danger*, *The Idiot* (Jeff Award), and *Lookingglass Hamlet*. As an actor he was recently seen in *Hard Times*, *Manuscript Found in Saragossa*, and *Argonautika*. His film work includes *Since You've Been Gone* for Lookingglass/Miramax and *Humanoid* with Dark Harbor Stories. He lives in Chicago with his wife Kerry and daughters Saylor and Emerson Finn. **Stuart Dybek**'s book *The Coast of Chicago*, adapted by Laura Eason for the Walkabout Theater, played at the Lookingglass Theater in Chicago in 2006. His *I Sailed with Magellan*, adapted by Claudia Allen, played at Victory Gardens in Chicago in 2007. **Paul Edwards** is a Charles Deering McCormick Professor of Teaching Excellence and associate professor of Performance Studies at Northwestern University. He has received the Joseph Jefferson Award and Citation, the After Dark Award, and the Leslie Irene Coger Award for stage productions, and the Lilla A. Heston Award for essays on performance history. **Laura Eason** is the author of more than fifteen plays— both original work and adaptations. More than ten of her full-length plays have been produced at theaters across the country. Her work is published by Broadway Play Publishing, where she was named playwright of the year in 2007. In New York, she is an Affiliated Artist and Kitchen Cabinet member of the Obie-winning New Georges, a playwright member of the

Women's Project Lab, and a second-year member of America-in-Play. For six years, she was the artistic director of Lookingglass Theatre Company in Chicago, where she is still an active ensemble member. **Frank Galati** won two Tony Awards for his adaptation and direction of Steppenwolf's production of *The Grapes of Wrath* on Broadway. Although he is known primarily as a director of epic plays and musicals such as Steppenwolf's *Homebody/Kabul* and Broadway's *Ragtime*, he is an equally adept actor and adaptor, receiving an Academy Award nomination for Best Screenplay for *The Accidental Tourist*. He directs his new adaptation of Murakami's *Kafka on the Shore* and appears in *The Tempest* at Steppenwolf this season. He is also an associate director at the Goodman Theatre and professor of performance studies at Northwestern University. **Jana Harris**'s most recent books of poetry are *Oh, How Can I Keep on Singing, Voices of Pioneer Women* and *We Never Speak of It, Idaho-Wyoming Poems, 1889–90*, both published by Ontario Review Press (Princeton). She is founder and editor of Switched-on Gutenberg, one of the first electronic poetry journals of the English-speaking world. She teaches creative writing online at the University of Washington. **Virgil Johnson** is currently designing stage productions of *Dangerous Beauty*, *Amadeus*, and *Don't Dress for Dinner* for Chicago-area theaters. His costume design for Giuseppe Verdi's *Macbeth* will open the 2010–2011 season of the Lyric Opera of Chicago. Mr. Johnson is a professor emeritus of Northwestern University. **David Kersnar** is a founding ensemble member of Lookingglass Theatre Company. At Lookingglass he conceived and directed *La Luna Muda*, *Through The Looking Glass*, and *Brundibar*, which was co-produced with the Chicago Children's Choir and Lively Arts. Kersnar has performed with the company in *The Secret in the Wings, Summertime, Her Name Was Danger*, and *The Great Fire*. He served twice as artistic director and is currently the education and community program's master teacher. Kersnar founded and currently instructs with the Lookingglass Education and Community Program and served as its director from 1992–1997. His film and television credits include *U.S. Marshals, Since You've Been Gone*, and *Early Edition*. Kersnar lives in Chicago with his wife Christie and his sons, Drew and Kyle. **Martha Lavey** has been the Steppenwolf Artistic Director since 1995. While leading one of the most acclaimed theater companies in the world, Martha turns in heartbreakingly honest work in such Steppenwolf productions as *Lost Land, The Memory of Water* and *I Never Sang for My Father*. She holds a doctorate in performance studies from Northwestern University. **Emily Mann** is a multi-award-winning director and playwright, starting her nineteenth season as artistic director of McCarter Theatre, where she has overseen over ninety productions. She wrote and directed *Having Our Say*, adapted from the book by Sarah L. Delany and A. Elizabeth Delany with Amy Hill Hearth at McCarter and on Broadway. She has been nominated for three Tony awards, including Best Play and Best Direction, and a Drama Desk award. **Bruce Norris** has an ongoing collaboration with Steppenwolf, where his plays *The Pain and the Itch*, *We All Went Down to Amsterdam*, *The Infidel* and *Purple Heart* (also in Galway, Ireland) were commissioned and produced. Additional plays include *The Actor Retires* and *The Vanishing Twin* produced at Remains Theatre and Lookingglass Theatre, respectively. In 2002, *The Infidel*, was produced at Philadelphia Theatre Company. His play *The Unmentionables* will be part of Steppenwolf's 30th season of new work and will feature ensemble members John Mahoney, Laurie Metcalf, and Amy Morton. Also an actor, Norris appeared on the Steppenwolf stage in *Closer* and can be seen in the films *School of Rock*, *The Sixth Sense*, and the upcoming *Homecoming*. **Anna D. Shapiro** has directed some of the most memorable Steppenwolf productions in recent years, including *August: Osage County* (for which she received a Tony Award), *Three Days of Rain*, *Drawer Boy*, *I Never Sang for my Father*, *Man from Nebraska*, and *The Pain and the Itch*. Outside of Steppenwolf, she has directed at the Atlantic Theatre Company, Manhattan Theatre Club, Huntington Theatre Company, and Paper Mill Playhouse, among others. Shapiro is also head of the graduate directing program at Northwestern University. **Mary Zimmerman** is a member of the Lookingglass Theatre Company and is an Artistic Associate of the Goodman Theatre in Chicago, Illinois. She has earned national and international recognition in the form of numerous awards, including the prestigious John D. and Catherine T. MacArthur Fellowship (1998). She has won more than twenty Joseph Jefferson Awards for her creative work and received a 2002 Tony Award for Best Direction for *Metamorphoses*. Other acclaimed works include *Journey to the West*, *The Secret In The Wings*, *The Odyssey*, *The Arabian Nights*, *The Notebooks of Leonardo da Vinci*, and *Eleven Rooms of Proust*. She is the director and co-librettist of the 2002 opera *Galileo Galilei*, music by Philip Glass, commissioned by the Goodman Theatre.

Subscriptions
Three issues per year. **Individuals:** one
year $24; two years $44; life $600. **Insti-
tutions:** one year $36; two years $68.
Overseas: $5 per year additional. Price
of back issues varies. Sample copies $5.
Address correspondence and subscriptions
to *TriQuarterly*, Northwestern University,
629 Noyes St., Evanston, IL 60208-4210.
Phone (847) 491-7614.

Submissions
The editors invite submissions of fiction,
poetry and literary essays, which must
be postmarked between October 1 and
February 28; manuscripts postmarked be-
tween March 1 and September 30 will
not be read. No manuscripts will be re-
turned unless accompanied by a stamped,
self-addressed envelope. All manuscripts
accepted for publication become the
property of *TriQuarterly*, unless other-
wise indicated.

Reprints
Reprints of issues 1–17 of *TriQuarterly*
are available in full format from Kraus
Reprint Company, Route 100, Millwood,
NY 10546, and all issues in microfilm
from University Microfilms International,
300 North Zeeb Road, Ann Arbor, MI
48106.

Indexing
TriQuarterly is indexed in the Humanities
Index (H. W. Wilson Co.), Humanities
International Complete (Whitson
Publishing Co.), Historical Abstracts,
MLA, EBSCO Publishing (Peabody,
MA) and Informa-tion Access Co.
(Foster City, CA).

Distributors
Our national distributors to retail trade
are Ingram Periodicals (La Vergne, TN);
B. DeBoer (Nutley, NJ); Ubiquity (Brook-
lyn, NY); Armadillo (Los Angeles, CA).

Publication of *TriQuarterly* is made
possible in part by the donors of gifts
and grants to the magazine. For their
recent and continuing support, we are
very pleased to thank the Illinois Arts
Council, the Lannan Foundation, the
National Endowment for the Arts,
the Sara Lee Foundation, the Wendling
Foundation and individual donors.

THE MASSACHUSETTS REVIEW

LAYLAH ALI

an especially queer issue of
the MASSACHUSETTS REVIEW

A QUARTERLY REVIEW *of* Fiction, Poetry, Essays, and Art, *since 1959*
massrev@external.umass.edu | www.massreview.org

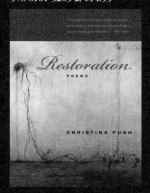

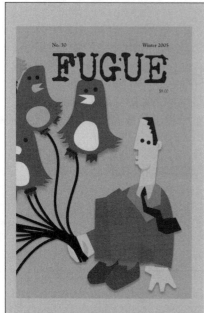